BABE RUTH

&

The American Dream

KEN SOBOL

BABE RUTH
&
The American Dream

Introduction by Dick Schaap

Random House 🏠 New York

Grateful acknowledgment is made to the following for permission
to reprint previously published material:

John Kieran: For his untitled poem "With vim and verve . . ."

I.H.T. Corporation: For twelve poems by Grantland Rice. Copyright ©
New York Herald Tribune.

Ring Lardner, Jr.: For an untitled poem by Ring Lardner, "We leave
tonight . . ."

Pictures in the photo section were obtained
from the following sources:
Acme Newspictures: 6, 14top, 15top
National Baseball Library: 3top, 4, 5top, 7, 10, 11, 12
Pacific & Atlantic Photos, Inc.: 5bot.
United Press International: 1, 8-9, 14bot., 15 bot.
Wide World: 2, 3bot., 13, 16

Library of Congress Cataloging in Publication Data
Sobol, Ken.
Babe Ruth & the American dream.
Bibliography: p.
1. Ruth, George Herman, 1895-1948. 2. Baseball.
GV865.R8S72   796.357′092′4 [B]   74-9051
ISBN 0-394-49233-1
Manufactured in the United States of America
First Edition

For my Parents

Contents

Acknowledgements

BABE RUTH WAS the most accessible of heroes and sometimes it seems as if every second American over the age of forty encountered him personally at one time or another. There is no room to list those persons who told me of their occasional experiences with Ruth, but I am grateful to them all.

I owe a great debt to Frederick Lieb. A fine sportswriter on whose work I have often drawn, he is also one of the few survivors of the generation of journalists who began working in New York around 1910 and who raised sportswriting to heights unequaled before or since. His vast knowledge of the period this book covers and his patience in answering my endless questions were invaluable aids.

Many other people who knew Ruth well talked to me at length: Earle and Ruth Combs, Jackie Farrell, the late Frank Frisch, Larry and Margaret Gardner, Mike Gazella, Harry Hooper, Mark Koenig, Grace Monroe, Ben Paschal, Roger Peckinpaugh, Bob Shawkey, Ernie Shore, Elmer Smith, Lloyd and Beth Waner, and Joe Wood helped my reseach greatly. The late Ephraim Colledge, Frederick Fried, Jane Pennock, Lou Perini, Oliver Pilat, and Paul Welsh also personally contributed important information.

Bill Adler first suggested the subject, Phil Spitzer and Stephanie Erickson encouraged it. Eliot Asinof, Bob

x ACKNOWLEDGMENTS

Broeg of the *St. Louis Post-Dispatch,* and Lawrence
Ritter pointed out avenues of investigation which had
not occurred to me. John Redding and Clifford Kach-
line of the National Baseball Library at Cooperstown,
New York, made many helpful suggestions, and Richard
Arnold of the York University Library in Toronto sup-
plied material from his private collection. The New
York Yankees graciously allowed me to poke around
Yankee Stadium. And the assistance of R. J. Smalling of
Ames, Iowa, who keeps a record of the whereabouts of
all former (living) major league players, saved me a
good deal of time and effort.

Julie Macfie Sobol read the manuscript at every stage
and contributed enormously to its development. The
comments and encouragement of Jane Jacobs also
helped me over some difficult stretches. And finally I
must acknowledge the pleasure, as well as the information, given to me by the sportswriters of the teens and
twenties. They were the best; I hope some of their élan
rubbed off on me.

K.S.

Introduction

The man is dead, and so are his most noble records, yet Babe Ruth remains the personification of professional sports in America. He embodied all that was good about pro sports, and most of what was bad. He was living proof, and is still mythic proof, that through sports a man can rise from common, vulgar beginnings to wealth, to fame, to a position of influence and impact attained only by movie stars and singers and a handful of Presidents. He was Marilyn Monroe up from the sticks, Sinatra up from the streets, Eisenhower up from the farm. He may have been bigger than all of them, and more imperfect.

Babe Ruth was living proof that through sports a man could rise from common, vulgar beginnings, and remain common and vulgar. The myth of Ruth has tended to ignore that fact. The myth focuses upon Ruth pointing to the spot where his next home run will land, or upon Ruth visiting sickly children in hospitals and promising a home run to each, or upon Ruth gorging himself on hot dogs and soda pop and, a few minutes later, feasting upon pitchers as though he were starved and they were his only meal.

In recent years, journalists have chipped away at the Ruthian myth, revealing the man underneath, exposing the coarseness, detailing his obscenities and his whoring and his syphilis, making clear the fitting coincidence that the man who inspired the title role in *The Babe Ruth Story* also embodied the title role in *The Hairy Ape*. This process of erosion is a necessary one, if it is done as it should be done, if it is done as Ken Sobol has done it so tellingly in this book—not with venom, but with compassion.

For Ruth was shaped by sports, just as sports was shaped by him, and if some of his non-culinary appetites were grotesque and even repulsive, they sprang from the milieu as well as from the man. Just as professional sports abundantly rewards the gifted athlete, it likewise abuses him. It subjects him to flattery, cajolery, temptation, chicanery and downright lying—to him and about him. Every great athlete who is adored, no matter how mindless he may be, has to wonder at some point exactly how he would be treated by his admirers if he didn't possess his athletic skill. Unless he is totally moronic, he must at least occasionally sense the sea of insincerity that engulfs him. Of all public figures—politicians and performers are his only peers—he is the least prepared to become a public figure; he is not taught public speaking or public presence; those are not the tools of his trade, and he must absorb them by osmosis, if at all. He is expected to live up to myths he did not create, myths spawned by writers and nurtured by the public.

No man had to live up to a greater myth than Ruth did, and the fact that he survived at all under the pressure of being Babe Ruth is immensely impressive. The fact that he survived for so long is astounding. There have been dozens, perhaps hundreds, of athletes as talented as Ruth, or almost as talented, whose names never became household words because the pressure killed their skills, in high school perhaps, or in college, or in sandlots, or in the infancy of a professional career.

Ruth fought Ruthian pressures and, on the playing field, flourished. Roger Maris and Henry Aaron had to beat only a ghost; Ruth had to beat the real thing—himself. It should not surprise anyone that the greatest professional athlete in the history of American sports was a man with distorted sexual, moral, social and financial values—no more than it should surprise anyone that the greatest amateur athlete in the history of American sports was a drunken Indian.

DICK SCHAAP

BABE RUTH

&

The American Dream

1

The Hero in his Glory

EARLY ON THE clear, sunshiny morning of October 11, 1927, Babe Ruth, Lou Gehrig, and Christy Walsh, Ruth's business manager, along with several aides, an equipment manager, a trainer, a chattering crowd of well-wishers and hangers-on, Mama Gehrig, two showy call girls with whom Ruth had spent the previous night, and an excited swirl of passersby irresistibly caught up by the magnetic presence of the Babe, swept into the great hall at Pennsylvania Station in midtown Manhattan. Ruth wore his inevitable camel-colored coat and cap and puffed on a big cigar, sending up clouds of smoke into the already thick haze. Cries of "Hurray for Babe" and "Good luck, Babe" echoed through the cavernous hall. The shoeshine boys stopped polishing and looked up. Bustling businessmen, clerks and secretaries on their way to work turned and began hurrying toward the commotion, wondering what it was. When they came near enough to see, they too shouted to the Babe. "Hiya, keed," Babe boomed back, grinning widely, comfortable amid the adulation, as always perfectly at ease in a crowd.

By the time he reached the platform where the train waited, Ruth was in the center of an ever-increasing crowd. Admirers pressed around him, trying to shake his hand, requesting an autograph for their kids, or just wanting to say hello. As he walked he signed everything

1

they thrust at him—backs of tickets, train schedules, detachable cuffs, and steno pads, inscribing each with that exquisite, flowing, feminine script with which he wrote his name. "Hiya, keed," "Hiya, sis," "Hiya, doc," he repeated again and again, at the same time pushing an aisle through the crowd for his flashy companions. Spotting an acquaintance, he winked broadly and showed the girls to him. "A couple of beauts, eh, keed?" he called, while the girls giggled.

Eventually Walsh worked his way through the crowd to Ruth's side and shouted that they had to get moving. "That's all, folks, gotta go," Ruth cried in his gravelly baritone. With a friendly slap on the behind and a large tip he sent the girls packing. Giving Mama Gehrig a big squeeze, he promised to look after her Louie and make him write every day. Climbing the steps to the car, he turned and waved his cap at the engineer and the porters, then gave a final salute to what was left of the well-wishers. As the whistle tooted he could be seen leading the others toward the dining car.

The Sultan of Swat was going on tour—right across the heartland of America. As he had sifted through a multitude of offers and schemes in the closing weeks of the 1927 season, Walsh's Yankee trader's instincts had inclined more and more toward a barnstorming tour. The money was there, it could be extracted quickly, and Ruth would be doing the thing that he did most easily. Besides, Walsh had found over the years that people would pay more to see Ruth play baseball than anything else. "Babe Ruth's coming to town," was printed in bright crimson script across the top of his special tour stationary. "Coming out to the thousands who cannot come to him!"

Walsh was confident that the fans of America's national game would break down the gates to see the Babe after his sensational season. What a year it had been—a new record of sixty home runs, a batting average of .356, 164 runs batted in. Ruth alone had hit more home runs than any other whole team in the American League, including the rest of the already legendary 1927 Yankees, if you took away Gehrig. The Babe had led New York to the pennant by nineteen games over Philadelphia, then to a four-game sweep over the Pirates in the World Series, in which he had personally broken nine all-time records. Only two years after a catastrophic 1925 season, which had encompassed Ruth's collapse after contracting syphilis over the winter, a midseason suspension, the largest fine in baseball history, and a rotten year at the plate, Ruth had miraculously come back to scale even greater heights than before. Those "Is the Babe Washed Up?" headlines now seemed nothing more than a bad joke.

The train pulled out of Penn Station around nine o'clock. Three hours later, after a leisurely second breakfast, Ruth and Gehrig were standing on the steps of the State House in Trenton, posing for pictures with Governor Moore. They had taken off their coats and looked every inch the prosperous young businessmen in their dark, well-pressed suits and vests. Gehrig hung back uncertainly, but Babe hopped up the few steps to the low porch entrance where the governor stood, almost blocking him from view with his huge body. "Meet Lou Gehrig, Gov," Ruth boomed. The governor smiled broadly and replied that he was pleased to welcome them to New Jersey and proud they had selected the Garden State as their first tour stop. "Glad to be here," replied Ruth. Gehrig, as usual, blushed and murmured something too soft to hear. "The keed don't say much," Ruth explained. In front of them, the photographers called for more handshakes. Ruth and the governor waved, shook hands, waved again, and shook hands again.

The publicity session over, Ruth and Gehrig were driven to the local ball park. In the game, which was scheduled for two o'clock, the Yankee stars were to join a Trenton semipro team against the Brooklyn Royal Colored Giants, a collection of black all-star ballplayers. The Giants had driven down from New York in their team wagon, and they were already on the field when Ruth and Gehrig trotted out to the thundering cheers of several thousand spectators. "What do you say, Bo?" Ruth called cheerfully to the nearest Giant, who grinned and waved in reply.

While Ruth limbered up, acknowledging the screams of the crowd over his every move, his black opponents watched him narrowly. Subversive notions about his racial origins ran through their minds. Speculation about Ruth had long been common among black players. His heavy features, swarthy complexion, pipestem legs, and enormous torso and belly—an unusual body structure for a Caucasian—along with the conflicting stories about his parents' origins, had even led some of them to assume he might be a secret brother.

The Giants' pitcher, a skinny, jet-black fellow determined not to be intimidated by the reputations of the men he was facing, put everything he had into his first fastball to the Maharajah of Mash. Ruth watched it almost into the catcher's mitt, then whipped his big bat around at the last second and smashed the ball far over the right-center-field fence. Hundreds of screaming, jubilant boys leaped from the stands to escort him around the bases, clinging to his legs, climbing up his arms, shoving autograph books at him, racing around his path in wide circles; it took ten minutes for Babe to travel the bases, and another ten to get the field cleared again. In the third inning Ruth did it again, and so did the kids. His third home run, in the seventh inning with two men on base, ignited a celebration so enthusiastic that the field could not be cleared at all, and the game was called. The final score was 9–4 in favor of the Trenton team. Gehrig, slightly overwhelmed by the feverish atmosphere, had been limited to a single and a double.

The next afternoon found Ruth and Gehrig anticlimactically back in New York, playing with another semipro team at Dexter Park in Brooklyn. (As far as Walsh was concerned, any activity that took place beyond the confines of midtown Manhattan should be called barnstorming.) Their opponents, again, were the Royal Colored Giants, now on their home grounds. The crowd was even larger and wilder than the previous day's had been. By game time an enormous mass had spilled out onto the field and with every passing minute was edging its way further and further into the playing area. At the close of the second inning the outfield had contracted by thirty feet all around. A revolving mob of boys darted in and out of the crowd, stealing everything not under lock and key: Ruth's bats vanished as soon as he glanced away from them; Gehrig's glove was nearly ripped off his hand; base hits to the outfield became a race for possession between the fielders and dozens of spectators; the bases themselves disappeared by the fifth inning. Ruth, who had begun the game playing first base, found that his only safety was on the mound, and so he went in to pitch in the eighth, allowing Gehrig to fight his way into the infield to take his place at first. An inning later the last of the forty-five baseballs that Walsh had brought along had vanished, and the field was swamped with thousands of struggling, half-hysterical, autograph-seeking young men and boys. At that point a police riot squad, judiciously summoned by Walsh, charged into the park and battled its way through to Ruth and Gehrig in the infield. Circling them, the police gradually wedged out a path to the dressing room, where Ruth, with a quick final wave to the mass of kids hanging off the dugout roof and wooden rafters, relievedly plunged into the security of the locker room. Ruth's team had been leading 3–1 when the game ended, but neither he nor Gehrig had homered.

On October 13 the tour left New York again. They were on the train for good now, heading west, although their first stop, Asbury Park on the Jersey coast, was actually east of Manhattan. There, for the third time in three days, Ruth and Gehrig faced the Royal Giants before a wildly excited overflow crowd. To Walsh's dismay, the local bigwigs sprang a time-wasting surprise— an award-giving ceremony in which every politician and civic leader of Monmouth County seemed to have included himself and a full complement of photographers. Between their speeches and the usual mob of

boys racing back and forth across the field at every opportunity, the game crawled along at something less
than a snail's pace. This time, however, Walsh had train
schedules to worry about.

Finally he decided to hurry things up. Using a dodge
often employed by the Yankee management while the
team was on spring exhibition tours, he grabbed a boy
and sent him racing out to first base with an autograph
book. Before the boy had reached Babe a dozen more
kids had picked up the cue and were charging across the
field with their pieces of paper. In another few minutes
the number had reached several hundred, and the situation was out of control. After a decent interval, Walsh
called in the cops, and the tour hurried back to the station. For the record—and Walsh always kept accurate
records of these things—the score had been 6–5 in favor
of Ruth and Gehrig's team. Babe had hit one home run,
making a total of four in less than three games against
the black stars.

The train pulled out, its ultimate destination Lima,
Ohio. Ruth headed for the dining car, slapping the grinning porters on their backs and calling loudly for food.
Walsh and Gehrig joined him, and while Christy explained the next day's plans to Lou, Ruth wedged his
big belly against the cramped table and proceeded to
stuff himself with food and drink. The waiters thought
they'd seen it all, but now they watched with bulging
eyes as Babe ordered triple portions of the best on the
menu and ravenously shoveled it in, sometimes with his
fork, sometimes with his fingers, hardly seeming to taste
the mountain of food as he wolfed it down. Calling for a
pitcher of fruit juice, he produced a fifth of gin and
emptied it into the pitcher, then drank the entire con-
tents as the meal progressed. The waiters just shook
their heads, wondering how any man could survive that
kind of gorging. But if that was what Ruth wanted,
that's what he would get. The size of his tips guaranteed
that.

After the bicarb, Ruth played poker or blackjack in

his drawing room or the lounge of their private car. On a trip with Walsh the stakes were necessarily low, since the skinny, dour-faced promoter abhorred risking his money. (Or giving it away. Walsh customarily left his house with his pockets empty of everything save carfare, the easier to refuse anyone who tried to borrow from him.) This time he had managed to bring along the only man Ruth knew who was tighter than himself—Gehrig. ("That guy thought every dime he owned was a family heirloom," laughs one former teammate.) Gehrig did not even gamble, and none of the flunkies wanted to go high with Ruth, either. Which, as everyone except Ruth admitted, was probably a blessing for the Bambino. He was a mediocre gambler with a predilection for bluffing that rarely fooled a good player. Everett Scott, for one, took him for thousands of dollars every season. Scotty had started getting rich off Ruth back in Boston, when they had been young kids breaking in. After both ended up on the Yankees and Ruth started pulling those huge salaries, he really went to town. And Mike Gonzalez, a catcher with the Cards, claimed to have doubled his year's wages, which would have been around three or four thousand dollars, playing poker with Ruth during a northbound spring-training exhibition tour in 1923.

The train reached Lima on the morning of October 14. The town looked like a hundred similar towns Ruth had played in over the years, with its neat, New England style town square, small two-story brick factories, and quiet, tree-dotted residential streets. Now the leaves were just turning red and orange and starting to drift down to the lawns and the crisp feeling of autumn was in the air. At the train station dignitaries from every corner of Allen County waited with a thousand or so kids to greet the two sluggers. A brass band broke in to a march as the heroes alighted and shook hands with the local bigwigs. Cigars being among the native products, Ruth was presented with several boxes, one of which he opened and made use of, to the delight of the manufacturer.

A short time later, at the ball park, the tour assumed

the structure that Walsh had planned back in his Seventh Avenue offices. Ruth and Gehrig now became the captains of opposing teams—named the Bustin' Babes and the Larrupin' Lous—which, fleshed out with local stars, would play each other throughout the remainder of the tour. Walsh had even brought a selection of ill-fitting uniforms—black for the Babes, light gray for the Lous. When the game was over and the crowd dispersed, Walsh pocketed the relatively meager proceeds (under two thousand dollars), and made a mental note to skip rural Ohio next time around.

Back on the train, life began to settle into the numbing routine of all road trips. Ruth ate and played cards, Gehrig wrote letters to his mother, watched the card games, or read the papers, and Walsh took care of correspondence and accounting, cut out local newspaper stories for his files, and plotted future money-making schemes. By the next morning the train was chugging through the gently undulating Missouri countryside. Out the windows, those who cared to look could see an endless procession of recently harvested fields fenced off by what midwesterners still referred to as "bob wire." Occasionally the grain elevator of a small town would appear suddenly and then sink back into the prairie. Often a Model T or a farm truck would run alongside the train on a parallel dirt road, or occasionally a paved one, for a few minutes, then turn off or fall behind.

When they did stop at one of the small towns, Ruth would invariably send someone out to scare up some food —half a dozen hot dogs, half a dozen Cokes, whatever else was available. Sometimes he met the public at the stops as well. If news had come ahead that the Sultan of Swat was on the train, or if the porters or engineer slipped the word to a friend as they pulled in, a crowd quickly collected. Ruth generally tried to avoid them, but occasionally they got a glimpse of his massive figure moving about in the car. And once in a while he came

out and called to the fans, or even signed autographs for
a short spell.

Gehrig, too, stayed out of sight. Being on the road
without Earle Combs, Ben Paschal, Benny Bengough,
Tony Lazzeri, and the rest of his buddies was somewhat
of an ordeal for the shy, awkward young man. Babe's
crudeness, particularly his constant swearing, made
Gehrig uncomfortable. And Ruth's cavalier and often
brutal opinions of women, whom Gehrig respected from
afar with all the passion of a newly pubescent teenager,
made the latter's skin crawl.

Gehrig's greatest dream was to learn to talk to girls
without making a fool of himself. He would give almost
anything to achieve the social ease so many other guys
possessed. Many of his close friends on the team were
married to attractive, vivacious women, some of whom
were approved of even by Mama Gehrig. And the goings-
on of the Yankee bachelors demonstrated very clearly
what he was missing in that area. The younger Yankees
delighted in kidding him, planning imaginary assignations
and going out of their way to point out beautiful women
who they claimed were dying to meet him. Once Mark
Koenig and Bengough laughingly refused his hesitant request to find him a girl on the grounds that he wouldn't
know what to do if he had one. The incident embarrassed him for years.

The tongue-tied awe in which Gehrig held the other
players was purely social, however. Physically he was a
more imposing figure than any of them, even more than
Ruth had been in his youthful heyday. Like Babe,
Gehrig was an abnormal physical specimen; he had an
enormous chest and overdeveloped thighs, almost like a
weightlifter's body. His suits had to be altered to fit, and
even the baggy Yankee uniform looked about to burst
under the strain of his physique. When he swung his bat
he seemed to be exploding with a ferocious, cooped-up
force that would obliterate anything in its way. If a pitcher facing Ruth trembled for fear of losing the game
on one pitch, against Gehrig he was afraid of losing a

limb. Ruth uppercut his swing, driving the ball out of sight in a great arc, but Gehrig swung straight and level, smashing line drive after line drive so hard that you could almost imagine you saw the ball flattening out against the wood before it screamed back into the field.

Although his "aw, shucks" bashfulness led outsiders to assume the contrary, Gehrig was in fact perfectly aware and inordinately proud of his physical uniqueness. He liked to study himself in a mirror, flexing his muscles slowly. The exquisite care with which he treated his body owed as much to ego nourishment as to health and professional motivations. His ramrod posture, crushing grip, and constant exercising seemed to be attempts to compensate for his agonizing social deficiencies. His record of doggedly playing in 2,130 consecutive games, despite broken bones, illness, and exhaustion that would have led any reasonable person to forget the whole idea, was the accomplishment of a man driven by a monumental vanity. (And of a man with a strong need to distinguish himself from the rest of the pack—particularly from the overwhelming shadow of Babe Ruth.)

On to Kansas City and Omaha the caravan rolled. In Kansas City they stayed over in a hotel before making the short trip to Omaha the following day. It was a stop to which both Ruth and Walsh were looking forward. For the latter it represented their first real chance to pick up some promotional fees on the side. For Ruth, the stop meant that some relatively high-class broads would be available. And for everyone, some decent shower facilities.

At the station waited the usual mob of boys, local dignitaries, sports and gossip columnists from all the papers in the area, and just curious folks. After a short welcoming speech by a pompous chamber-of-commerce big shot, Ruth was whisked out to a children's hospital. There a hall full of sick kids—cripples, incurables, county wards, and charity cases—were treated to more excitement than they had ever known. Many of them probably did not even know who the huge, thick-necked fat man was, but the crowds of photographers and the anticipation of the nurses had made them half hysterical with excitement, too.

Ruth sat in the middle of the ward, surrounded by kids, dangling one or two on his knee, posing for the hordes of cameramen climbing over each other like a troup of Hungarian acrobats. He picked out a bashful little girl, clucked her under the chin, and asked "How you doing, sis?" An emaciated eight-year-old boy shyly held out a cast for Ruth to autograph. "How about here?" Babe asked, and the boy nodded, his throat too dry to speak. Hospital attendants and smiling dignitaries helped Ruth to hand out baseballs and candy. "You coming to see me, ain't you, sonny?" Ruth said to a boy in a wheelchair. "I'm gonna hit you a home run, so you be there." The boy could only gasp in reply. "They'll be there," a middle-aged nurse assured him. "This is a wonderful day for them, Mr. Ruth." Another kid was put in Ruth's arms for the photographers, and then Ruth and his entourage, shepherded by Walsh, headed for the front door.

The next stop was the news room of the *Kansas City Star*. Here Ruth took off his jacket, rolled up his sleeves, put on a green eyeshade, and sat down at the sports editor's desk. "Babe Ruth Edits Star Sports Page," the next day's headline would read. Under the headline would be a photo of Ruth hard at work, a pencil behind his ear and copy in his hand, with a caption along the lines of "Noted Behemoth of Bash toils over unfamiliar task, says putting out a sports page is harder work than he thought. Next time he'll have more respect for the energetic efforts of the gentlemen of the press."

After a hectic but, as always, substantial luncheon at the hotel, Ruth and Gehrig were taken to the ball park. On the field that day the Bustin' Babes and Larrupin' Lous were nervously warming up, one eye on the ball, one on the dugout, watching for Babe and Lou. Ten thousand fans had been jammed into the park for an hour. The crippled kids, guests of the Knights of Columbus, the game's sponsors, were installed along the near right-field line at ground level. Suddenly a tremendous roar announced the arrival of the stars. Boys piled out of their seats and onto the field, shouting for autographs, but the ushers shooed them back.

Two hours later the game ended with the customers satisfied. Ruth's team had won, and both Babe and Lou had homered. The kids had had their chance to run around, and every person there could say, for the rest of his life, that he had seen Babe Ruth play in person. The admission price—$1.00 for grandstand seats, $1.65 for the boxes—was money well spent.

The next day the scene shifted to Omaha. The usual hospital visit came first, but at the ball park festivities departed from their normal routine. Here, before an overflow crowd of fifty-five hundred, the local grange had arranged a ceremony at which Babe was to be formally introduced to Lady Amco of Norfolk, the world champion egg-laying hen, known as the "Babe Ruth of Chickens." That morning, true to form, it had layed an egg for the 171st consecutive day.

Babe, Lou, an announcer, and the farmer who owned Lady Amco walked out to first base, where that day's egg, wrapped in a pink ribbon and set in a jewel box, was presented to a sheepish-looking Sultan of Swat. Gehrig, grinning widely, bent down to examine the thing, which was inscribed "From the Queen of Eggs to the King of Hitters." Babe gingerly handed the box to Walsh, acknowledged the cheers coming from the rickety grandstand, and turned to go back to the dugout—only to find the farmer holding out toward him a squawking white chicken. Grasping it reluctantly, he tried to hand it to Gehrig, who quickly backed away. "Hold it closer, Babe," a photographer called. Babe complied briefly, then thrust the creature back toward its owner and made his retreat.

The event predictably caught the attention of newspaper editors throughout the country, although some big-city journals became confused by the wire service reports and implied in their stories that Lady Amco had layed 171 eggs that day.

Once the feathers had cleared from the field, the game began, with Ruth playing for a team called the Brown Park Merchants, and Gehrig joining the Omaha Printers. Babe, perhaps inspired by Lady Amco's example, smashed two stupendous home runs over the right-field fence. Gehrig did less well at the plate but thrilled the crowd when he came in to pitch in the late innings and struck out Babe with a high hard one with the bases loaded.

That night, October 16, they were back on the train. Ruth had brought some girls along and disappeared with them into his drawing room. Gehrig wrote an amused letter to his mother, commenting that they were going backwards again. Des Moines, Iowa, two hundred miles east, was their next stop.

After the unusual events of Omaha, Des Moines proved to be merely routine. They autographed balls for charity kids, attended a smoker, met the bigwigs, and played before a crowd of about the same size as the one in Omaha. The game itself was dull, and both Ruth and Gehrig seemed a bit sluggish. The *Des Moines Register* headlined its story: "Ruth, Gehrig, Fail to Hit Homers."

The tour switched directions again the next day, toward the northwest. They arrived just in time for a half-day celebration in their honor at Sioux City. In the parade Ruth demonstrated his ability on horseback. As with all things involving physical coordination, he performed effortlessly, riding as if he had been born in the saddle. He also tried to get Gehrig up on a pony, but Lou wasn't having any of it. On this occasion they met their first Indians, all decked out in ceremonial robes and headdresses. Ruth had toured through the West before, but Gehrig was wide-eyed at everything. "He ain't never seen no real redskins," Ruth explained to reporters.

They were really in the outback now. And while the

crowds were not as large, they were more devoted and more respectful. They came from hundreds of miles around—kids riding in buggies, families making a day of it on the train, truckloads of teenagers who hadn't been to the city in two years, old-timers who recalled seeing Christy Mathewson or Honus Wagner or some other legendary figure when he had been through years before, Elks Clubbers,. Mason and Grange members, young future farmers of America. They wore overalls, chewed grass, their hair was in their faces, and they came to see the greatest hero they could ever imagine passing through their quiet lives.

A few years earlier Ruth and Bob Meusel, the Yankee right fielder, had barnstormed through central Iowa, and a social reporter in Perry had noted that ". . . Reservations [for the game] had been made from Collins, Cooper, Jefferson, Adel, Des Moines, Yale, Coon Rapids, Spencer, Madrid, Boone, and all the nearby towns." This year it had been no different. The citizens might never get to see Chicago, or even Kansas City, but now they had seen Babe Ruth. Up close. They'd seen him grin and wave, take a deep breath and swing his bat. And someone they knew or someone sitting near them, or, believe it or not, they themselves, had gotten his autograph or touched his uniform or run around the bases with him after he'd hit one out.

After Sioux City the procession wended its way through the corn belt, cutting across Nebraska, passing through quiet prairie towns dead to the world by seven-thirty at night, crossing rivers no one had ever heard of. They were on the way to Denver. Ruth ensconced himself in the dining car, acknowledging the obsequious attention of the waiters, handing out tips larger than they had ever received before. Finally Walsh, driven out of his customary reticence by the generosity of Ruth's gratuities, for which he was paying, chastised the Babe for throwing money away. "Shut up, you cheapskate," Ruth told him. But it wasn't anything serious.

Denver provided more of what they had already ex-

perienced: excited and worshipful kids; proud fathers
hoisting their sons on their shoulders to see over the
crowd; officious, eager-to-please local notables; reporters wearing trenchcoats and dangling cigarettes from the
corners of their mouths, imitating what they assumed
was the manner of Ring Lardner, Damon Runyon,
Grantland Rice, Heywood Broun, and the rest of the big
names. Indians said "how" to the great white Sachem of
Slug, and the horseback-riding experiment was repeated,
with the same results. Again, Ruth and Gehrig visited
some sick children and attended a banquet, where Ruth
made a brief speech.

Walsh, who had been carefully feeding copy to the
press, now decided that it was time to release some hard
news. Babe Ruth, he revealed, was at this moment the
second most heavily insured man in the United States.
Only Rodman Wanamaker, heir to the Wanamaker fortune, was worth more to his beneficiaries. Wanamaker
would cash in at five million, but Ruth wasn't far behind. The Yankees' policy on him, spread out over a
period of several years, added up to three million.

Leaving Denver on the evening of October 19, the
tour began its arduous final haul over the mountains and
salt flats to California. They would be traveling all of the
next day and night. Both Ruth and Gehrig were grateful
for the breather. Although only nine days had passed
since they had brought Penn Station to a temporary
standstill with the excitement of their departure, it
seemed like an entire season. In that time they had
played nine games, involving fifteen different teams,
crossed twelve states, met an endless blur of governors,
mayors, representatives, councilmen, local heroes, charity volunteers, lodge officials, Indian chiefs, children, and
animals, shaken hands and given autographs until their
fingers were numb, and eaten bucketsful of real Midwest
home-style granite beefsteaks and rubber chicken—and
even Babe's stomach was beginning to protest.

Not much more than a vague whirlwind of faces and
things stayed in their memories. One place looked pretty

much the same as another. The one constant factor was
the presence of kids. They were everywhere—peering in
through the windows of the train and the hotel, sitting
on fences and rooftops, hanging in trees overlooking the
parade routes and ball parks, lying in hospital beds,
pounding their gloves in the stands, rushing out between
innings to leap on Ruth and Gehrig. At every stop a
spectator could see a dozen or so get trampled and fall
out at the edge of the crowd, then suddenly forget their
injuries and plunge back into the battle to reach the
Yankees. "Hey, Babe, hey, Babe, hey, Babe," they cried
from all sides, waving their autograph books and franti-
cally trying to get his attention. And the lucky kid who
did, who got the Babe to sign, or even received a ball
from his huge, calloused hand, achieved a triumph that
would last him at least until adolescence.

Now and then certain kids were singled out to receive
special attention. Back in Sioux City or Des Moines, no
one could remember which, an undersized seven- or
eight-year-old boy wearing patched overalls and carrying a tattered, worn first-baseman's mitt had suddenly
left the stands and dashed across the infield to Ruth in
the middle of an inning. As the crowd held its breath,
the Babe, with his never-failing showman's instinct,
stopped playing, lifted the little boy up on to his shoulders and carried him back to his seat, where he presented him with an autographed ball. The standing ovation
went on for several minutes.

The tour arrived in the San Francisco Bay area at
two-thirty on the afternoon of October 21. The local papers had been issuing daily progress bulletins to drum up
interest ever since Kansas City, so there were a thousand
or so fans jammed into the Oakland station to meet the
train. Among them were Mayor Rolph and Police Chief
O'Brien; the usual clutch of aldermen, county commis-
sioners, and political hangers-on; a delegation from the
Bay Area Knights of Columbus, which was partially
sponsoring the visit along with the *San Francisco Chronicle*; numerous sportswriters; and hordes of boys playing

hookey. After Ruth received the keys to Oakland, Ruth, Gehrig, Walsh, the mayor, the police chief, and an ever-increasing clot of dignitaries and fans struggled down to the ferry. Here Gehrig got his first view of San Francisco Bay, which he described as "beautiful."

On Saturday the real grind began. The morning was spent handing out baseballs and handkerchiefs to deserving boys and girls at the Knights of Columbus headquarters. A luncheon followed, at which Ruth and Gehrig were delighted to find a number of current and retired major leaguers, many of whom would be playing in the weekend games. Tony Lazzeri was there, as were Jimmy Reese, a Yankee farmhand, Lefty O'Doul, Duster Mails, and Ping Bodie, who had played for New York in the early twenties. Bodie owed Babe a lot. He had become famous in sports columns for a quip about the Babe's way of life. During spring training of 1920 he had been asked with whom he was rooming. His succinct answer was: "Ruth's suitcase."

The first game at Recreation Park in San Francisco drew thirteen thousand fans, the largest crowd yet on the tour. In a ceremony at home plate before the game, Gehrig presented O'Doul with a check for one thousand dollars, his reward for being named the most valuable player in the Pacific Coast League that season. Since Gehrig had received nothing more than a handshake for winning the most valuable player award in the American League (Ruth was ineligible under the then-existing rules, having already won it once), he might have felt a certain irony. And he certainly felt nervous. But with his introduction written out on a card, he managed to stumble through his duties.

The major leaguers split up to join the two teams, but the game was a sloppy one, and the last innings degenerated into the by-now customary mob scene. When the game was called the Larrupin' Lous were ahead 10–7. Gehrig hit one home run, but Ruth was shut out.

Sunday morning, after an extended blowout in Ruth's hotel suite the previous night, the teams got back on the ferry for an early game before a packed house in Oakland.

Ruth again went homerless, but Gehrig partially made up for it with a tremendous blast over the right field fence, and led his bleary-eyed squad to a 6–3 victory.

Back in Recreation Park that afternoon, another full house watched the King of Clout smash two home runs to Gehrig's one. In the late innings the stars took turns on the mound, mainly to escape the surging kids. The final score read Bustin' Babes 15, Larrupin' Lous 4.

The next morning Walsh had scheduled a game at Marysville, a farming community about 120 miles northeast of San Francisco. Because it was the smallest town on the tour, Walsh had made some pricing concessions, reducing general admission seats to twenty-five cents and boxes to one dollar. Despite that attractive price, and the half holiday declared by the local board of education, tickets went slowly at the Valley Fruit Store box office. It appeared that the thousand-dollar guarantee Walsh demanded might not be posted. Fortunately, according to the *Marysville Appeal Democrat,* a group of civic-minded businessmen came up with the necessary cash, and the kids of Marysville, two thousand strong, got their chance to see the Maharajah of Mash and his sidekick.

No sooner had they finished signing autographs in Marysville than Walsh rushed them down to Stockton to play an afternoon game. In that town Ruth and Gehrig joined the Angel's Camp Miners and the Local Stars respectively. This game was notable for two reasons: Babe bashed the first ball ever hit out of Stockton Park, and one of the town players performed so brilliantly that his name was mentioned in papers as far away as San Francisco. "Ernie Tascano, local busher, connected for two homers, both inside the park," noted the *Chronicle.* In Stockton, as elsewhere, a swarm of kids innundated the field in the late innings, ending the game early. The Babe's team won, 15–4.

Both Ruth and Gehrig were ready for a long rest, but the tour had another week to run. Early on October 25 it limped into Sacramento. At the children's hospital there Ruth probably muttered to Walsh that he needed the beds more than the patients. But by game time, with a man-sized lunch and two pitchers of beer inside him, he felt better. Both he and Gehrig belted balls out of Moreing Park, while several thousand spectators cheered wildly. The Lous won the game, 9–7.

The tour struggled down through California: San Jose on the 26th, Fresno on the 27th, the next day lush Santa Barbara, where they played in a cold, clammy drizzle against a team from the U.S.S. *Colorado*, San Diego the day after that. In each town the school board declared a holiday, Babe "edited" the local newspaper, and he and Lou climbed into their dress suits for one more smoky evening banquet. But they staggered on, shaking hands with an endless sea of semipro stars, grand exalted commanders, sports editors, and crippled kids. Signing autographs, leading parades, giving baseball opinions, eating local dishes—and watching the calendar move with excruciating slowness toward October 31.

On the evening of the 29th, a calm, balmy night, the tour came to rest in Los Angeles. Ruth perked up immediately. It was like coming home. Los Angeles, which to Ruth meant Hollywood, was a place in which he could feel comfortable. L.A. was high living, publicity crazy, superactive, full of great broads, and always pushing everything to excess. You could do any crazy thing there, right out in the open, and only become more popular for doing it. Only the winter before, during a vaudeville tour, Ruth had actually been arrested in Long Beach for violating child-labor laws. When he had called up some kids from the audience, a headline-seeking sheriff had stopped the performance and run him in. No one took the charge seriously, of course. Many people, in fact, professed to see Walsh's fine hand behind the whole thing.

After that vaudeville tour Ruth had stayed over in Los Angeles to make a movie, entitled *The Babe Comes Home*, for First National Pictures. Anna Q. Nilsson, a popular, middle-rank romantic lead, was his co-star. Koenig and Meusel visited him on the set. "He couldn't act worth crap," is Koenig's remembered opinion, but that didn't stop him from having a fantastic time.

The studio gave him a sumptuous dressing room with a big star on the door, a limousine and chauffeur to run him around town, and all the starlets he could handle. Women were all over the place—in the dressing room, in the car, in the hotel suite. Absolutely beautiful broads. "Broads with skin like milk," as Ruth was fond of repeating. Cases of champagne were scattered all over the same spots, with the empties stuffed under the beds or between seat cushions. The party went on all day and all night, not breaking stride even in transit from one locale to another.

Despite the studio's red-carpet treatment, or maybe because of it, Ruth ended up paying for much of the fun. Living up to their reputation as high rollers, the sports of Hollywood picked off every extra penny that the Babe could lay his hands on. During spring training of that year Walsh sadly admitted to Yankee pitcher Bob Shawkey that Ruth had spent virtually all of his fifty-thousand-dollar fee before the shooting was even completed.

As for the picture itself, opinions differed. When it opened in New York in February 1927, critics shrugged it off with a patronizing here-comes-another-sports-hero-making-a-fool-of-himself attitude. Koenig and the other players scoffed at it from a technical point of view, pointing out that, like all baseball movies, it got everything about the game wrong. The catchers wore rings while they were catching, rosin bags lay directly in the baseline, the umpires stationed themselves in positions from which they couldn't possibly see the plays, and so on. But *The Babe Comes Home* wasn't really much worse than other comedies of its genre. Its box-office failure was due mainly to Ruth's unbending wood-enness and not especially attractive appearance.

After seeing Ruth's performance, the studio bosses

were smart enough not to give him another chance. Their practiced eyes had seen that he was simply not movie material and that no updating of script formula could help him. Unlike Jack Dempsey and Johnny Wiessmuller, his two main rivals for popularity in the sports world, both of whom became big hits on the screen, the camera seemed to reveal a fundamental deadness in Ruth. He projected no sense of who he was, no feeling of dynamism, no trace of the confident power that emanated from him when he was surrounded by large crowds. But that wasn't really surprising. Ruth always had difficulty when he was on his own, without mobs of admirers to respond to.

But now, this time around, he was back in the role which suited him. After his great year, the Sultan of Swat had crossed the nation in triumph, carried on the shoulders of tens of thousands of adoring subjects. The weekend games in Los Angeles would wind up the tour in the greatest possible burst of brilliance. It would be an extravaganza that no one would forget—the biggest baseball show ever to hit the West Coast.

And it was. Thirty thousand people jammed into Wrigley Field to see the semifinal game of the record-breaking tour. Douglas Fairbanks and Mary Pickford, John Gilbert, Clara Bow, Marion Davies and old man Hearst, Buster Keaton. De Mille, and dozens of other top names were spread out in the boxes from first to third. (None of their names meant anything to Ruth.) Seated as close to the royalty as they could get were scores of flashy starlets and would-be starlets and their handsome boyfriends, heads continually swiveling, eyes darting everywhere, glancing around to see if they were being seen. As always, kids dominated the grandstand and bleachers, sustaining a commotion loud enough to deafen half the neighborhood. The Hollywood Legion Band marched in the infield, flag bearers presented arms, drum majorettes twirled two flaming batons at once. California Lieutenant Governor Buron Fitts threw out the first ball. And after the game

Babe climbed up to the top of the stands, from which he hurled a hundred gift baseballs—donated by A.C. Jones, president of the Piggley Wiggley Company —to the massed youngsters on the field. It was a day fit for Hollywood.

In comparison to the audience, the game itself was anticlimactic. Gehrig hit two homers to Ruth's none, and the Larrupin' Lous, which now included a few southern California major leaguers such as Charlie Root and John Rawlings, whipped the Bustin' Babes 5–2. But no one cared. When the activities ended, several thousand boys stood happily on the playing field and cheered their throats raw as their hero made his triumphant way down to the dugout.

The tour officially ended the following day with a game in Long Beach against a team which included George Sisler. After the tumult of Wrigley Field, neither Ruth nor Gehrig could get very worked up about it, and when Walsh encouraged a mob of youthful hero-worshipers onto the field, the stars were only too glad to let them halt the contest. Both Ruth and Gehrig were at the end of their stamina. All they wanted was to go somewhere comfortable and lie down.

Babe remained in Los Angeles for a few days, partly to receive congratulations as the guest of honor at various functions, including the annual Wampus Baby Stars Dinner, partly to sign a few endorsement packages, but mostly to let his hair down after what to him had been the austerity of the trip. While he more or less disappeared from public view, Walsh released a mass of headline-grabbing statistics. In all, Ruth and Gehrig had played, in less than three weeks, twenty-one games in nineteen different cities in eight different states.

According to his calculations, they would have traveled 8,000 miles after completing the return trip and played before more than 200,000 cash customers. Ruth had signed 5,000 autographs and Gehrig slightly fewer. For the record, Babe had come to bat 99 times, delivering 61 hits, of which 20 were home runs, for a batting average of .616. Gehrig's figures were 89 times at bat, 55 hits, and 13 home runs, giving him an average of .618. Both men had played every position except that of catcher.

After the country had a chance to digest those figures, Walsh let the press in on Ruth's financial report for 1927. The barnstorming tour had netted him around $30,000. (Gehrig had received $10,000.) When that sum was added to his other emoluments. Ruth's projected income for the year was as follows: $70,000 in straight salary from the Yankees; $5,500 as his winner's share of the World Series pot; $25,000 from the newspaper columns and related publishing enterprises; and $50,000 for starring in *The Babe Comes Home*. All together, a total of $180,500. To fans all over the country, that inconceivable amount proved once again that there had never been a guy like Ruth.

Had Walsh chosen to reveal the full amount of Ruth's earnings, the fans would have been even more awed. Including personal appearances, endorsements, long-term investments, his ten-percent cut from Yankee exhibition games, and other "quiet" money, Ruth's income must have come close to $300,000. But even if he could have made public those extra sources, Walsh might well have chosen not to do so. Even an adoring fan might begin to wonder if one man, a baseball player at that, could possibly be worth that much money.

At a press conference at the Hotel Roosevelt, Ruth and Gehrig were asked what they intended to do with their tour earnings. Ruth replied that Walsh had convinced him to invest it in an annuity fund so that he would be taken care of in his old age. Off the record, Walsh commented that of all the transactions in which he had guided Ruth, getting him to put away just a small percentage of his income to insure his future solvency had been the most difficult.

Ruth also answered the reporters' question for his teammate. "The keed's giving it all to his mother," he said. The Gehrigs—Lou, Mama, and the slightly doddering Papa Gehrig—had just moved into a new apartment at 133rd Street and Broadway. Mama would find good use for the money.

The reporters asked how they were going to spend the rest of the off-season. "I plan to play a lot of basketball," replied Gehrig. "I ain't doing a thing," Ruth roared. "Except you know what!" Further questioning elicited the printable response that Ruth was contemplating a winter of shooting pool, playing cards, taking in some fights, working out at Artie McGovern's gym down on Vanderbuilt Avenue, and generally resting up for the next season.

"I ain't no kid no more, you know," the Babe pointed out in conclusion, winking broadly at the reporters. "I got to take care of myself."

2

Bad Beginnings

IN THE FALL of 1968, the City of Baltimore decided to tear down the block of South Emory Street, which contained number 216. A group of prominent citizens immediately protested. Few of them had ever actually seen the street, which runs a few short blocks through the shabby old waterfront district south of the new University of Maryland Medical Center, but they all knew what was on it. Somewhere in that Catfish Row of tiny, ancient, brick row houses was Ruth's birthplace. And if that wasn't a Baltimore landmark worth saving, nothing was.

The house, which is really one of four addresses in a single, three-story Federal-style row house, had sat unremarked for many years—for its entire existence, in fact. The Babe had made no sentimental pilgrimages to his place of origin (not surprising in view of the fact that he had never actually resided in the house, it having been his grandfather's home). After his death Claire Ruth, his widow, had come by to take a few photographs, but she had not been followed by busloads of tourists. No historical marker adorned the front, and if the neighbors were aware of what the house had produced, they kept the knowledge to themselves.

By now the place had become a shambles of broken windows, sagging walls, and refuse, long since abandoned to rats and roaches. Its only inhabitants were old drunks who staggered in out of the rain and young addicts looking for a quiet place to shoot up. Across the street a gas-and-electric company installation had wiped out several blocks of old warehouses and tenements, and the high-rise institutions and utilities of downtown Baltimore were rapidly encroaching from the north. Besides, the neighborhood had been solidly black for almost fifty years, and by this time rated at the bottom of even the ghetto sections. Most of its inhabitants were elderly, often illiterate, and not infrequently crippled, mutilated, or just plain sick in the head. Any clear-sighted citizen could see that the whole area was destined to be razed soon. If the Ruth boosters wanted to save the house, they would have to move fast.

A Committee for the Preservation of Babe Ruth's Birthplace quickly formed, with the enthusiastic support of Mayor Thomas D'Alesandro, the Baltimore Oriole Boosters, the Chamber of Commerce, the Citgo Dealers of Greater Baltimore, and other public-spirited groups. Paul Welsh, a genial, service-minded executive of the McCormack Spice Company, was named chairman and took charge of organizing the effort. (Welsh, as it happens, did not know Ruth, or even much about him. He was simply a dedicated Baltimorean—although, like most of his associates, he lives in the Maryland countryside.)

Despite the initial optimism, the task proved tougher than expected. The problem, as Welsh and his colleagues soon discovered, was that nobody in Baltimore seemed to care about preserving the Babe's birthplace. Although they tried a number of fund-raising schemes —selling reproductions of a well-known painting of Ruth, issuing Babe Ruth commemorative coins and histories of his life, creating a "714" club which offered for one hundred dollars, the "sponsorship" of a small wall plaque commemorating one of Ruth's lifetime total of home runs—not many people were interested. In the first five years of the committee's existence only 220 of the home-run plaques were subscribed to, and almost no one collected the coins. But the committee wasn't composed of top business brains for nothing; eventually their efforts paid off, as several local corporations and civic groups, as well as organized baseball, were induced to take up the slack. The necessary money was raised. Structural renovations, costing approximately $130,000, were completed in early 1973. The building, numbers 212–218 S. Emory Street, was completely rebricked and repainted. Its windows and doors were reframed, the foundation recemented, the roof resealed. Today, it shines as it never did since its birth, a splendid example of an early nineteenth-century half-block row house.

Inside, the walls separating the original houses were ripped out, and the interior redone in a kind of Danish modern museum style. Small exhibits and meeting rooms are tastefully mixed, much in the manner you would expect in a gallery devoted to Persian miniatures. A stairway, the railing of which is made of Louisville Slugger duplicates of Ruth's bats, leads to a second-floor balcony and a circular projection booth. The new walls are painted a gleaming white, the carpet is a rich green. When the home-run plaques are fully subscribed they will cover all three walls of a central room. Pictures of Ruth in action will be everywhere in evidence, and changed often. There will also be autographed balls, old uniforms, and other baseball paraphernalia.

The original outlines have been left standing only in the section of the shrine which demonstrates how the place looked when Ruth was born. But even there the fireplace, walls, and stairs have been newly rebuilt, and the period furniture that has been installed—a sideboard, an overstuffed wing chair, an antique table— looks rather nice. Old-fashioned, but comfortable. Not a bad place to live even today. The kind of place that would be called an elegant townhouse if it were somewhere else.

Unfortunately, the rest of the neighborhood still conforms to what it has been for generations. The other house on the short block has conspicuously not been renovated. It remains a squalid, half tarpaper shack, half crumbling brick wreck of a building, with windows of chicken wire and roaches two inches long. A rotting wooden stairway leads up the side, and garbage and empty wine bottles are its main decorative touches. It is lived in, of course. With so many houses being torn down, living space is scarce. Welsh and the other members of the committee don't like it, but there's nothing they can do about it just now.

The surrounding streets also remain the same—a bewildering tangle of alleys and pavement lined with long rows of brightly colored, incredibly tiny (six feet by eight feet is a large room) two-story disintegrating brick tenements, more like cages than houses, a sort of pastel Bogside. Old people sit on many of the two-step stoops, staring vacantly at nothing in particular. Broken glass and rusting junk cover the footpaths like a hall runner. The sidewalks are broken and uneven. Not a single tree is visible for blocks. The view from any street corner, in any direction, is abruptly terminated by another row of tenements slicing through at an odd angle, leaving the impression of an enormous prison complex or a concrete maze from which there is no hope of escape.

And the people in the streets are the same kind of people who always walked the streets in the tenderloin, as it was called three generations ago, when Ruth was born there—the same kind of people who live in every desperately poor slum in any generation. For every child there is a drunk or a crazy staggering along the street, exposing himself or pissing on the side of a house. For every hard-working mother there are a half dozen who have given up hope. And for every healthy body there are ten people with rotting teeth, marled eyes, crooked bones, or illnesses that they don't even know enough to recognize.

Anger and frustration are palpably present in the streets. Women fight; furious men barge out of back-yards raging incoherently, old winos flare up, mothers beat their children, kids smash windows and bottles. Irrationality is everywhere. Stupid, unpleasant things happen for no reason, without the slightest warning. (As Paul Welsh and I left the Ruth house a ragged, drooling middle-aged man limped down the street toward us, urinating no-handed as he lurched along. He stopped, insisted upon shaking Welsh's hand, then limped on.) But that, of course, is the way slums are. Even slums where national heroes are born.

The Baltimore waterfront was no more enticing in the 1890s than it is today. Geographically, it began at the wharves on the western side of Back Basin, in the southern tier of the city. From there it extended west for about two miles to the gigantic Baltimore and Ohio railyards at Camden Station. Immediately to the north, across the grimy B & O tracks, lay the major mercantile establishments and the fashionable hotel and theater center. Beyond that began the burgeoning middle- and upper-class residential sections, virtually a foreign country to waterfront residents. To the south the city petered out into the backwater of Federal Hill—once a thriving commercial district, but long since moribund. The line between the good and bad parts of town (literally the right and wrong side of the tracks) ran east and west along Lombard Street or Pratt Street, depending upon how fastidious one was. But no one in a position to choose spent any time south of Pratt Street.

Life on the waterfront consisted mainly of a battle for survival—commercial and personal. Victims of street and industrial accidents wore a frequent trail to City Hospital, which, in H. L. Mencken's description, sometimes resembled a "battlefield." (Mencken was a reporter on the *Baltimore Herald* papers from 1899 to 1906, and on the staff of the *Sun* papers from 1906 on. His memoirs constitute the best description of Baltimore in those days.) "Razor parties and drownings" accounted for much of the area's social life. Fire broke out often and burned until the horse-drawn engines managed to clear a path through the confusion. Garbage, animal and human waste, and stagnant water lay where it fell or was thrown. Dead bodies were another feature of the neighborhood, courtesy of the city morgue, which was located at the end of one of the municipal docks. On a good day you could see a half-dozen floaters drying out in the sun, their condition depending upon how long they had been in the water before being fished out.

On February 6, 1895, Kate Ruth, nee Kate Schamberger, gave birth to a son on the third floor of the house on South Emory Street. The boy was named George Herman Ruth, Jr., after his father. Both parents were of mainly German descent, with some Irish blood on the side of George Herman Ruth, Sr., and both had lived all their lives within a few blocks of the wharves. George Ruth was then in his early twenties, and his wife not quite twenty. In *The Babe Ruth Story,* Ruth's as-told-to-Bob-Considine autobiography (actually ghostwritten by sportswriter Fred Lieb), Ruth mentions an older brother named John, who died very young. But the Baltimore city registry records show that John was born after Babe. In subsequent years six more children appeared in the Ruth household, but only one of them, Mayme, born in 1900, survived to adulthood. The others died in infancy or soon afterward from the usual childhood diseases, exacerbated by malnutrition and wretched care. Not much is known about them, and they seem to have made little impression on their older brother.

Most of the boy's early life was spent in a flat above a saloon at 426 Camden Street, in the very depths of the worst part of the waterfront area. In articles about Ruth the saloon is usually referred to as his father's saloon, but it is unclear whether the senior Ruth actually owned it or just worked there. Apparently it was a typical waterfront dive, filled with riffraff from all over the world, the scene of innumerable bloody fights and drunken collapses.

Mayme, the only person alive today with any first-hand knowledge of the family, paints a picture of a happy household in which everyone got along fine and cared deeply for one another. From all other accounts, however, the Ruth household seems to have been an angry, violent, desperately poor place, tense with all the frustrations of extreme poverty and shabbiness. Kate Ruth, daughter of a penniless German immigrant upholsterer, was a plain woman given to frequent hysterics, plagued by ill health, and emotionally unable to cope with the overwhelming problems facing her.

Martin Weldon, a sportswriter who wrote a biography of Ruth in the 1940s, reports that people remembered her as "a pleasant woman, but apparently not a particularly devoted mother. Often ill, . . . mainly she left the boy to shift for himself." Lee Allen, in his chapter on Ruth in *The American League Story,* quotes a cousin of Mrs. Ruth: "When the boy was home, she used to strike him over the head and otherwise abuse him." Other snippets of memory, containing similar comments, can be found in many of the magazine pieces done on Ruth while he was alive, particularly in the 1930s.

Most of her time was spent tending bar in the saloon. George, Jr., was on his own almost from birth. He could find his own food on the floor and learn to talk as best he could from the screams of family arguments and the curses of his father's customers. Ruth himself provides the best testimony in this regard. *The Babe Ruth Story* flatly states: "I hardly knew my parents." And although Kate Ruth lived until her oldest son was seventeen years old, nowhere in the book, or in any other place, did Ruth ever make even a pro forma protestation of his mother's affection for him or his for her. For a man whose mind ran almost exclusively to sentimental cliché throughout his life, that omission is the most telling of evidence. What little care the boy received came from his maternal grandparents. He spoke German before he spoke English, and in fact he barely understood the latter until he started school.

George Ruth, Sr., is a less shadowy figure than his wife, but nowhere in all the millions of words written about Ruth is anything good said about his father. Although he and his oldest son were so closely matched physically that a stranger might have mistaken them for twins, the only other visible marks of his paternity were his son's bruises and scars. The elder Ruth, a sallow-faced, heavyset man, was considered a heavy-drinking brawler by all who knew him, a man whose first impulse was to trample anything that got in his way. His uncontrollable temper, combined with near illiteracy, made him a failure at every job he attempted— butcher, gripman, carter, installer of lightning rods, and finally bartender and saloonkeeper. His frustrations exploded in every direction, more often than not at his wife and children. According to Weldon's informants, he was often seen beating his son with a billiard cue. And while Kate would wail and shriek, there was no stopping her husband when he got started.

A short news item in the *Baltimore Sun* of August 26, 1918, sums up George Herman Ruth, Sr., as well as anything could. The story is actually a report of the elder Ruth's death, which resulted from a fight with his brother-in-law over the mistreatment of a sixteen-year-old girl who was staying with the Ruths. The brother-in-law, Benjamin Sipes (Kate Ruth was dead by then, and Ruth had married a woman named Martha Sipes), told the police and reporters what happened: ". . . Ruth emerged from the side entrance of the saloon and approached him. Sipes said Ruth walked up and hit him on the cheek. He reeled and another blow felled him. While on the pavement, he says Ruth kicked him, but he managed to get up and struck Ruth." That blow knocked Ruth down, and in falling he smacked his head against the stone curb, fatally fracturing his skull. Since Ruth had started the fracas and Sipes was a much smaller man anyway, the police called it justifiable self-defense and brought no charges against him. People who knew George Ruth nodded when they heard about it. Most of them felt he was lucky to have survived this long.

Well, it was a tough way for a kid to start life. "Ruth . . . was the product of a childhood so bleak that it was almost no childhood at all," wrote Roger Kahn, and every other biographer and historian has agreed with those sentiments. "The adults he looked up to and sought to imitate were the Chesapeake Bay steve-

dores and oyster dredges who frequented the saloon.
. . . His earliest mental images were of scouring
the congested streets for scraps of contraband and
food, of running from cops, of prowling in gangs and
fighting other gangs, of dodging the legs of plunging
truck horses," comments Weldon. Lee Allen, the former
historian at the National Baseball Library, adds: "By
the time he was seven he could chew tobacco and swear
like a sea captain's parrot." Ruth himself, as transcribed
by Considine/Lieb, had made the most poignant statement about his early life. "I was a bad kid," are the first
words of *The Babe Ruth Story.* It goes on to affirm:
"When I wasn't living over it [the Camden Street
saloon] I was living in it, studying the rough talk of the
longshoremen, merchant sailors, roustabouts and waterfront bums. . . . I had a rotten start and it took me a
long time to get my bearings."

From all accounts, life for the young boy seems, as it
does for most "abandoned" children, to have been a bewildering mixture of abrupt changes and inexplicable
demands both at home and on the street. Unexpected,
incomprehensible storms of anger broke over his head
no matter where he went—from his parents, from adults
he pestered in the streets, from storekeepers, from older
boys. New brothers and sisters appeared at home and
died off before he even got to know them. The family
repeatedly changed living quarters within the neighborhood; between 1895 and 1906, various sources, including the city directory, record at least nine different addresses for the Ruths. One dislocation followed another
with a speed that must have left the boy bewildered.
And there was still worse to come.

On June 13, 1902, Kate Ruth packed her son's
threadbare clothes in a cardboard suitcase, and the sev-
en-year-old boy and his father climbed aboard the Wilkens Avenue electric trolley. Something less than an
hour's ride brought them to the southwestern outskirts
of the city. Alighting at the corner of Wilkens and Caton
Avenues, in the midst of cow pastures and vacant fields,

they faced a set of gray, prisonlike brick and stone buildings surrounded by a high wall. Inside the gate, a large, scruffy playing field could be seen to the left of a three-story, factory-style stone building. In the field a number of boys, all wearing identical dark denim overalls, marched about in military drill, led by a few no-nonsense-looking men dressed in the full-length black gowns of the Xaverian Order. The sign on the front gate read "St. Mary's Industrial School."

Keeping firm hold of his arm, George Ruth dragged his son through the gates. The boy was terrified. Even at seven he knew a reformatory when he saw one. But his screams made no impression on either his father or the superintendent. As a teenager, Ruth told Louis "Fats" Leisman, a "classmate" at St. Mary's, that he had cried his head off that day, and when his father left he knew that "it would be a long time before he saw any of his relations again." Leisman, a well-known figure on the fringes of Baltimore sports life for many years, recorded the conversation in a disingenuous, sentimental, clumsily written but completely convincing memoir of his "school" days with Ruth written in 1956, entitled *I Was with Babe Ruth at St. Mary's.* (Years earlier, another former inmate of St. Mary's told Fred Lieb a very similar story about Ruth's first days at the school.)

Whether or not the teenage Ruth was speaking in hindsight is impossible to know, but his foreboding was proved exactly right. There is no evidence that any member of his family ever did visit him during all the years that he spent behind the walls at St. Mary's. If Leisman's memory is to be trusted, he recalls mentioning to Ruth in 1912 that he hadn't seen his ill mother in two years. Ruth's reply, undoubtedly laundered by and put into proper English by Leisman, was "You're lucky, Fats. It's been ten years since I've seen my father."

Poignant as that statement sounds, it is somewhat misleading. In fact, Ruth did not spend his entire middle childhood and adolescence in St. Mary's. In 1919 a fire destroyed much of the institution, including the administration and records building, but Ruth's own account indicates that he was taken home only a month after that traumatic leave-taking in June. In November 1902 he was returned to St. Mary's, and then released a few weeks later when his family moved to a new house in South Baltimore. After a year at home he went back to St. Mary's and remained there until 1908. In that year he was removed again, then sent back several months later to stay another three years. By 1911 an overworked, increasingly sick Kate Ruth had become too weak to help out in the saloon and George, Jr., was again taken out and put to work behind the bar. After his mother died the following year he went back once more, to stay inside until his final release in 1914. Although Ruth himself was never quite sure of the specific dates, Leisman corroborates the later ones, and there is no reason to doubt the general accuracy of the others.

At least it is certain that he was in and out of St. Mary's several times during those years. One day his father would appear and sign him out; then another day would arrive when he would get back on the Wilkens Avenue trolley, sentenced to another indefinite stay. He was given no hint of impending release, and he probably received as little warning when he was being sent back. From all indications, he was returned whenever the family got fed up with having him around, and sprung when his mother's unpredictable temperament indicated a desire to see him or when his father needed help around the bar. "Kate used to cry and ask her husband to get him out," says the unnamed cousin interviewed by Lee Allen. But once he was out, she quickly lost interest in the boy.

And during the nine years Ruth spent at St. Mary's no one ever walked through the shiny iron gate and up the front drive to greet him on the one Sunday a month visitors were allowed. Perhaps the best evidence of this is that Ruth, as an adult, never mentioned the subject to anyone. His autobiography also ignores it. Leisman's teenage conversations with Ruth, remembered forty years later, are the only words that exist on the subject. And while they sound rather low-grade literary ("Babe would kid me: 'Well, I guess I am too big and ugly for anyone to come to see me. Maybe the next time.' But the next time never came."), Leisman is emphatic about the situation they describe. Since we know from former teammates that no relatives or friends ever came to see him play with the Baltimore Orioles after he left St. Mary's, and that only once in his career as a star with the Red Sox did his father attend a game, Leisman is probably right.

A great deal has been written about St. Mary's, all of it sentimental and laudatory. Not surprisingly, most of its eulogists have never even set eyes on the place, even if they wrote before it was razed in the 1950s. If they had, they might have tempered their enthusiasm. Founded in 1866, supported by the City of Baltimore and the Xaverian Order, the institution's official name was St. Mary's Industrial School for Orphans, Delinquent, Incorrigible, and Wayward Boys. There being a substantial number of such unfortunates in Baltimore (many of its boys combined elements of all four categories), the school was quickly filled to more than capacity. Soon after it opened, the St. Mary's population reached seven hundred, ranging in age from five to twenty-one, the legal age of release. It remained around that number until 1907, when the addition of a new dormitory wing brought the total up to more than eleven hundred.

St. Mary's served two purposes: to get the juvenile delinquents off the streets (and out of the sight of better-off Baltimoreans) and then to do what it could do to straighten them out. In the eyes of the municipal government there was no doubt that the first goal was paramount. The 1880 Baltimore Sesquicentennial Memorial Volume referred to the home as a "moral hospital, which treats poor maimed souls and deeply wounded spiritual natures in the same incisive way . . . that our surgeons use in dealing with the wounds and inposthumes of the body." The Annual Catalogue and Report of the institution, in a preface repeated many times over the years, inclined more toward the second approach: "Thus many young unfortunates are cast upon the world, and would most likely be lost, if we extended not to them the hand of charity. Hence, it is easy to see that the best institutions which can become substitutes for family government, are industrial schools." In practice, the two aims were complementary. The head brother was as much a warden as a headmaster. And when he used the term "government," he did not mean "democracy."

St. Mary's may have been many things to many people, but no one would have denied that first of all it was tough—tough as nails, a medium-security prison for children. High walls surrounded the campus, and guards patrolled the gates day and night. "Release," the official term for getting out, meant precisely that. There were only two ways out—through the front gate in the official custody of a responsible adult, or over the walls in one's own custody. When a boy tried the latter course, as happened regularly, the school truant officer and the guards charged off in pursuit. And since the boy usually headed straight for his old neighborhood, he was usually recaptured in a day or two.

Physical punishment and mortification of the body formed the basis for order at the school. Severe "problem cases" were put in solitary confinement. Less serious falls from grace received military-style punishment, which often meant long hours and days of standing in one place in the yard, regardless of the weather, or marching endlessly in one of the school drill squads. (A side result of this regime was that the drill squads were noted throughout Baltimore for their precise discipline. In the great sesquicentennial parade, St. Mary's boys were given pride of place ahead of even the military academies.)

Tough as the kids were at St. Mary's, the brothers were tougher. Especially Brother Mathias. God help you if the the wrath of Brother Mathias, the prefect of discipline, fell on your head. Brother Mathias was a broad-shouldered, long-faced giant of a man, six feet six and nearly three hundred pounds, with a palm that could strike like thunder against the side of a boy's head. Challenging his authority was tantamount to spitting out the communion wafer before the Holy Inquisition.

Judging by the stories told both by Catholic propagandists and by many sportswriters (two occupations which frequently merge), the good brothers ruled by reason and example, rarely raising their voices, and then only to gently admonish their adoring charges. But one anonymous alumnus of St. Mary's, talking to Tom Meany in the 1920s, just shook his head in wonderment over the image St. Mary's had gotten since his and Ruth's time. "You know," he said, "either Babe's gone soft or I've gone nuts. But I hafta laugh when I hear that place mentioned as the 'home.' All I know is that there was guys with guns on the walls."

The curriculum at St. Mary's was divided between devotional and vocational training. Although they accepted occasional "Hebrews and other non-Catholics," the brothers made a strong effort to cement the souls of their charges as firmly as possible in the mortar of the Church. All boys attended chapel every morning, as well as High Mass on Sundays and other holidays.

The Saints' Days were rigorously observed. Catechism and confirmation studies were mandatory. And statistics worthy of an IBM computer were kept on the measurable degrees of devotion. In 1911, at which time the school boasted a population of 1,128 boys, the Chaplain's Report affirmed that in the previous year there were "30 Baptisms, 101 First Holy Communions, 126 Confirmations, 114 received into the Sodality of B.V.M., 227 received into the Holy Name Society, 17,951 confessions heard, 58,314 communions received —and the moral conduct of the boys has improved over fifty percent."

One of those Hebrews who allegedly received the benefits of St. Mary's schooling was a belligerent Russian-born youngster whose name had been anglicized to Al Jolson. Who can forget the heartwarming scenes in *The Jolson Story* of a young and frightened Jewish boy being selected for the chapel choir by the prescient and understanding Father McGee? Certainly not the popular Catholic press, which has long since featured and embroidered the story as an example of brotherhood and tolerance. The actual facts present a somewhat different picture. As far as can be ascertained, Jolson's brief stay at St. Mary's occurred sometime in 1897 or 1898, when he was eleven or twelve. Apprehended by the police in the Baltimore railroad station on one of his many runaways, he was committed to St. Mary's as a wayward boy and did not take kindly to the experience. In his own words, spoken to his wife while they were taking a look at the old place in 1948, quoted in Michael Freeland's recent biography: "The gate's open. It was always shut when I was here. Once I hit a boy on the stairs, coming down from chapel. They put me in solitary. That's bad enough. But to look out the window—watch the others playing—well, honey, I screamed and hollered until I ran a temperature." How long the boy soprano stayed at St. Mary's is unclear, but it was no great length of time. As soon as the police located Rabbi Yoelson in Washington, he came to take him out. If Jolson's reminiscence in 1948 did not have such a ring of authenticity, a good case could be made for dismissing the whole episode as fantasy. It appears definite that he was briefly locked up in Baltimore at some time during this period, however, and it was common policy to send such cases to places like St. Mary's.

(In the twenties and thirties Ruth often informed interviewers in apparent seriousness that he had first met old Al at the "home," and remembered him well from that time, a somewhat unlikely occurrence in view of the fact that Babe had just turned three at the time of Jolson's supposed incarceration. In some Jolson biographies a third figure is added to this friendship of future greats—none other than Bojangles Robinson, the great black dancer. To picture the three of them frolicking through a high-spirited childhood at St. Mary's Industrial Home for wayward white Catholic boys challenges the imagination of the most dedicated brotherhood romantic.)

The principle on which St. Mary's based its academic program is described in an article on the institution entitled "They Reared Babe Ruth," in the *Catholic Digest* of September 1938: "Many of the boys do not have the mental capacity to absorb their studies. The brothers have found that education, as it is standardized today, often sweeps over these boys and they become discouraged at their own helplessness. The brothers do not force studies on such cases. Instead they are placed in one of the school shops to learn a trade."

Most of the boys did struggle through grade four, at least formally confronting such elementary school subjects as reading, geography, math, Bible history, American history, and spelling. After the fourth grade the great majority left the classroom for the shops to begin learning their trades. For those boys who might benefit by further exploration into academic discipline, the annual report proudly acknowledged the availability of reading, physiology, and rudimentary bookkeeping up to a sixth-grade level. And on the rare occasions when a boy managed to impress the brothers with his intellectual promise, he was sent to Mount St. Joseph, a nearby academic high school.

Not much was expected in the classrooms, nor was much achieved. The classes were overcrowded. Materials were obtained from out-of-date stocks, which were of poor quality to begin with. Minimal lighting and uncomfortable, stiff, high-backed desks virtually piled on top of each other further discouraged the students. Few of the teaching brothers had any more than devotional qualifications, anyway. Pictures of the old classrooms show the walls plastered with religious icons and edifying moralisms to the exclusion of any other teaching aids. "A young man idle is an old man needy" seems to have been the reigning favorite. To have profited academically, or even to have reached a level equal to that of an average student on the outside, would have been a herculean task. Those who accomplished it must have been few and far between.

The main effort at St. Mary's was directed along vocational lines. Over the years the school had built up a substantial plant consisting of several factory-size buildings. They included a bakery, carpentry shop, print shop, shirt and shoe-making establishments, a greenhouse, a farm, a laundry, and training centers for painting, plumbing, and masonry. Virtually all of the school maintenance work took place there. Repairs to the institution were made by the boys, clothes were washed in the laundry, and publications were printed by the print shop. Besides these duties, the trainees also performed jobs for outside businesses, which contracted for them with the school.

That all sounds quite commendably like the work-study programs found today in many colleges and high schools. But in real life it meant eleven- and twelve-year-old boys spending several hours a day in hot, noisy, cramped factories, full of dangerous machinery, for little material reward. "Sweat shop" might be a more reasonable description of the training shops, at least as far as the younger boys were concerned.

The trade to which any given boy was assigned presumably depended to some extent upon his aptitudes. Often, however, he was simply put where there was a vacant place. Ruth, who, if his adult capacities are any indication, had emerged from the classroom barely able to read or write, was shunted off to the shirt factory with other boys who showed no noticeable promise for the more difficult trades. He spent several years making cuffs on the third floor, known around the yard as the "high city tailor" to distinguish it from the second floor, called the "low city tailor" and devoted to the production of collars. Leisman did a bit better, spending his time in the print shop, learning how to set type. The best-off boys were the ones who managed to get themselves assigned to the greenhouses.

Rising at six, the boys washed, attended chapel, ate breakfast, and were in their classrooms or at their machines and work benches by eight. They worked or studied until lunchtime, then, after a break, returned to their tasks. At certain specified hours of the afternoon, depending upon the boys' ages, they finished for the day and were excused to play until supper. After supper they attended chapel again and were expected to be in their beds by eight. Interspersed in those hours were various devotional duties and such extracurricular activities as existed—mainly playing in the band or singing in the chapel choir.

If he wanted to, a boy could work overtime to pile up extra credits for candy at the commissary, a little stone building open one hour each evening. That represented the one possibility of an extra treat that St. Mary's offered. On Sundays and holidays the discipline relaxed slightly, particularly when they coincided with the monthly visiting days. And many of the boys were released to their families during Christmas and other special times of the year. (But George Ruth, after his first year, was never one of them.)

Aside from those concessions, the rules were inflexible: work until the afternoon, spend at least two hours out of doors regardless of the temperature (the brothers were firm believers in the efficacy of exercise to dispel unhealthy thoughts), sit down to dinner in one of the huge dining halls, say your prayers, and then to bed.

It wasn't so bad; after all, as any sensible person would have argued at the time, three square meals a day, clothes on their backs, an opportunity to learn a trade, and few chances to get into bad trouble was a good deal more than most of the St. Mary's boys would have received on the outside.

But St. Mary's was still a prison. Those boys who entered with reasonably secure psyches might receive some valuable training and survive well enough. But for the others—the neglected, sick, half-wild incorrigibles who had been thrown in as a last resort—it represented nothing less than a death camp of the spirit. If you could meet them halfway, the brothers probably wouldn't hurt you, and conceivably might help. But if you were unable to meet them halfway—if you didn't even know where halfway was or how to get there—only a miracle could allow you to emerge a whole person.

Understaffing in particular destroyed any possibility of meeting the most pressing need of many of the boys —an adult with whom to establish and maintain a warm, personal relationship. Ruth always made a great deal out of his supposed intimacy with Brother Mathias ("It was at St. Mary's that I met and learned to love the greatest man I've ever known," although sometimes he slipped and opted for Brothers Herman, Gilbert, or Paul as the greatest influences in his life), but the chance that any very close relationship actually existed between them is almost nil. Brother Mathias had to serve as a father-figure to a thousand boys. His disciplinary duties, as well as the absolute necessity of maintaining an even-handed attitude, precluded a very close relationship with any particular boy. He may have had a profound influence on Ruth, but it is more likely that that influence grew in proportion to Ruth's distance, in time, from the school—and in proportion to sportswriters' demands for heartwarming copy about his past. (In Robert Smith's *Baseball,* to quote one example among thousands extolling Ruth's father-son relationship with Brother Mathias, he states: "Hour after hour the big man and the slender [?] boy would play the game [batting fungoes for fielding practice] in the school yard. . . ." But what were the other eleven hundred boys supposed to do while their leader played with his protégé? Somehow it just doesn't seem likely.) The men who knew Ruth during his first few years in the majors do not recall any glowing testimonials along that line.

The boys at St. Mary's lived in an undifferentiated herd. Each one of the three sleeping dorms consisted of a huge central chamber on each floor, in which scores of steel frame beds were lined up head to foot in long rows across the room. In those rooms no possibility of privacy existed—merely going to the bathroom meant passing dozens of wisecracking boys. Any kind of nightmare, minor illness, personal humiliation, or private misery was necessarily revealed to a large crowd of interested outsiders, or else bottled up inside. The normal sexual curiosities and explorations of teenage boys became a group endeavor or were rigorously suppressed. There was nothing, not even the smallest personal touch, to differentiate one boy's few square feet from another's. A bunk in an army barracks would have seemed like a private suite by comparison.

Everyone ate together in huge dining rooms. They attended chapel and school in large groups, and stood in long lines for everything from confession to candy. Blue shirts and overalls were mandatory for everyone, all the time. Outside, every corner of the not-very-extensive grounds could be seen from somewhere else, and there was always another person or persons nearby no matter where a boy went. Except for required religious silences or solitary quarantine, almost every moment of the day involved a crowded, noisy, and ritualized activity. To go off and think quietly by yourself, or even to read a racing form or dirty book in peace, was next to impossible. Not even the toilet stalls had doors on them, the better to protect against evil thoughts or deeds in those situations.

The boys dealt with the problem in many ways: by misbehaving, fighting, running away, and the countless other methods kids have always used to draw attention to themselves. Another solution was in the ascription of nicknames to each other. "Fats" Leisman, in the course of his history, mentions boys nicknamed Congo, Skinny, Ike, Lefty, Loads, Reds, and Yellow, and refers to only three boys by their given names. Ruth's nickname, given to him soon after he first entered St. Mary's, was "Nigger," along with its usual variations of "Nig," and "Nigger Lips." Leisman customarily called him the last of these. (Earle Combs recalls a former St. Mary's boy coming into the Yankee locker room once after an exhibition game to shoot the breeze with the Babe. He jokingly asked Ruth if he remembered how they always used to call him "Nig" back in the old days. But Ruth emphatically denied any memory of the nickname and changed the subject.)

There was one activity that made up for a lot of the hardship, however. The boys could always play baseball. Virtually everyone at St. Mary's, from Brother Paul, the head brother, to the newest five-year-old incorrigible, was loony about baseball.

The brothers, recognizing the value of outdoor activities and the morale-building nature of the game, encouraged the boys to play in every spare moment. Competition was organized for every age group. Eight-year-olds played against eight-year-olds, dorms against dorms, and the varsity and junior varsity ("sophomores" and "freshmen") against other Catholic schools and reformatories. Much of the recreation budget went into uniforms, equipment, and the like. There was even a travel allowance, used to transport the various school teams to the diamonds of other schools for big games. During Ruth's last years at St. Mary's there were forty-three separate teams in existence, each with its own uniforms. Everyone played—a boy could no more not play baseball at St. Mary's than not eat. (Those inevitable few who did not find baseball the most engrossing pastime ever invented, or who were hopelessly clumsy, must have suffered the agony of the damned. But no mention of such unnatural creatures has ever been discovered in connection with St. Mary's.)

Baseball madness was not limited to this obscure reform school on the outskirts of Baltimore, Maryland, of course; the entire nation was crazy for the game. The 1880s found a floodtide of baseball enthusiasm sweeping almost every square inch of American territory. Baseball traveled with the homesteaders and prospectors up every new mountain and into every virgin valley. Probably the two most recognizable signposts of the firm establishment of a new community were a whorehouse and a ball field, one as rough as the other. By the turn of the century baseball had become part of the national self-image, a sign of the peculiar American character. In "Birches," Robert Frost could yearn wistfully for "Some boy too far from town to learn baseball," but he wasn't likely to know any.

As the frontier closed, the playing of baseball came to serve as a civilized substitute for the action of the Wild West in the imaginations of Americans. It was no coincidence that Bat Masterson—Bat Masterson of Dodge City, colleague of Earp and Tilghman, hero of the Comanche uprising at Adobe Walls, the man who stopped the Gray County War just when it seemed likely to depopulate southwestern Kansas merely by sending a telegram threatening to come in person—spent his last twenty years as a sportswriter and sports editor with the *New York Morning Telegraph.* Nor was it surprising that Zane Grey had been a professional ballplayer before he found his true métier, and between grinding out western potboilers wrote equally exciting boys' baseball adventures.

So they played baseball at St. Mary's, as they did everywhere else. Nothing was as important to the boys, and possibly to the brothers as well. After all, the Baltimore Orioles of the 1890s had been the most glamorous of all baseball teams up to that time. Men such as Wee Willie Keeler, Dan Brouthers, Uncle Wilbert Robinson, John McGraw, Kid Gleason, and Hughie Jennings were among the greatest of heroes in the eyes of Baltimore citizens, rivaled only by Grover Cleveland and Teddy Roosevelt. Baltimore was a big league city until 1903, and even after its bitterly contested demotion to the minors it remained a passionately committed baseball hotspot. And possibly no people in Baltimore were hotter for the game than the boys and brothers of St. Mary's Industrial School. They didn't have other pleasures to divert them.

One of these boys was this tall, muscular, moon-faced kid nicknamed "Nigger Lips" Ruth. A dumb kid, who spoke mostly in monosyllables and swearwords, who could barely read or write his own name. Not a bad kid at heart, generally good-natured and gregarious in a crude, conventional way, although given to childish rages when things went wrong and unable to accept criticism without sulking or starting trouble. A kid who often seemed to be somehow out of tune with everyone else, who never seemed to be able to absorb instructions, to whom something came naturally or didn't come at all.

All in all, a boy with more than the average share of problems, probably destined to end up no different than his father, or in jail, or in some other kind of trouble. The first time a cop crossed him, or a bookie demanded his money, or he was bounced from a job, would be the beginning of the end. There were kids like him in gutters and jail cells all around the country.

Except, the brothers observed, this boy could play baseball. He could do things on a ball field that no one at St. Mary's had ever dreamed a kid could do. Other good athletes had passed through the gates at the institution, including at least three future major leaguers besides Ruth, but none of them remotely approached his ability. No one even tried to coach him. Just running out onto the field he seemed to be traveling on a different plane from the other boys. His body reacted in ways that bordered on the supernatural. No ball could be hit past him, no throw was too hard for him to scoop up with a graceful flick of his glove. From the first he seemed to have every move down pat, no matter what position he played.

And if skill wasn't enough, he had stamina as well. A sickly mother and drink-fattened father had somehow produced a child with the strength of a real-life John Henry. He could not be worn down. He never got tired. Long after every other boy had fallen from exhaustion, Ruth would be as fresh as the moment he had begun.

At first the prodigy was usually put behind the plate, where he could use his amazing throwing arm against baserunners attempting to steal. Equipment being in short supply, he was outfitted with a right-handed catcher's mitt despite being a lefty. When a baserunner took off for second, Ruth would catch the pitch, shift the ball to his right hand, shake off the glove, shift the ball back to his left hand, and then rifle it down to second, almost always in time to nail the runner. It appar-

ently never occurred to him that such a complicated series of motions before releasing the ball should make
catching the runner all but impossible. And although
many people are inclined to dismiss this exploit as one
more press agent's invention, early pictures of Ruth
wearing the right-handed glove bear it out.

And when he stood up at the plate and swung his bat,
the first reaction of the kids in the field was to dive for
cover. Even the soft, lopsided mushball used until it dis-
integrated by the St. Mary's nines became a cannon shot
when Ruth connected. Several times during his St.
Mary's career he hit balls that carried well over four
hundred feet on the fly, an accomplishment few major
leaguers of the time could boast. In later years big
league ballplayers were to stand in open-mouthed awe
as incredible blasts from Ruth's bat soared over their
heads. The incredulity of teenagers from visiting teams
seeing the same thing must have been enormous.

Around the age of seventeen he transferred his talents
to the mound. None of the other inmates has recorded
his sentiments at batting against the new pitcher, but
they could not have been especially happy at the prospect. No more than a half-dozen major league stars
could throw a ball with more speed on it than the ones
Ruth threw from the mound at St. Mary's. (Three
weeks after leaving St. Mary's, at the age of nineteen, he
struck out Home Run Baker and Eddie Collins twice
each in an exhibition game against the world champion
Philadelphia Athletics.) If a boy got on base it was due
either to a lucky swing or a loss of concentration on
Ruth's part. In his last full season at St. Mary's, George,
Jr., did not lose a single game—no small accomplishment in view of the erratic fielding, umpiring, and playing conditions common at that level of baseball.

At St. Mary's Ruth must have also had an early taste
of the exhilaration that stardom brings. Being the best
player in an institution single-mindedly devoted to playing baseball clearly set him apart from all the other
boys. For the first time in his life he became the center
of someone's attention. During his last years at St.

Mary's, the coaches at other Catholic institutions, including the exclusive Mount St. Joseph, often begged the brothers to let their star be briefly transferred to their rolls in order to pitch for them in important games. The brothers, intent on protecting their own roster and also aware that once they let Ruth go they might never see him again, always found excuses to keep him at home. But all that flattering attention certainly did not escape the boy's notice.

The presence of an audience somehow seemed to transform George's personal crudities into uproarious crowd-pleasers. A piece of film taken during his playing days at the institution (incorporated into *The Glory of their Times,* a compilation of film clips following the narrative of Lawrence Ritter's book) shows him hotdogging for all he was worth at the plate—licking his fingers, pulling up his sleeves, ominously eyeing the pitcher, and throwing frequent glances back at the stands to see how the boys were taking it. And, of course, the boys seemed to holler like mad every time he did it.

By 1913 Ruth's abilities were drawing comment even outside the world of Catholic high school athletics. News of local prodigies traveled fast in Baltimore, a hotbed of professional baseball. Employees, former players, and even fans of the Orioles (then a triple A team playing in the International League) kept a sharp eye out for any youngster with potential. One of these unofficial scouts tipped off Jack Dunn, the battle-wise Oriole manager, about a big, smoke-throwing left-hander at St. Mary's Industrial School. Tom Meany divides credit for the discovery between Joe Engel, a Washington Senator pitcher who had seen Ruth on the mound in a game against another reform school (Engel's alma mater), and Brother Gilbert of St. Mary's, who is said to have written to Dunn about the boy.

The tip could have come from any of a dozen different sources, but more than likely someone at St. Mary's had been tossing Ruth's name around. By the 1913 season the boy was thought to be approaching twenty (actually he was only eighteen, but a mistake in recording his date of birth, not corrected until many years later, had added an extra year to his life). It was time to do something with him. He hadn't learned much at the school, but there was no point in continuing the struggle. In many ways he had outgrown St. Mary's. For in those days the boy was a giant—six feet two, almost one hundred ninety pounds of hard muscle. His boundless energy was becoming difficult to contain. Even clothes for his oversized frame were difficult to find. And on the ball field he now played so differently from the other players that it was like watching two separate teams.

In any event, Dunn and the brothers made contact, and the Oriole manager motored out to St. Mary's. One popular account has him signing up Ruth immediately after watching him skating in the icy yard during February of 1913 or 1914. But it is unlikely that such a shrewd operator would take a chance on an unknown quantity merely on the say-so of a few tipsters and a brief observation of his sliding skill. Apparently he did express interest in the big kid, as well as in some other boys whose names he had come across in various reports, and suggested that if a game could be set up for him to observe, maybe something would come of it.

So a game was arranged, with Mount St. Joseph's as the opponent. Both Leisman and Ruth recall a good deal of finagling taking place around this time, because Dunn was also interested in Mount St. Joseph's star pitcher, probably a boy named Bill Morrisette. (Ruth gives his rival's name as Ford Meadows, but that name never appears anywhere else. Morrisette, who definitely attended Mount St. Joseph and later pitched for Philadelphia and Detroit of the American League, is the more likely candidate.) The Mount St. Joseph manager apparently did not want to lose his star just yet, because he tried to avoid the confrontation. In the end, however, a game was played, with Morrisette and Ruth as opposing pitchers.

Leisman's recollections of the hubbub surrounding

this game are quite precise (he apparently checked with other surviving spectators before setting down his account), and he recalls that the tension began to build as soon as the game was scheduled. The boys talked about nothing else. The school and its grounds were given a thorough cleaning and the bleak concrete grandstand was festooned with decorations. It was undoubtedly the most important game ever scheduled at St. Mary's, and the institution was determined to live up to the great moment.

The pressure on Ruth must have been too great. One morning two weeks before the game, the boys in Dormitory One found his bed empty. Some time during the previous night "Nig" Ruth had gone over the wall. Brother Gilbert and the school guards set out in pursuit and, to the relief of the boys, brought him back a few days later. A punishment of five days' standing in place during recreation time was levied on the miscreant. But that period ended in plenty of time to prepare for the big game, and apparently Ruth came to his senses.

With Dunn and a large crowd of outsiders watching, and the boys of both schools screaming their heads off, Ruth pitched St. Mary's to an 8–0 victory, striking out fourteen. (Almost certainly this is the game which appears in *The Glory of Their Times* film.) By the time the last batter went out, Ruth's future was settled.

In order to pluck the underage boy out of St. Mary's, Dunn was obliged to sign papers making him his legal guardian. But that was only a formality, as was his salary of six hundred dollars a year. Dunn planned to take a good look at him during spring training of 1914. If he worked out he would get a new contract. If he didn't— well, that was the boy's problem. The kid was a little strange, a little overexcitable and hard to fathom, but what Dunn cared about was whether he could pitch. You had to expect a bit of initial craziness from someone who'd been brought up the way he had. On February 27, 1914, Ruth walked through the gates of St. Mary's for the last time, at least as one of its inmates. Twelve years earlier he had entered as an ignorant, un-

disciplined product of the slum streets. He was leaving
in much the same state. But now he was a Baltimore
Oriole—if he could make the team.

It didn't take long for Dunn to decide that the kid had
talent. In fact, from the first moment he walked out to
the mound to face an International League lineup, the
manager knew he had a star on his hands. George, or
"Babe," as the Oriole players had nicknamed their new
teenaged teammate, didn't seem to notice any difference
between the pros and the kids he had pitched against at
St. Mary's. He just mowed them down like tenpins, veterans and rookies alike. Dunn was so pleased with his
find that he made out a new contract for him, calling for
a salary of eighteen hundred dollars for his year's work.

But that increase ironically presaged a distressing turn
of events for Dunn and his team. In a very short time,
unforeseen financial troubles had made Ruth too expensive for the Orioles to keep. The problem was that the
new Federal League (an "outlaw" third major league,
established to compete with the two existing major
leagues) had installed a team in Baltimore. The Feder-
als found fertile ground among fans who still bitterly remembered their city's relegation to minor league status.
"Jesus, I remember once, we were fifteen games or
something in the lead and we had nineteen paid admis-
sions at a game," says Ernie Shore, like Ruth, a rookie
pitcher on that team. "The same day the Federal League
team, they played across the street, had ten or twelve
thousand."

As the season progressed and attendance levels failed
to rise, Dunn's bank account plummeted. The fact that
the payroll might be in danger forced him to act. He reluctantly put up for bids his top three prospects—Ruth;
Shore, a lanky, raw-boned twenty-three-year-old from
East Bend, North Carolina, with iron nerves and a
rifle-like arm; and Ben Egan, a catcher. Connie
Mack of the Athletics, impressed by Ruth's performance against his club in spring training, had already
expressed his desire to buy him for next season, but

Dunn needed the money now, and Mack couldn't raise it. So when Joe Lannin, the Red Sox owner, jumped in with an offer for the three youngsters, Dunn quickly accepted it. Ruth, Shore, and Egan were officially sold to the Red Sox on July 10, 1915, for the sum of eighty-nine hundred dollars.

The Boston Red Sox—holy Christ! That was all Ruth could say. A little more than three months earlier, George Herman Ruth had solemnly shaken hands with Brother Paul and left St. Mary's with some guy named Dunn. Now he was Babe Ruth, standing under that funny, white, upward slanted dugout roof in a place called Fenway Park in Boston, Massachusetts, while big leaguers called Speaker, Hooper, Wood, Gardner, and a bunch of other names he couldn't remember brushed by as they went about their business. He'd heard some of those names back in Baltimore, but he didn't know anything about them. And they sure didn't know or care much about him.

The manager was a stocky, no-nonsense man named Bill Carrigan. He reminded Ruth of a smaller Brother Mathias. He didn't waste any time, either. On July 11, one day after Babe's arrival, he handed him a ball and told him he was pitching that day's game against Cleveland. "Don't be nervous, kid," he said. "I'll be catching. Just do what I say." But the kid didn't need any reassurance. Why should he be nervous about Cleveland? He didn't even know where it was.

Babe looked around the stadium as he warmed up. The lopsided park had a strange, deep left field that slanted up a kind of hill to a high wall, then cut sharply back for a short stretch in dead center, made a right-angle turn back toward him, looped away again around in right field, and came back once more to end up in a short right-field foul line. It was like nothing he'd ever seen before. Only a few thousand fans were sprinkled around the seats that day, some in their shirtsleeves leaning on the thin metal pipes that separated one box from another, others lounging with their feet on the seats in front of them in the bleachers. The temperature had risen to the mid-seventies, a light breeze blew in from left field, and the atmosphere seemed lazy and unconcerned, almost like a picnic. Ruth was too new at it all to be much worried on a day like that.

The first Cleveland player to face the rookie was Jack Graney, an outfielder. He didn't look so tough to Ruth. None of them did, except for a smooth-swinging guy named Joe Jackson, who batted third. After him came an old guy named Lajoie, who crossed his back leg behind his front one before he stepped in to a pitch. He was supposed to be good, although Ruth had never heard of him, either.

In the game Babe had no trouble with him. For six innings he had no trouble with any of them, scattering five singles and giving up only one run. But in the seventh he weakened and they got three hits, including a real screamer by Jackson, and scored a couple of runs to tie the score at 3–3. After he had retired the last hitter, Carrigan told him he'd done a good job, but now he was putting in a new pitcher to finish the game. "Nice game, kid," said a couple of the regulars. When Speaker drove in a run in the bottom half of the seventh and then Dutch Leonard held Cleveland scoreless the rest of the way, Babe officially racked up his first major league victory. And he felt pretty damned good about it.

A couple of days later Ernie Shore got his chance. He pitched brilliantly, holding Cleveland to five hits in a 2–1 win. Carrigan, having room for only one new starter in his rotation, chose to go with Shore. He put Ruth on the bench, told him to watch and learn, and more or less forgot about him. In mid-August he called the kid into his office, handed him train fare, and instructed him to report to the Red Sox International League farm club at Providence. They were fighting for the pennant and needed some pitching help. But he told Babe not to worry. He'd get his shot in spring training next season. Carrigan said he saw no reason why Babe shouldn't be a Red Sox regular in 1915. In fact, he was counting on him. And Babe had no doubts, either. He knew he could pitch in this league. In his mind he was already a major leaguer.

3
Breaking In

BABE HAD BEEN lucky to come to Boston. Of all the major league cities, Boston, with its monuments, imposing banks and civic buildings, quiet, grassy squares, clanging trolleys, and narrow, crowded, bustling business streets resembled his home town most closely. Boston Common was just like Druid Hill Park in Baltimore. In the better sections the same kind of sedate town houses stood behind stone gates, hidden by old, leafy trees. He'd never been in one, but maybe he would some day.

When he walked down to look over the harbor he saw a waterfront slum full of brawling seamen, grog shops, and warehouses, just like the Baltimore tenderloin. The same kind of things—ranging from prizefights in smoky back rooms of saloons to riots over working conditions —went on there. The micks had a lot more going for them here than their counterparts in Baltimore, of course. Here they had their own mayor, and the old-line families had to divide the city's spoils with them. But all in all it wasn't too different from where he'd grown up. As much as he could feel at home anywhere, he could feel at home in Boston.

"Gee, yes, it was a fine place to be," says Larry Gardner, in those days the Boston third baseman. In 1915 it was fine to be alive, finer to be a ballplayer, and the finest of all to be a member of the Red

Sox. That year the team that Ruth had joined took the cream off the top. They were the best in the game, one of the best teams ever. They were what baseball was all about. Even the resonant all-American ring of their names seemed drawn from some shiny-eyed boys' baseball adventure. How could an outfield composed of men named Tris Speaker, Harry Hooper, and Duffy Lewis fail to live up to the greatest expectations of its adoring fans? They were as swift as birds, as sure-handed as cardsharps, the finest defensive outfield ever put together. And clutch hitters at the plate, dangerous men, hard to get out, they were feared by every pitcher in the league.

Gardner, who had driven in the winning run after Fred Snodgras's fatal muff in the seventh game of the 1912 World Series, second baseman Jack Barry, formerly of the Athletics' famous hundred-thousand-dollar infield, and young Everett Scott, a smooth-fielding newcomer at shortstop, held down the infield. Crafty Bill Carrigan was catcher, as well as team manager. And the pitching—Jesus, what a pitching staff: Dutch Leonard, Ernie Shore, Ray Collins, George Foster—all big winners at one time or another in those years. Smoky Joe Wood was washed up, but still good for an occasional start, and on the bench future Hall-of-Famer Herb Pennock and Sam Jones sat half forgotten, not yet good enough to break in to the regular rotation. Fastballers, spitballers, curveballers, junkthrowers, lefties, righties, overarm, underarm, sidearm—Boston had them in all sizes and shapes, enough to staff two more major league teams.

Off the field, in 1915, the veterans separated into two distinct though amicable cliques. One centered around Speaker and Wood, inseparable pals, both dashing abrasive, quick-tempered products of the last frontier— bad men to cross, and good men to have as friends. Wood was a matinee-idol type from Colorado, always perfectly turned out, tall and slim, with slicked-down hair and piercing eyes. The stockier Speaker looked more rough at the edges, more like the tough, muscular Texas roughneck, ready to flash a grin or start a fight on equally quick notice. Tris was a hard drinker and a compulsive gambler, always intent on getting into the action, and Wood wasn't far behind. Wherever they went there was always something going on.

Harry Hooper and Duffy Lewis formed the other social nexus. Both had grown up in the San Francisco Bay area in the late eighties and nineties, and both were graduates of St. Mary's College in Oakland. Hooper, an intelligent, independent young fellow interested in what went on in the world, had intended to make a career for himself as an engineer. But a chance meeting with a Red Sox scout on a Sacramento street brought him to Boston. The dapper Lewis was the team fashion plate, a light-hearted, light-stepping man always ready for a laugh. Bubbly, talkative little Larry Gardner and Ray Collins, old friends and classmates at the University of Vermont, were also close to Hooper and Lewis. (Harry and Larry courted the same young lady for a time, in fact. She was a dilly, too. Tall and slim, with fine, clear features, well educated, a good athlete in her own right, and firmly convinced of her right to say whatever she thought whenever she thought it. Larry ended up marrying her—or vice versa.)

There were other college boys on the roster, too. A decade earlier Christy Mathewson of the Giants and Eddie Collins of the Athletics, from Bucknell and Columbia respectively, had seemed like oversensitive minnows in a pool of drunken, ignorant, rowdy piranhas, but those disreputable days were slowly passing. Not all ballplayers were bums anymore. The Red Sox in particular featured a number of educated men, perhaps because of some subtle influence from the centers of culture in the area. Jack Barry had attended Holy Cross and even taught school in the off-season. Pitcher Marty McHale was another engineer, with a degree from the University of Maine. Shore came from Guilford College in North Carolina, and Jake Stahl, a first baseman, from the University of Illinois.

Player-manager Bill Carrigan combined traits of both the old-time tough guy and the new educated man. An alumnus of Holy Cross, an astute businessman (he owned a bank in Lewiston, Maine, and a chain of movie theaters in that area), he was at the same time harder than the hardest of his players. Stocky, muscular, a bit under six feet tall, with an open Irish face, only thirty years old when he became manager in 1913, he could sometimes be one of the boys, sometimes a whip-cracking taskmaster. The Boston sportswriters nicknamed him "Old Rough," and it was a good description of his character and methods. He took no back talk. When the team played or traveled he laid down strict orders, and he expected them to be carried out. His brand of baseball was a throwback to the cutthroat old school—when he instructed a pitcher to stick one in the ear of an opposing batter, that batter went flat on his back on the next pitch, or the pitcher coughed up a fifty-dollar fine.

The rest of the team was composed of the usual mixture of farm boys, Silent Sams, tough guys, drinkers, town-painters, and rookies like Ruth who didn't fit in anywhere yet. There was the occasional problem case like lanky Carl Mays. Mays was a moody, misanthropic midwesterner who caused dissension from the moment he arrived, but who was allowed to stay because he was too good a pitching prospect to lose. There were quietly intelligent, compassionate youngsters like Pennock, a skinny kid from a small town near Philadelphia who appeared to be more suited to life as a county-seat magistrate than that of a pitcher in the rough-and-tumble atmosphere of professional baseball, and veteran hardcases like Heinie Wagner, a sometime coach and special friend of Carrigan's. There were good guys, bad guys, indifferent guys, ignorant guys, crude guys who spit tobacco juice on the rug, scared kids who came and went so quickly that the regulars hardly noticed them, heavy-drinking old-timers playing out their strings, clubhouse boys, trainers, club officials, groundskeepers. A bunch of guys as diverse as can be, given that they were all white, small-town, usually Anglo-Saxon or Irish turn-of-the-century jocks.

The Red Sox spent their spring training at Hot Springs, Arkansas, which was always a plus in the men's eyes. Who ever had a better place to recover from the rigors of winter? Not only did it boast the famous hot mineral baths which many players swore by, but its atmosphere was like a perpetual state fair. Hot Springs was both a resort spa and the gambling center of the lower Mississippi River, a Saratoga and Phenix City rolled into one. The arrival of the ball teams (the Pittsburgh Pirates also trained there), along with the opening of bucolic Oaklawn Park racetrack, with its gleaming green and white grandstand, signaled the onset of a dizzying social swirl. Anyone who had an interest in the sporting scene—sloe-eyed shady ladies, southern-style hustlers swinging malacca canes and showing spotless spats, gangling, overalls-clad hero worshippers sneaking a day off of their farm jobs, good old local boys who seemed to spend twenty-four hours a day bowing to their womenfolk or guzzling straight bourbon, the fast-action element from Little Rock, Pine Bluff, and Fort Smith, not to mention vacationing hotshots from the big towns east and south—converged on the resort and set up shop. (The closest modern version of it might be Tuscaloosa, Alabama, the month before the opening of the professional football season, when Joe Namath graces and stimulates the heart of Dixie with his presence.)

The players themselves did not usually keep up as frantic a pace as that of the local sportsmen. But they didn't devote all of their energies to baseball, either. Daily practices began at 10 A.M. on the Hot Springs field. That was some field, as they often remarked. They dressed at the hotel, then went down a long hill and walked along the railroad tracks until they reached a scraped-off diamond in the middle of a pea patch. The stands around it were four or five rows of wooden planking, with a lot of chicken wire behind them. Small, unpainted frame houses, almost shanties, with gardens full of squash and rutabaga that came right up to the backstop, lined the third base side of the field. The housewives could hook a rope from the chicken wire on the backstop to a tree or fence in their yards and hang their wet laundry on it. But all in all the players liked the atmosphere, liked waving hello to their neighbors as they worked in their gardens and patting the kids on the head when they brought back foul balls.

After 2 P.M. the early spring chill started to set in and the teams headed back up the weedy tracks to the Hotel Majestic. As they passed through the fancy lobby, with its velvet drapes and rows of plush sofas, they nodded to the old ladies and gentlemen sipping tea and mint juleps as they worked up enough energy to take another dip in the baths, and winked at the other kinds of ladies and gentlemen cruising around with their minds on other things.

Most of the players joined the old codgers in the baths after practice. The rest of the day was their own. There was plenty of time to play the ponies, tear up the Arkansas mud ruts in new flivvers (Hooper and Lewis bought a Stutz in one of those years, and sent chickens and goats squawking and squealing with their death-defying thirty-five-mile-an-hour plunges up and down the surrounding hills), read a book (*Penrod and Sam,* by Booth Tarkington, was a big favorite in 1915), put on a pair of plus fours and play the newly popular game of golf, catch Charlie Chaplin or the *Perils of Pauline* at the Springs Nickelodeon, make plans to get up early the next morning to go fishing, or just sit around the lobby waiting for dinner. If they had to resume training, there was no more painless way to do it than in the warm March sunshine of Hot Springs.

The days passed quickly when the team felt it was going places. In 1915 most of the top players were coming off good years, and Carrigan was counting on a couple of highly regarded new pitchers to go with Shore, last year's rookie sensation. (He had finished the year with a 10–4 record.) Ruth was one of them, of course, but the newcomer from whom most people expected the greatest things was Mays, up from Providence, where he had pitched the team to a pennant. Tim Murnane, Boston's reigning baseball writer, had singled him out as the man to watch. That screwy sidearm delivery of his could be expected to fool a lot of hitters this year, in his opinion.

Carrigan was equally pleased with Ruth even if the sportswriters ignored him. The kid needed a good deal of polishing and would probably never learn to study the hitters or position his fielders, but Carrigan could take care of those problems from behind the plate. And if he couldn't mold a kid with Babe's natural talent into a first-rate pitcher, he would hang up his spikes for good. In Carrigan's mind there was no doubt that Ruth would be one of his front line pitchers.

As the days passed, the regulars began to agree with Old Rough. Ruth was going to be a good one. He was strong as an ox, although sometimes his thick trunk seemed too heavy for those spindly, thin-ankled legs of his. But he was fast. Sometimes his curve ball snapped across the plate so quickly you couldn't tell it from his fastball. He was a potential powerhouse at the plate, too. And while his new teammates laughed at his batting style, which consisted of an all-out lunge at nearly every pitch, they had to admit that when he connected he really gave the ball a ride. Of course, he didn't have no science, as Ring Lardner's Jack Keefe might have sneered. Only his lightning-quick reflexes allowed him to recover after he'd misjudged a pitch and hit it anyway. But he hit as if he had a personal grudge against the ball. He never even knew where he was hitting it; you might just as well ask the ball to direct itself as ask the kid to shorten his swing and place a hit somewhere.

There were certain other aspects to Ruth that drew the players' attention as he pranced around the practice field. In the first place "he looked like a nigger," as one of the old-timers delicately phrased it. That drew a lot of quiet comment. His nickname caused some smiles. And his temper was quickly marked, too. Joe Wood, his fabulous arm gone at the age of twenty-six, bitterly struggling through the start of what looked like his last season, came near blows with him over an errant throw.

Like many "green peas," as Hooper called them, he seemed determined to be known as a sport, handing out money to every bum with a good story, trying to screw every woman in town, soaking up flattery like a sponge from the touts who at the first race on opening day had spotted him for an easy mark. He picked up bicycles left leaning against front-yard trees, rode them helter-skelter over the ruts in the street, whooping "Hey, look at me, look at me!" until he fell off, and left them where they lay. He roared around town in borrowed autos and forgot from whom he'd borrowed them. He'd never been on a horse or held a hunting rifle in his life, but now he cantered through the patchy fields playing Buffalo Bill and sat in marshy blinds at dawn waiting for the ducks to settle on the water. (And he could really shoot, too. His eyes were like telescopic sights.) But what the hell —everyone was entitled to blow off a little youthful steam. Most of the other players hadn't been much different.

Gradually, however, qualitative and quantitative differences did emerge. One thing the players soon noticed was that his personal habits were as primitive as any of them had ever seen. There was no lack of crude ignoramuses in the league, but this kid was a virtual caveman. Since Babe and Shore had been teammates during their one season at Baltimore, Carrigan put them together as roommates, but the polite, easygoing southerner soon rebelled. In *The Babe Ruth Story* Shore is said to have demanded a change because Babe insisted on sharing his toothbrush. (An assertion that caused much laughter when it was published among people who had known Ruth. "He must have thought it was for something else," was a typical comment.) According to Fred Lieb, who actually ghostwrote *The Babe Ruth Story,* what Shore really said was that he refused to stay in the same room with a man who didn't know enough to flush the toilet after he used it. Lieb felt that such graphic details were inappropriate for an inspirational book, however, and so made a substitution. Ruth's lack of toilet training was not the only thing that bothered his roommates. Not only did he invariably sleep in the nude, but he never wore any underwear after he got up (a habit which continued to the end of his playing days). And he sweated like a pig, too.

Watching him eat, especially in the morning or late at night, caused many players to lose their appetites. At the same time he was swallowing enormous mouthfuls of steak or catfish, he was bellowing for more, reaching out to snatch at the waitresses' aprons as they hurried through the hotel's ornate polished-wood dining salon. His frequent loud belches and farts and his even louder laughter over such clever tricks made his table companions fervently wish they had chosen another restaurant. He didn't even seem to know what silverware was for. He lacked the most elementary notion of dietary care, and no one could convey to him what even common sense should have dictated. (After watching him slug down six ham and cheese sandwiches and six bottles of soda pop for an after-midnight snack, Hooper warned him to take it easy. "About what?" Ruth wanted to know.)

Some of the more tolerant players tried to strike up conversations, to draw him out a bit, but he wasn't much to talk to, either. Mainly his conversation was limited to three areas of interest: baseball, gambling, and the cruder forms of sex. The last was his favorite. Comparing cock lengths, or debating the size of some broad's tits in the stands that day, were among the few subjects he could become involved in. (In many of the southern towns in which the team played exhibition games the town fathers roped off a special section, usually in right field, for the local whores to sit in. Babe soon became an expert at the good and bad points of the girls set out for inspection.)

But he preferred doing to talking, and spend a great part of his spare time wearing out the women of the town. He didn't seem to differentiate between any of

them. Hardened pro or eager amateur, they were all just
something to be laid. "He'd stick it in anything that had
hair on it," was one teammate's pungent comment.

Ruth reminded Dutch Leonard, who raised grapes in
California during the off-season, of one of those rare gigantic bunches of mutant grapes a grower finds hanging
from his vines every once in a while. A story that illustrated his insatiable appetites was soon circulating
throughout the league. It seems, so the story goes, that
on a road trip, his roommate (usually given as Shore,
but occasionally someone else) was awakened one night
by Ruth entering the room with a local girl. They proceeded to go at it while the roommate dozed fitfully with
a pillow over his head, silently cursing his bad luck at
drawing Ruth for a roommate. The grunting and sweating
lasted all night. The next day the red-eyed roommate
asked Ruth just how many times he had done it. Babe
didn't know for sure, but he had smoked a stogie after
each time. His roommate counted seven cigar butts
crushed into the windowsill.

He had occasional companions but still no real
friends. The other guys involuntarily drew back from
him, and in any case Babe seemed to be a loner by nature. He pulled up a chair as soon as a road-trip card
game started, and often snapped a towel at someone's
bare ass in the shower, but outside of things like that the
players seldom had much to do with him. He always
seemed to be rushing off to meet some woman. Which
was okay with the others. His stories about whom he
had just screwed, while repetitive, were always good
for a laugh when he returned.

His teammates' wives knew what he was like from
their husbands' reports and from personal experience,
and it didn't appeal to them. "He was a mess," says
Margaret Gardner, Larry's wife. (Sixty years hasn't soft-
ened her opinion of him. In their apartment in a new
building overlooking Lake Champlain in Burlington,
Vermont, Larry tries to shush her, but she pays no attention.) "He was foulmouthed, a show-off, very distaste-
ful to have around. The kind of person you would never

dream of having over to dinner. I suppose he was likeable enough in his way, but you couldn't prove it by me.

"Once, on a train, he came up to me and started talking in that loud voice of his about how I had gotten him in trouble," Mrs. Gardner goes on, shaking her head. "I asked why and he said earlier on the trip he had seen a woman who he thought was me, and he had come up behind her and whopped her on the head, but it had turned out to be someone he didn't know. He thought that was the funniest thing he'd ever heard of."

Grace Monroe, then the giddy, glamorous young wife of a prominent Boston boxer, Jo-Jo Avile, came from a very different environment from Margaret Gardner's, but she experienced the same feelings when she knew Ruth in the twenties. (She lives in Queens now, and her hands shake because of a nervous disorder, but she's still a striking blonde with a great figure. You can still see why Ruth whistled and demanded of her husband, "How do *you* rate *that?*" when he first met her.) "I doubt that he appealed to many women," she says thoughtfully. "He certainly didn't appeal to me. He was so blustery and loud. And he used so many swearwords it embarrassed you. And believe me, I don't embarrass easy. He didn't ever seem to want to be with women, anyway. He'd always rather be with the men, talking about fighting or something like that. Somebody I knew who knew him real well used to say he was a 'man's man.' Well, he certainly wasn't a woman's man—I don't care how many women he slept with."

But in those early years in Boston no one gave his antics such serious thought. Carrigan had him under pretty firm control in the clubhouse, anyway. And despite everything, both the players and their wives managed to put up with him when they had to. After all, he was just a kid. In his own crude way he tried to be friendly enough, and no one had to associate with him off the field.

But he was sure full of surprises. When the team returned to Boston in April 1915 to start the season, Babe had another one for them. It now turned out that he was a married man. In October of the previous year, George Herman Ruth, Jr., of Baltimore, and Helen Woodford of South Boston, had been joined in holy matrimony at Ellicott City, Maryland, a small town west of Baltimore. And not only did Babe have a new bride, but her face looked vaguely familiar to the players. Most of them could have sworn they'd seen her somewhere before.

In fact, they had seen her many times. For the past year Helen had worked as a waitress on the early shift at Lander's Restaurant, a thriving coffee shop on Massachusetts Avenue, not far from Fenway Park, where the players occasionally stopped for a snack. Rather pretty in a unspectacular way, about five feet three inches tall with brown hair and eyes, she seemed to be a nice, quiet girl without anything especially noticeable about her—except perhaps for her distinct Maritimes accent (her family had come to Boston from Nova Scotia not many years before). She was very young, sixteen years old at most, quite naive and not particularly bright—just another poor girl from a working-class family out on her own at too early an age, who probably knew her way around the back seat of a car but not much else.

Ruth took a fancy to her, however. He had spotted her on his first morning in Boston in July 1914, when he and Shore had wandered into the restaurant in search of a meal. His loud, awkward joshing annoyed the older girls, but Helen liked it. She thought he was really goofy. He was always fooling around, loosening the salt-shaker tops and all that kind of stuff. He might not have had the polish of a Harvard professor, but he was a big, strong, energetic galoot, and she wasn't likely to interest a professor, anyway. He took her out, bought her nice presents, and threw his money around all over the place. What more could she ask?

In the space of the few weeks Ruth spent in Boston that July and August she became his official girl. After he went down to Providence he came back a few times to visit her. Once he actually took a taxi the whole way. "Did you ever hear of anything that crazy?" Helen

asked her girl friends. But she was certainly flattered.
And she liked walking out on the arm of an older man,
especially a ballplayer. It made her feel important. Nobody recognized him yet, but he said they would soon
enough. He wanted her to come to the park when Old
Bill—that was the manager, a real good friend of Babe's
—put him in another game.

When Babe popped the question ("She used to wait
on me in the mornings, and one day I said to her, 'How
about you and me getting married, hon?' "—*The
Babe Ruth Story.*) she was more than ready to say
yes. Soon after the season ended Babe rushed her off to
Maryland, where the law required no frustrating three-
day delays between obtaining a license and finding a
preacher. Since both were legally underage, Ruth presented a waiver signed by his father, and Helen simply
added two years onto her age to make herself eighteen.
Father Thomas Dolan of St. Paul's Roman Catholic
Church performed the ceremony.

What prompted Ruth to rush into wedlock at the age
of nineteen, only seven months after his release from St.
Mary's, remains a mystery. It may have stemmed in part
from a longing for some kind of stable home life such as
he had never experienced, if only in the form of a permanent address and someone waiting for him when he
staggered home after a night out. Another factor may
have been that marriage sounded good. It was something other people aspired to, so why shouldn't he? And
having a wife meant that there would be at least one
person always handy to keep things moving. He would
never have to be alone. In any event, he just made up
his mind, and once he did that there was no stopping
him.

The newlyweds moved into an apartment on a quiet,
tree-lined street in Cambridge when the season started.
As Ruth's 1915 contract called for thirty-five hundred
dollars a year, they had none of the financial problems
that beset most young couples. Babe told her to go out
and buy all new furniture—he only wanted new stuff.
With the help of her mother she spent weeks shopping.

Babe didn't seem to care what anything cost, although she couldn't always tell how he would react. Sometimes he would arrive home after a road trip with an expensive present for Helen, then take her out to dinner and tip the waiter a thin dime. The next time she would get nothing, and their waiter would receive a larger bill than he'd even seen from a Cabot or a Lodge. But it was important to him that Helen look good, and he was willing to pay for it. He had become a flashy dresser himself, with his camel coats and caps, forty-dollar suits, a drawer full of silk shirts and monogrammed handkerchiefs (which he never used), and Florida shoes.

Their home life was erratic at best. Ruth was out all the time. He couldn't sit still. Sometimes he took Helen along, but more often than not she was left to her own devices. Babe was out gunning a new car past the startled eyes of dignified pedestrians on Commonwealth Avenue, or drinking with a bunch of hangers-on, or paying a boisterous visit to a new old acquaintance at one of the South Boston whorehouses. He would concoct elaborate, preposterous excuses for having to go out alone, and convince himself that Helen always believed him. (Once in New York he told her that he was dining with President Harding that night. He got all dressed in his tuxedo and came home three-quarters drunk, with his clothes covered with booze and food stains from a rowdy stag party. Some of his excuses were less picturesque, but most were equally unlikely.)

He might arrive home for a quick 3 A.M. change of clothes and take off again, or just not bother to come home at all. On occasion Helen would come along to a party, have too much to drink, and have to be taken home. And, of course, she faithfully attended all the Red Sox home games, and once in a while accompanied him on a road trip. A couple of years she went along to Hot Springs as well, but much of the time she was left to herself.

To Ruth's teammates in those early years Helen seemed something of a nonentity. She would give them a cheerful smile and say hello if they greeted her first, but she rarely had anything further to say. Mostly she appeared shy and unobtrusive. She certainly never made demands on Babe. You hardly knew she was there, was their unanimous verdict.

At first the other Red Sox wives seemed to intimidate her. She chose to sit apart from them at the games and seldom worked up the nerve to approach them at other times. Babe waved to her occasionally during a game but never seemed to notice that she was not with the other women. (Later on, however, according to Herb Pennock's wife, Jane, she did sit with the other wives, although none of them ever became specially friendly with her.)

To most of the wives Helen was so ordinary as to be almost invisible. Margaret Gardner's only vivid memory of Helen concerns an incident during a road-trip hop between Cleveland and New York. As she and some other women, whose identities she has now forgotten, sat chatting and looking out at the farms and hillsides of the Mohawk Valley, Helen approached their group and sat down in an empty chair on the fringe. They tried to include her in the conversation. Somehow the subject of schools came up, and to their surprise Helen told them that she had attended Smith College. Since the others all knew her to have been a waitress, they merely smiled and replied, "How nice." "I suppose we could have been friendlier," Mrs. Gardner admits. "But, really, she never had very much to say. You hardly noticed her. And she was so young."

One thing they couldn't help noticing was the way Ruth treated his wife in public. Sometimes he was all affection, but more often he seemed to consider her a nuisance. Fred Lieb remembers her intruding once while Ruth was holding forth to a group of sportswriters. "I told you to get your ass out of here," he snapped. And when Ruth paid his lustful compliment to Grace Monroe, he ignored the fact that Helen was standing by his side.

But they had some great times, too. During spring training of 1916, the Gardners found themselves at a carnival with the Ruths. Babe contrived to have the ferris wheel stalled while he and Helen were at the top. Bellowing uproariously, waving his cap, he rocked the carriage back and forth while the lights on the ground swam faster and faster before Helen's terrified eyes and she screamed bloody murder in a voice that could have been heard halfway to Little Rock. Later the two couples passed through the monkey house, where Babe started leaping up and down, scratching his armpits and making gorilla noises, to the dismay of Mrs. Gardner. When one of the apes began to respond Helen thought it was hysterical. "Look, Babe, he knows you," she cried.

Well, life with Babe wasn't quite what every young girl dreamed of. But Helen supposed she loved him and he loved her, deep down. She could still be romantic about things. She was still a teenager, and still had a teenager's resilience. And she had every material thing she could want. Eventually she might get fed up and start to rebel, but for now she was too new at the game to do anything but wait quietly on the sidelines.

In the meantime, Ruth had not been neglecting his profession. "He was already the best lefty in the league," is Harry Hooper's estimation of Ruth in 1916. Gifted with great endurance, unfazed by the reputation of any of the batters he faced, and a good man in the clutch, he was soon a bulwark of Boston's great staff. ("He was probably too dumb to know the difference," laughs Hooper. "But he was one of the few men who could throw a fastball past Cobb with any regularity.") He won nine games in August and September of 1915, finishing with an eighteen and six record as the Red Sox beat out Chicago in an exciting race. He didn't pitch in the Series, however. Shore, Foster, and Leonard mopped up Philadelphia so efficiently that Ruth wasn't even called upon to warm up.

The following year he came into his own. In 1916 he won twenty-three games, lost twelve, and led the league in earned run average with a figure of 1.75. He was soon considered the ace of the pitching staff; in that

year's World Series against the Brooklyn Robins he
pitched the second game, winning a fourteen-inning
struggle 2–1. (Mays, who had won eighteen games during the season, pitched the first game because Carrigan
wanted to start with a righty.)

"You should have seen him that day," says a former
teammate. "He was just unbeatable." As he had so
many times before that season, Babe just stood solidly
out on the mound, his baggy uniform flapping in a brisk
wind while the strangely angled shadows of Fenway
Park grew longer and longer around him. Before every
pitch he stared down at Carrigan with a vacant but intent expression on his flat face, then wound up in a com-
pact motion, kicked his right leg, heaved his heavy upper body forward, suddenly snapped his left arm around
and flung the ball past the always surprised hitter.
Strike, strike, strike—the same fastball every inning,
getting stronger as they game wore on, all concentrated,
unshakable power up on that little hill sixty feet away.
He gave up a home run in the first inning, then pitched
thirteen straight scoreless frames, allowing only five singles the rest of the way. When the Red Sox finally got a
run to win it for him in the bottom of the fourteenth, the
rest of the team looked more worn-out than Ruth.
That's the kind of pitcher Babe was when he was on his
game.

At first little notice was given to the fact that the new
star pitcher coud hit, too. In August 1915 he was leading the Red Sox in batting with an average of .360 (he
finished the year at .321), and in home runs with four,
but neither the players nor the sportswriters took those
statistics seriously. After all, he'd only been up fifty
times, so his average meant nothing. As for the home
runs, well, they weren't really part of the game. A home
run was almost invariably the result of a defensive mistake, such as failing to cut off a line drive or playing a
hitter improperly. The Red Sox had only hit eight home
runs all season, excluding Ruth's, and all of them were
inside the park. Admittedly Babe's soared right over the
heads of the fielders and into the seats, so you couldn't

write them off as fielding mistakes, and one of them had sailed clean over the right field stand at the Polo Grounds—only the second time that feat had ever been accomplished, but so what? Everything Ruth did was a curiosity. It didn't mean much in baseball terms. And when Carrigan tried him as a pinch hitter in 1915 and 1916, he didn't set the world afire. More often than not, in fact, his eagerness to belt one out caused him to screw up. In 1916, after a game in which he had struck out on three straight bad pitches in the bottom of the ninth with the winning runs on base, a *Globe* reporter complained bitterly about his misguided efforts to "send the ball out of the park instead of between two fielders."

But those were minor problems. Ruth was a pitcher, and a darn good one. "Boston's best," one paper called him before the 1917 season. And with phrases like that in the air, it did not take Babe long to awaken to the fact that he was a star. With his new status came more money ($5,000 in 1917, plus his $3,900 Series share), increasing flattery, classier women, and even greater irresponsibility.

"Christ, his head swelled up like a balloon the minute he became a star," Hooper recalls. If he had been hard to take before, now he became unbearable. Speaker had been sold to Cleveland a year earlier, and now he considered himself the top player on the team and tried to live up to what he felt was the part. He lectured the players on their failures in the field, burned the umpires' ears off with comments on their blindness, and rode the opposing players with a newfound belligerence. Several times particularly insulting outbursts brought him to the verge of blows with various other players, and catcher Chester Thomas in particular. But the men soon found he was more a shouter than a scrapper. Frequently he would provoke other players, then back off when they stood up to him. More often than not, the guys noticed, he left himself a path of retreat or started something when someone in authority was due on the scene at any moment.

The sports pages picked up upon his new attitude.

After one poor performance on the mound, a *Record* writer blamed his ineffectiveness on "recorditis, thinking more of piling up a long string of victories [than of the game itself]." Edward Martin of the *Morning Globe* gave Ruth some pointed advice in print on May 25, 1917: "Ruth has added something to his repertoire which he might just as well eliminate before it gets chronic," he wrote. "It is nagging the umpire behind the plate. Babe puts on a stubborn child sketch every time the arbiter calls one wrong. His conduct today was at times painfully distressing."

But Martin was talking to the wind. Ruth wouldn't listen to anyone, least of all a sportswriter. Shore was about the only one who seemed able to reach him after one of his frequent rages. Carrigan had retired by then, and Jack Barry, the new manager, had no control over Ruth. Besides, as long as Babe was pitching well, there wasn't much Barry could do. And he was pitching like a demon. By the end of May his record was ten wins, one loss, and the fans were eagerly speculating about the possibility of thirty wins.

On June 23, however, he finally pushed his luck too far. Starting against Washington at Fenway Park, and facing Ray Morgan as leadoff hitter, he threw four pitches, all of which were called balls by umpire Brick Owens. Ruth took each call as a personal insult. He stood glaring down from the mound, hands on hips, muttering bitter denunciations at Owens, making sure the crowd knew he was angry. After the third called ball he lost control and screamed a half-dozen insults toward the umpire. Owen's cheeks turned scarlet. Ruth threw a fourth pitch and the umpire cried, "Take your base." Morgan threw the bat aside and started down toward first base, but a rising roar from the stands caused him to look back. Ruth was charging down toward the plate, swearing at the umpire, his eyes flashing almost like a lunatic's.

Exact accounts of what happened next vary from observer to observer. In the Ruth/Considine/Lieb version, Ruth says, after the fourth ball, ". . . I just went crazy.

I rushed up to the plate and I said, 'If you'd go to bed at
night, you so-and-so, you could keep your eyes open
long enough in the daytime to see when a ball goes over
the plate.' " After some further shouting, Ruth was
thrown out of the game. Then "I hauled off and hit him,
but good. It wasn't a love pat. I really socked him—
right on the jaw. Chet Thomas, our catcher, Barry, and
other players tore us apart and hustled me to the clubhouse!"

Martin, in the *Globe,* reported the incident as follows: "Then in rushed Ruth. Chester Thomas tried to
prevent him from reaching Owens. . . . 'Get in there
and pitch,' ordered Owens. 'Open your eyes and keep
them open' chirped Babe. . . ." After some additional
dialogue, "Babe started swinging both hands. The left
missed the arbiter, but the right struck him behind the
left ear. Manager Barry and several policemen managed
to drag Ruth off the field."

But Hooper, who had a good view of the mess from
right field, remembers quite a different scene: "After
the guy walked, Ruth ran down to the umpire. He was
mad enough to punch him but he was really looking
around, waiting for someone to hold him back. He
couldn't seem to let the punch go. If he actually did
swing at Owens, it was after he was damned sure there
were people around to pull him away."

Whatever the exact nature of the Brick Owens incident, league president Ban Johnson had no choice but to
take some action against Ruth. No one could be allowed
to take a sock at an umpire. But dealing with a hothead-
ed star was as complicated a task then as it is today.
After sitting on the case as long as he could, Johnson let
Ruth off with a hundred-dollar fine. (He also promised
a suspension at some unspecified time in the future, but
no one took that seriously.)

Ruth "apologized" in the papers, and assured everyone he had learned his lesson. He might not have
escaped so lightly had the remainder of the game not
provided one of the high points in baseball history. After Ruth was ejected. Shore came in and proceeded to

pitch a perfect game—only the third of the century. In the ensuing hoopla Ruth's display of bad sportsmanship was easily forgotten. (But he never quite regained his early season form after that, finishing the year with a 23–13 record.)

Despite such incidents, or maybe partly because of them, Babe soon became a news item. Boston had few enough popular celebrities, and the low personal opinions some sportswriters held of Ruth did not prevent them from exploiting his printable characteristics. Personality tidbits about Ruth soon began to appear in the Boston sports pages. A pen portrait of his ugly mug appeared in one of the *Evening Globe's* Daily Graphix Puzzles ("Find the two hidden fans in this picture.") In mid-1917 his car scattered a hay wagon all over a country road, but after the police recognized who was at the wheel, "everyone enjoyed a hearty laugh," according to a local columnist. A few days later a *Globe* writer observed "the elegant Mr. Ruth," emerging at a "decided windward tilt" from one of his "favorite caravansaries."

And when Ruth came to the sudden conclusion, over Helen's protests, that the time had come for him to purchase a country home, the papers carried that decision in detail. He had always wanted to own land, Ruth grandly informed the reporters. His deprived childhood had left him with that desire. The country house turned out to be a white clapboard colonial mansion with two large wings off the already substantial main structure and several barns, fodder bins, work sheds, and other outbuildings, located in Sudbury, about twenty miles west of Boston. (When the Ruths arrived to take possession they found their new home full of old furniture, hooked rugs, and various other antiques, some of which dated well back into the previous century and possibly earlier. Ruth paid a local carter to pile up all that crap and haul it away. He wanted new furniture.)

By 1917 even the New York columnists were occasionally mentioning Babe. The semiofficial tip-off on a player's rise to the top was the appearance of his name in Grantland Rice's syndicated column. If you were singled out in "Sport Light," you were said to be on your way. You had that something extra. Ruth's name had appeared before in the column in lists of Red Sox pitchers, but in early 1917 the "poet of the pressbox," as he was widely known, found Babe worthy of a full-blown quatrain. "He can hit himself / And, to add to the glim,/ He can keep the others / From hitting him," ran the less-than-immortal lines. In fairness to Rice, it should be acknowledged that this particular verse was the contribution of a poetic fan, rather than his own effort. Still, it carried a certain glory. Not many players rated a solo rhyme in "Sport Light."

The papers also reported Babe's tendency to abuse his body. As early as July 1915 he had incurred what was to be the first of an encyclopedic catalog of avoidable accidents and illnesses. On the Fourth of July of that year, enraged over some trivial irritation, he treated the bench to a swift kick and in doing so gave himself a badly cracked toe, which put him out of action for a week. Wrenched knees, bruised hands from slugging walls, skin abrasions ignored until they grew into abscesses, self-lanced and subsequently infected boils, sore throats magnified into bronchitis, and every kind of stomach ailment followed in rapid succession as the years passed. What could a reporter do with a story like that—except write a funny bit about how it happened this time, and give full play to Ruth's assertions that he had learned his lesson and would never let it happen again?

By the end of the 1917 season, however, the doings of Ruth or any other baseball player no longer seemed very consequential. The country was at war. Mobilization had begun to alter the fabric of American life. Huge black headlines alerted the nation to victories and defeats in obscure, unpronounceable European places. American names were added daily to the gruesome casualty lists. Alarming threats to democracy arose even on the country's doorsteps—U-boats spotted in our estuaries, spies and saboteurs in our industrial plants, labor unrest and the influence of the diabolical Bolsheviki on the rise. In the neighborhood groceries even the American housewife was threatened; sauerkraut, schnitzel, frankfurters, potato salad, and other insidious products of the Germanic palate were doing their best to undermine the war effort. There was no respite in the struggle against the middle-European enemy.

In the midst of all this excitement baseball suddenly seemed less important. The sports pages, taking their cue from the National Commission—baseball's ruling body, which consisted of the American and National League presidents and a "neutral" club owner—did their best to buoy up the public's interest in the game. Sports editors attempted to point out the relevance of ballplaying experience in the making of a good soldier. Where else but on the ball field had the American doughboy developed his competitive spirit? A popular cartoon showing a soldier "batting" a German in the head with his rifle butt, "pitching" a grenade, and "sliding" into a trench made the rounds of many of the nation's sports pages.

In Ban Johnson's less than balanced opinion, baseball's contribution to the national morale was of the greatest importance, and it raised a good deal of tax revenue as well. Johnson and the owners therefore argued that the national game was one enterprise that deserved an exemption from the Wilson administration's wartime restrictions on inessential activities. And to demonstrate the strength of baseball's good faith and importance to the war effort, the National Commission ordered major league teams in 1918 to perform military drills before the games, substituting bats for rifles. Johnson even offered a five-hundred-dollar prize to the best drill team; it was won by the St. Louis Browns. (The Brooklyn team, showing its traditional iconoclasm, told him what he could do with his bat and ignored the whole thing.)

Despite the efforts of the baseball brass to shunt it to the sidelines, the war refused to go away. The Selective Service Act of 1917 required every man between the ages of twenty-one and thirty to register for the draft. It was extended a year later to men between eighteen and forty-five years of age. Except for those men who were physically unfit, had families dependent on them, belonged to pacifist religious organizations, or were engaged in jobs essential to the war effort, they were all eligible to be chosen for military service. And although Johnson's arguments in behalf of exempting baseball players because of their indispensible occupation appeared perfectly logical to him, the War Department seemed to consider it frivolous.

Many of the younger ballplayers, like many young men all over the nation, enlisted before they were called up. This led to an element of contradiction in the National Commission's attitude, for while it was lobbying in Washington for essential-industry status, each departing player was saluted to the skies as living proof of baseball's patriotism. Then, as now, however, baseball officials were not much given to irony, and saw no conflict.

The Red Sox, like most other teams, lost a substantial number of players. Barry, Lewis, Shore, Pennock, Leonard, Hal Javrin, the second baseman, and several minor players were all wearing Navy blue at the start of the 1918 season. (They had enlisted in Boston, where the Navy reigned supreme.) Dick Hoblitzel, the first baseman, went inland and joined the Army in April. A nucleus of a team remained, but the squad was far different from what it had been the previous year.

Ruth, who as a married man was exempt from the draft, chose to stay out, although his situation was not precisely what the drafters of the Selective Service Act had in mind when they exempted men with dependent families. Before his action is condemned or applauded, however, it should be pointed out that almost all the players who did join up were assigned to stateside morale-building duties, mainly coaching training-camp baseball teams, and got no closer to the front than the nearest Army or Navy canteen. This in no way reduced baseball's boasting about their contribution, of course. And those who actually did see some action, such as

Bob Shawkey, on a destroyer in the North Sea, or gained a commission, such as Ernie Shore, were hailed as baseball's versions of Sergeant York.

The 1918 season ended a month early. Although the Red Sox won their third pennant and third World Series championship in four seasons, this time there wasn't much to brag about. Boston's pitching staff, now led by Ruth, Carl Mays, Sam Jones, and Joe Bush, simply proved too strong for a drastically weakened league. Mays took twenty-one games, Jones sixteen, and Bush fifteen. Ruth, who was called on to fill in at first base and in the outfield, tired slightly under the strain of double duty and saw his record decline to thirteen wins and seven losses. He revived to pitch brilliantly against the Cubs in the Series, however, winning the first game 1–0, and the fourth 3–2. The two eighth-inning runs scored by Chicago were the only ones scored against Babe in twenty-nine consecutive innings of World Series pitching, going back to 1916, establishing a record that lasted until Whitey Ford broke it in 1961.

One additional statistic had illuminated a dull year in baseball. Ruth had tied for the league lead in home runs with eleven. He had faced inferior pitching, but still, who ever heard of a pitcher hitting .300 and driving eleven balls out of the park? The fans seemed taken with the big boy. All over the league, people were coming out to see him play, hoping he would hit one of his towering blasts into the stands. He was something new in the game—a big, strong, confident muscleman who stood up at the plate aiming for the seats every time, holding his heavy forty-two-ounce bat all the way down at the handle, overlapping the handle, in fact, waving it delicately back and forth over his shoulder as he waited for the pitch, his right foot ready to lunge smoothly forward and plant itself in a line with second base as he whipped the lumber around with all of the strength in his straining body. None of the art and science of batting for this kid—no place hitting, no studying the pitcher or the fielders, no shortening up with a two-strike count. He wanted the whole thing every time, and the crowds seemed to want it, too. As the war moved toward a crisis, little attention could be given to this new phenomenon, but many fans and sportswriters filed in the backs of their minds questions on the subject of Babe Ruth. When the war ended and baseball got back to normal they would see just how significant was the new approach of the wild man from Baltimore.

For the Red Sox, the 1918 season was the culmination of a continuous shuffling of personnel over the war years. Speaker's acrimonious departure for Cleveland after the 1915 season had begun the exodus. (After selling the center fielder to the Indians for fifty-five thousand dollars, a vindictive Joe Lannin informed the sportswriters that no baseball player was worth half that amount—especially a has-been like Speaker. Tris vindicated himself by hitting .386 the next year for his new team.) Smokey Joe, too, dropped out of baseball at that time, although he later switched to the outfield and rejoined Tris at Cleveland. Larry Gardner left a couple of years later, first moving to Philadelphia and then on to make a Boston threesome on the Indians. Ray Collins was released in 1915, George Foster in 1917.

Although they had no inkling of it at the time of their enlistments, the careers of Barry, Shore, Lewis, Leonard, Javrin, and Hoblitzel were also virtually over. Only Barry would ever play for the Red Sox again, and then only for a few games in 1919. The rest were washed up. By 1921 all except Leonard would be out of baseball as active players. (Shore had felt something pop in his shoulder in the last month of the 1917 pennant race. Like Smokey Joe, the moment before it happened he was on top of the world, and the moment after, a prime candidate for the baseball glue factory. Lewis and Barry had simply slowed down with age, while Leonard never really recovered from his year-long layoff.)

The man who had molded Ruth into a top-notch pitcher was gone, too. Bill Carrigan had been making noises about retiring throughout the 1916 season, but the guys were certain that he was just putting the squeeze on Lannin for more money. They should have known better. Carrigan never bluffed. After the last game of the 1916 World Series he toured the locker room, shook hands with his players, told them he was glad to have known them and wished them the best of luck in the future. Still bitter over the sale of his best player a year earlier, tired of handling prima donnas, arguing with owners, and thinking for rockheads, the man who had molded the Red Sox into a great team decided to go home to Maine, where he could look after his business interests in peace. At the age of thirty-four, Carrigan, the most successful manager in the game, just up and quit.

Before the next season began Joe Lannin followed his manager out of baseball. The Speaker affair had left its mark on him, too. Besides, the club had not been all that profitable despite its first-place finishes, and Lannin figured he would never have a better time to unload it. Let somebody else have the headaches—he felt he deserved a long rest.

The men who replaced Carrigan and Lannin were both destined to make names for themselves in baseball, and to have profound effects on Ruth's career, although for diametrically opposite reasons. They were Edward Barrow and H. Harrison Frazee, manager and owner respectively. (Jack Barry's appointment as manager in 1917 had been only a temporary assignment, since he made no bones about heading into the Navy at the end of the season.)

Ed Barrow, who took over in 1918 as both field manager and general manager, was, the players agreed, just a bastard. Before his elevation to the Red Sox at the age of fifty, he had been in and around baseball for many years—as a sportswriter, as manager of Detroit for a couple of years at the turn of the century, and more recently as the iron-fisted president of the International League. A sturdy, bullet-headed, hard-faced storm

trooper of a man, he demanded instant and slavish obe-
dience from anyone working for him, and was capable
of cursing out the smallest mistake made by a subordi-
nate. As ruthless and as devious as a backroom politician, his word meant little if it got in the way of a profitable deal. Many young hopefuls encountered that aspect
of his character, and few emerged from a go-round with
Barrow with much of their wide-eyed idealism intact.

Ben Paschal, a promising young outfielder in the Boston farm system, was one of those who learned the hard
way. In 1920 he signed a contract with Barrow with the
understanding that he would be given a chance at the
big leagues that year—a promise Barrow failed to keep.
At the end of that year Barrow moved to the Yankees,
and Paschal found his contract mysteriously sold to the
New York organization. Since the Yankees had one of
the best outfields in the majors, his fate was sealed. Barrow held him in the minors for four more years as a
convenient reserve in case something happened to one
of his regulars. Paschal finally got his first real chance to
play in the majors in 1925, but by that time he was thirty years old, and the book on him was that he couldn't
hit left-handed pitching, even though he'd batted .360 in
eighty-nine games that year. He stayed on as a utility
outfielder for a few more seasons, but not even his
World Series checks compensated for the loss of his
chance to become a full-time major leaguer.

Above all, as the players soon realized, Barrow was
cheap. The team's profit margin, of which he usually
had a piece, was sacred. Squeezing blood from a stone
was an easier task than getting an extra penny from him
at contract times. He just did not budge once he had decided how little a player was worth. And since he held
all the cards, most players took what he gave them and
that was that.

Despite the opinions of those who worked for him,
Barrow always managed to enjoy a good press. The
writers seemed a little intimidated by him, and so always
characterized him as a baseball mastermind without
questioning his methods in print. Harry Frazee, on the

other hand, was drawn and quartered by reporters almost from the first day he arrived on the scene in late
1916, fresh from New York, a brash, big-city promoter
hoping to make a killing in baseball. A theatrical pro-
ducer by trade, he operated on the traditional Broadway
hit-or-bomb, boom-or-bust psychology; one season a
millionaire and everyone's pal, the next a failure and nobody's friend. And if that kind of philosophy were not
enough of a shock to the conservative world of baseball,
Frazee added insult to injury by quickly revealing the
fact that he knew next to nothing and cared even less
about either the game or the city of Boston. His cavalier
attitude toward baseball caused many bitter comments in the higher councils of the league. There had to
be something wrong with an owner who invariably referred to his general manager as "Simon," after Simon
Legree, even if it were an accurate appraisal of his character.

The players themselves didn't know what to make of
him. He rarely had much to do with them except at contract times, when he could invariably con them out of
their shirts. "He was always trying to put something
over on you," said Gardner, who was the first starter
whom Frazee got rid of after he took control. In his eyes
the players were nothing but small-town rubes. In theirs
he was the epitome of everything unpleasant about New
York. Everything about him—from his swarthy, levan-
tine face, short, thick, unathletic body, diamond rings
and flashy clothes to his wisecracking New York humor
—irritated them. (Even today one of his former players
refers to him as "nothing but a Jew.") And to top it off,
there were rumors of his involvement in a series of
crooked deals, including the fixing of the notorious Jack
Johnson–Jess Willard heavyweight championship fight
in Havana in 1915—a fight he had helped to promote.
According to Shore, around the clubhouse he often
bragged of the killing he had made on that tank job. In
short, there was something about Frazee to upset everyone. Just what the hell baseball was coming to when his
kind could buy into the game was a question often heard

in the clubhouse in 1917–1918.

Ruth, of course, cussed him out with the rest of them, but his heart wasn't really in it. Babe was far too impressed with himself, and too busy enjoying the obeisance of an ever-growing crowd of hangers-on, to spend time worrying about other people. Besides, he seemed to have a certain admiration for Frazee. Harry was big time, a high roller—the first real Broadway slicker Ruth had ever seen up close. When Harry wanted something he never let personal niceties stand in his way. Other people might describe his manner as arrogant, but Ruth always got along with him. And although neither would have recognized it at the time, they had a lot in common. They were both growing too big for Boston. The Big Apple was where they belonged, and where both would be before long.

4

Waiting for the Other Shoe

IN THE SPRING of 1919 Damon Runyon, Ring Lardner, Grantland Rice, W. O. McGeehan, and the rest of the big-time sportswriters in New York were feeling restless. They had it pretty good; newspapers all around the country carried their syndicated columns, Rice and McGeehan had pushed their salaries well past the $125-a-week level, and Runyon's and Lardner's incomes, supplemented by book, magazine, and playwriting sources, were close to three times higher. But there was one sense in which their success was not complete: they wanted heroes of their own and they'd never had them. Most of the great sports figures to whom they had devoted a decade of inventiveness—Cobb, Wagner, Matty, Mack, McGraw, Jack Johnson, Philadelphia Jack O'Brian, the light heavyweight champion, Tod Sloan, the great jockey, Pop Warner, Jim Thorpe—were already there when they arrived around 1910. They hadn't really helped create any sports legends in their own time.

The prospects in 1919 looked no better or worse than usual. Runyon, an avid fight fan, had hopes for a tough pug from a mining camp in Colorado named Jack Dempsey, who was to meet old Jess Willard for the heavyweight championship in July. But Runyon was a notoriously poor judge of young talent. Some of the touts along Broadway were peddling an untried two-

year-old colt called Man o' War, but they always had
some hot number to talk about. Rice was pushing golf as
a new mass sport, but without great success. And in
baseball—well, it just looked like more of the same.
Cobb had won his eleventh batting championship the
year before, Walter Johnson was still going strong, Grover Alexander of the Phillies would be back from service
and undoubtedly would pick up where he had left off.
Maybe, just maybe, that experiment the Red Sox were
trying with Babe Ruth—playing their slightly Neander-
thal lefty full time in the outfield—would be material
for their genius.

And in their way they were geniuses. For years before
they'd come on the scene, New York sportswriting had
been an academic, straightforward affair devoted to
scientific analysis of the game and dominated by men
such as Joe Vila, the arrogant, crotchey, Harvard-edu-
cated sports editor of the *Sun*. Vila had practically invented the analytic approach to sports journalism; because of his close friendship with Ban Johnson, who, as
the dominant force on the National Commission, virtually ran baseball, he had become the most authorita-
tive of all baseball writers. In the early years of the century he set the tone for New York sportswriting, and a
dignified tone it was.

But back in 1911 Bill Curley, a Hearst editor and talent scout, had decided to take a chance on a slight,
tight-lipped, squinty-eyed young man from Colorado
named Alfred Damon Runyon. The *New York American,* the most engaging and lively of the Hearst papers,
was looking for some new punch on its sports pages.
Runyon had come up in the freewheeling, shoot-from-
the-hip style of western journalism. Maybe what had
gone over big in Denver would also appeal to New York
readers. And while forty bucks a week was high pay for
a rookie, they were playing for high stakes. A popular
sportswriter was worth a mint to a newspaper chain.

In the space of three months, Runyon had turned
New York sportswriting on its head. No one had ever
seen anything like him. On July 20, for example, cover-

ing a game between the Giants and the St. Louis Cardinals, he began his story by informing the anxious readers:

> Toledo is in Ohio, a statement which may be immediately verified by reference to any well-ordered map, railway guide, or automobile prospectus.
> The score yesterday was 4 to 2 in favor of the Giants.
> It is a large and thriving midwestern city, with paved streets, tramways, and electric lights. It is noted chiefly for its imports of magazine writers considering the efficacy of the Golden Rule, as applied to municipal government, and for its exports of baseball players.

The story continued in that vein, providing only near the end a few crumbs of information with the details of what had actually happened in the game.

Two days later Runyon launched into his story of another Giants-Cards game with a straight-from-the-shoulder cry of triumph. "As for you, Roger Bresnahan, with your oily voice and city ways—take that! Zam! Bumpty bump-bump! (Noise of villain falling off the front stoop, bleeding from the nose)," crowed his lead paragraph. To the consternation of the old guard, the fans loved it. They didn't know what it was, but they wanted all of it they could get. By the end of the season Runyon had become the nation's leading baseball writer.

Lardner, although still based in Chicago at this time, also contributed to the demise of the old style of sportswriting. A pessimistic, enigmatic little man from a small town in Michigan, ill at ease with strangers and sometimes even with friends, he was given to compulsive benders that left him white and drawn for days afterward. "He'd show up in the pressbox looking like hell after one of his drunks," Fred Lieb, another of the new generation of sportswriters, remembers. "You'd ask him how he was and he'd murmur something about his troubles with 'old man liver' and then just drift away." In some way his imagination was even more wide-ranging than Runyon's. (The two men felt the rivalry and did not get along well.) His nationally syndicated column,

"The Wake," mixed bits and pieces of poems, letters, impossible prize contests, lunatic serials, detective stories, and baseball news in a dada-like assault on the reader. One typical item is a 1911 contest for The Best Play I Ever Saw, to which he wrote all the entries, and therefore won all the prizes. "The best play I ever saw was *Hedda Gabbler,* with Mrs. Fiske doing the Gabbling," was one of the winners.

He composed epic poems and mock Elizabethan tragedies using the Chicago players as characters. In the course of one of them, Frank Schulte, the Cubs' right fielder, is discovered ruminating about an upcoming road trip:

> We leave tonight to go due east,
> Where many games we'll play;
> We may not lose as many as
> We did when it was May.
> I'll write you from the different towns
> In whom to play we're booked in:
> From Boston, Philadelphia,
> From New York, and from Brooklyn.
>
> I've often been in New York town
> And certainly do love
> A town in whom the subway is
> Below and not above.

The epic continues in that vein, chronicling the ups and downs of the Cubs as they travel the stormy seas of the National League.

Granny Rice, a generous, cheerful, handsome southerner with a penchant for sentimental verse, and Bill McGeehan, a rambunctious, heavy-drinking San Franciscan who specialized in wild flights of exaggeration, joined New York papers at the same time Runyon did. With him they were destined to become the big three of New York sportswriting. Also in 1911, Chicagoan Franklin Pierce Adams, better known as F. P. A., in whose column in the *Evening Mail* the famous Tinker to Evers to Chance rhyme first appeared, moved to New

York. And Heywood Broun, Harvard '10, another fast man with a metaphor, signed on with the *World* and did his best to add color to the sports scene.

The new freedom attracted more creative talent, and by 1919 the new breed had been augmented by such aces as Gene Fowler, a brash, high-strung newshound from Denver with an eerie sense of where to find a big story; dour, drunken Westbrook Pegler, who had a cutting word for everyone regardless of race, creed, or color; and Arthur "Bugs" Baer, perhaps the greatest wit of them all. (Introducing Jimmy Walker at a testimonial dinner, Baer became carried away and praised the guest of honor as "a man who would fight by your side, a man who would lay down his life for you." After continuing in this manner for some time, he suddenly realized he had laid it on rather thickly. He paused, looked out over the mass of upraised faces expectantly watching him, and asked, "And who is this man? I do not see him here tonight.")

So the writing talent was there. Now all it needed was a suitable subject. As the writers dropped into their accustomed seats at Billy LaHiff's crowded, noisy watering hole on Forty-eighth Street to trade wisecracks and watch the Broadway crowd shuffle through on its seemingly endless patrol of the Great White Way, they drank a final prespring training toast to the coming year, and hoped that good copy awaited them.

The Red Sox had switched their spring training camp from Hot Springs to Tampa, Florida, in 1919. The New York Giants trained there also, and the reporters who followed them down to the sun got to take a close look at the man who would soon revolutionize baseball. They saw a loud, swaggering, twenty-four-year-old who carried a newly developed pot belly and an ego the size of Fenway Park, and who seemed to spend his time rushing from cathouse to racetrack to the ball field and back again. But that was all right with them. Many of them felt a certain kinship with the kid, since they looked on spring training as a well-deserved chance to get some hard partying done out of sight of their editors. And if Ruth developed into a strong hitter, his excesses would make good copy.

They had almost missed seeing him. Babe, now in his fifth year as a major leaguer, felt he deserved at least twelve thousand in 1919 (he had made seven thousand the year before). The proposed figure so far exceeded Harry Frazee's notion of what a ballplayer was worth that the owner clutched his chest, retreated to his Broadway office, and refused to endanger his health by listening to any more such wild demands. Ruth must be nuts, he exclaimed. Frazee didn't even pay his top stage stars that kind of money.

After an appropriate period of time he summoned to New York, for a salary conference, what he assumed would be the contrite player. Seated behind his gleaming antique desk, surrounded by posters from his shows and framed, autographed pictures of the Barrymores, Georgie Cohan, Eddie Foy, and the rest of his dear theatrical friends, he sat ready for Babe to meekly take his pen in hand and sign for a slight raise. But when his charismatic employee strolled in, nodding to the secretaries as if he owned the place and signing autographs for the office boys, Frazee realized with a sinking feeling that his act hadn't even penetrated Babe's consciousness. "What the fuck do I care about actors?" Babe asked bluntly when Frazee started the old routine. All he wanted was the money, and he'd hold out until the Fourth of July unless he got it. In the end the unhappy owner agreed to ten thousand a year for three years. How could he work on someone who didn't even know enough to be impressed by the Barrymores?

On a mild early April day, lulled by the breezes sweeping in off the sparkling waters of the Gulf of Mexico, half asleep from the late nights they'd been keeping, the sportswriters watched the big boy prance up to the plate in his first exhibition game, against the Giants. Swinging easily, he stepped into a fastball and connected with a resounding crack. The writers' heads jerked up. Folding chairs went crashing as they jumped to their feet to try to follow the ball's flight toward the right-field fence. When it had vanished into the palm tree tops sticking up beyond the confines of the park, they rubbed their eyes, shook their heads, and looked back in awe to the infield. There, Babe was just starting to round the bases—even he had stood still and watched the ball out of sight.

McGeehan's column the next day raved: "The ball sailed so high, when it came down it was coated with ice . . . a drive that would have rattled off the clubhouse roof at the Polo Grounds." Fred Lieb, together with Rice and a Red Sox publicist, wanted to measure just how far the ball had gone. They left the park and walked to the adjacent racetrack beyond the right-center-field fence where it had landed. Today, Lieb recalls the distance between home plate and the spot where it came to rest as 625 feet, almost all of which had been in the air, since the ground where it landed was not conducive to rolling. In his autobiography, *My Fifty Years in Baseball,* Ed Barrow gives the distance as 579 feet. Other estimates have it around 550. But whatever the measurement, it was by many lengths the longest blow anyone had ever seen.

Rice saluted Babe's prowess with a major poetic effort:

SON OF SWAT—BABE RUTH

When you can lean upon the ball
    And lay the seasoned ash against it,
The ball park is a trifle small,
    No matter how far out they've fenced it.
Past Master of the four base clout,
    You stand and take your wallop proudly—
A pretty handy bloke about,
    I'll say you are . . . and say it loudly.

(two additional verses)

But for all the excitement, it was still just spring-training stuff. The New York writers didn't yet see any great significance in Ruth's ability to slam an occasional ball out of sight. In the American League, Chicago, featuring Eddie Collins, Joe Jackson (the same Joe Jackson who had driven Ruth from the mound in his first major league start), Ray Schalk, Buck Weaver, Eddie Cicotte, and half a dozen other fine players, was the big news. Cleveland, another exceptional team, led by Tris Speaker, now the playing-manager, Larry Gardner, shortstop Ray Chapman, and pitchers Stan Coveleski and Jim Bagby, wasn't far behind. The Red Sox, even with Ruth playing full time, looked like a second division team, which was a pity since it would probably keep Ruth from getting the attention he deserved—at least in New York, which was where it counted.

But the Boston writers down there viewed the prospect of seeing the newly designated home-run king play every day as manna from heaven. The morose Mays was the only other young star left from the team's great days, and he wasn't exactly a colorful character. Babe was their savior. On his first day in camp the headline of the *Morning Globe* baseball page blared "LOOK WHO'S HERE—BABE RUTH ARRIVES!!" The writers soon created new appelations for Babe, such as the "Sudbury Farmer," and "Master of Ceremonies of Swat." The intersquad team for which he played in practice games was dubbed "Babe's Busters." When he sat out a game, the team was archly called the "Ruthless Sox" because it had disappointed the fans. The papers ran numerous photo features on Ruth, including one in the *Evening Globe* showing him staring blankly at a splinter of wood, with the caption "Ruth mourns one of his pet bats." And when the Red Sox played exhibition games against other major league teams in towns not far from Tampa, the writers joshed the rubes who failed to realize whom they had in their midst. "The Gainesville fans were all for the Giants," sniffed Edward Martin after one such game. "Apparently they had never heard of Babe Ruth."

His lack of renown didn't bother Babe as much as it bothered the Boston writers. The broads knew him, that was for sure. "They'd recognize that cock anywhere," he roared to the guys in the locker room as they took their showers. Jesus, there were some fancy whorehouses down here in Florida. Full of hot Cuban broads with dark eyes and skin like coffee. ("Make that like coffee *grounds*," snorts one former teammate, who had a more realistic view of the local ladies of the evening.) But in Ruth's eyes the places in Hot Springs had been nothing in comparison. The one thing he missed was the hot baths. Nothing beat them. But he liked the warm sunshine, soft ocean breezes, blue skies, and lush golf courses in Florida. He had become addicted to golf. Almost every day after practice he played nine holes or so, spraying the ball enormous distances in unpredictable directions, dropping new balls when he didn't feel like playing a difficult lie, losing patience on the greens and taking four putts from twenty feet, angrily heaving a club into a water hazard when a bad shot left him frustrated.

The greaseballs down at the dog track knew him, too. He'd dropped half his first month's salary backing the wrong mutts. How the hell was anyone supposed to figure out which one of those dumb dogs could run faster than the next? Anyway, who cared? He had a good time there. The boys were always glad to see him, and that was what counted. He liked those tall drinks they were always handing out, the ones with the salt on the rims.

As the 1919 season began, Hooper did his best to drill Babe in the rudiments of outfield technique but met with only sporadic success. Although Ruth had good speed for such a big man (his playing weight was now up to 220 pounds) and, of course, he possessed a strong, accurate arm, he was not likely to make anyone forget Speaker or Lewis. Hooper himself started out in center field, but he soon realized that Ruth would never fully grasp the procedure of calling for a fly ball and, in his own words, "began hearing footsteps" whenever he veered toward Ruth's territory. Before the season had progressed very far he switched himself back to right field, put Ruth in left, and then in center when Braggo Roth, another galloping elephant, joined the team, and hoped he would survive the year without being trampled to death during one of Babe's mad lunges after a ball.

At the plate Babe couldn't buy a base hit, let alone hit one out of the park. After fourteen games his average scraped bottom at .198, and his home run total was one. After one futile infield pop-up he stormed back to the dugout and smashed his bat to pieces against a supporting pillar. The papers, as quick to turn critical as they had been to celebrate, began demanding his return to the mound. Barrow consulted with Hooper and shortstop Everett Scott, who really ran the team while he concentrated on front-office duties, and allowed himself to be talked into continuing the tryout a while longer. (He did use Ruth to pitch occasionally in the course of the season, and Babe compiled an eight-and-five record.) That decision paid off, for Ruth finally broke out of his slump. By the middle of May his average was up to .290, and on May 23 he hit his fifth home run. "There ain't a pitcher in the league I can't belt one off," Babe bragged to Helen.

Baseball followers began to scan the sports pages for the two- or three-paragraph wire service summaries of out-of-town games to see what wonders the big boy from Beantown had performed that day. More often than not they found something to shake their heads over. On May fifth he started his first game on the mound and doubled in the winning runs to beat the Yankees 3–2. On the fifteenth he came in from left field to win a game in relief. On the twentieth he pitched against the Browns and slugged a grandslam home run to win 6–4. In Cleveland on the twenty-seventh the summary announced that "Ruth's triple was the longest hit ever made on the local field." Three days later he shut out the Athletics 6–0.

On the seventh of June, "With two out in the fifth Ruth hit the first ball pitched into the right field bleachers, where a boy stood up and caught it." The fourteenth saw him pitch thirteen innings and lose to the Indians 3–2, although he drove in one of Boston's runs

and scored the other. The next day Cleveland outfielder
Jack Graney, the first man Babe had faced in his first
game in Boston back in 1914, "caught a long ball hit by
Ruth on the embankment below the scoreboard."

They were talking about that blow in Cleveland for
weeks afterward. The wooden stands at Dunn Field
were a dead gray color in the deeper reaches of the outfield and when the ball cleared their plane it just seemed
to vanish into the bright sunshine. All you could see was
Graney running back toward the scoreboard in dead
center. The left-center stands measured 410 feet from
home plate and this ball was going lots farther than that.
Graney shouldn't have had a chance at it, but he had
been playing deep and the thing was hit so high he managed to catch up with it just in front of the wall. When
he made the catch he was so far away that the fans behind the plate could barely make him out. Ruth was already past second, tearing toward third. When the third
base coach Heinie Wagner held up his hands and told
him the ball had been caught, Ruth just stopped and
looked around in disbelief. Then he kicked the dirt in
disgust.

On July fifth, against Chicago, he slammed two home
runs, one into the right field seats, the other into the left.
A week later he hit his eleventh of the year, tying his
league-leading total of the previous season. On the sixteenth, after a Cleveland hitter tripled with the bases
loaded in the eighth inning to send his team ahead, Ruth
homered with the bases loaded in the ninth to win
the game for Boston. A few days later in Detroit
"Ruth . . . put the ball over the right field fence for
the longest hit ever made at Navin Field." In that same
week the Red Sox beat the Yankees and "the prime factor in their defeat was Babe Ruth and his extraordinary
bat. Ruth made one of his famous home runs in the
eighth inning, enabling the Sox to take the lead."

In the first week of August "The longest home run
ever made at the local park (Comisky Park in Chicago)
was hit by Ruth in the fifth inning over the right field

bleachers." And in the report of a game in Detroit, a significant new kind of statistic made its appearance alongside Ruth's name: "25,000 persons watched Babe Ruth add two more home runs to his total, and then drive over the run that won the contest."

The drawing power of Cobb, Speaker, Johnson, even young George Sisler (on his way to becoming the new Cobb) seemed to pale beside the mighty slugger from Baltimore. To the dismay of the old-timers, the crowds got more excited when one of Ruth's all-out flailings with the bat missed connections than they did when another player punched out a good clean base hit. As early as May, a wire service summary had thought it worth reporting that Cicotte had managed to fan Ruth twice in a game, and as the season went on his misses were as avidly chronicled as his hits. By the last two weeks of the season the sports fans of the nation were in an uproar. On September 20 he tied the all-time one-season home-run record of twenty-seven, which had been set by a Chicago White Stocking player back in the dark ages of 1884. When he finished the year with the unheard-of total of twenty-nine, four of them grand slams, the entire nation exulted. The New York writers cheered as loudly as the rest and wished he were playing in their back yard.

Babe reveled in the attention. At the start of each game he strutted out onto the field with his chest extended and chin up, making his way to the outfield with measured steps. He took his time strolling up to the plate, joking with the umpires, making the pitcher and the crowd fidget while he adjusted his uniform and went through a few practice swings, letting the tension build. When he hit one out he laughed at the downcast pitcher as he rounded the bases and tipped his hat to the crowd before he entered the dugout. As the cheers of the fans echoed around him he seemed to swell like a peacock.

The fans, especially the young boys, took to swarming all over him after a game, or when they spotted him on the street. Sometimes they practically pulled his clothes off his back before he got away. That threw him a little. Novelist James T. Farrell, then a fifteen-year-old bleacher addict in Chicago, watched one Ruth appearance in Comisky Park and recorded his impressions in *My Baseball Diary:*

> After the game, I watched the players come out of the clubhouse as I usually did. As I was leaving the ball park, I saw Ruth. A crowd of over a hundred kids had him not only surrounded but almost mobbed. They pushed, shoved, scrambled, and yelled so that Ruth could scarcely move. Wearing a blue suit and a gray cap, there was an expression of bewilderment on his moon face. He said nothing, rolled with the kids, and the strange, hysterical and noisy little mob slowly moved to the exit gate with Ruth in the center of it. . . . Ruth swayed from side to side, his shoulders bending one way and then the other. . . . Ruth and the kids left the park, with the big fellow still in the center of the crowd of kids.

The Red Sox players regarded Babe's new popularity with a slightly jaundiced eye; most of the 1919 team had been around too long to let a few home runs influence the way they felt about him. Some were jealous, of course. For several weeks during the first part of the season one of the players, a man with a loud, penetrating voice, delighted in making jungle noises and thicklipping "big baboon, big baboon," whenever he caught Ruth with his back turned. Babe didn't like it. The mere sound of his tormentor's voice seemed to get to him. After a game in New York, while Babe sat on a bench pulling off his sweat-soaked uniform, the player pulled his favorite trick again. Ruth exploded and stormed about the dressing room, slamming his fist into the walls and challenging the whole team. Most of the players shrugged and turned back to their lockers to finish dressing, but Hooper noticed that Babe had been brought to the verge of tears by his teammates' studied indifference. Feeling that Ruth deserved some compassion, he used his authority as team captain to order the man to knock it off. (He will not reveal the player's name, however.)

Not that Babe's swelled head had gone down any.

When Ed Barrow stood in front of Ruth in the Fenway Park dressing room and bawled him out for a series of curfew violations, Babe clenched his left fist and shook it at the manager. "You can't talk to me like that," he bellowed. "I'll punch you right in the snout!" Barrow's eyes narrowed as he studied Ruth for a moment or two. Then he stripped off his suit coat, rolled up his sleeves, and ordered the room cleared of everyone except Ruth. Hooper and Scott tried to reason with him, but the furious "Simon" wasn't having any of it. He could only mutter that when he got finished with the big bastard they would have to sponge him up. Babe looked around uncertainly, trying to work up a face-saving grin. The others took one last look at Barrow's glowering brow and twitching cheeks and quickly decided to clear out. Barrow looked around for Ruth, but all he saw was Babe's broad back as he ran out after the others. He wasn't going to fight a fifty-year-old man, for Christ sakes, as he later explained to skeptical teammates.

Late in the season, during a game at Dunn Field in Cleveland, he once again became embroiled with his old antagonist Brick Owens in a disagreement as to the quality of the latter's eyesight behind the plate. Owens threw him out of the game, and just as he had in June 1917, Ruth flew off the handle and threatened to punch the hell out of the umpire. This time, however, he waited until players from both teams had rushed out of their dugouts to head him off before hurrying down from the mound. He knew they wouldn't let him go too far. He pulled in more fans than the rest of them put together —they couldn't afford to let him get in trouble. He didn't have a damned thing to worry about.

For Harry Frazee, 1919 had been a terrible year. He had backed several wrong numbers in the theater, and although he had followed Barrow's advice and picked up first baseman Stuffy McInnis, catcher Wally Schang, and pitcher Joe Bush to beef up his roster, the ball club was proving to be as big a bomb as some of his shows. A sixth-place team, even with the home run king in the lineup, couldn't attract enough fans to help him much. On top of everything else, Joe Lannin, from whom he had purchased the Red Sox, had decided to call in his notes. If things went on this way, Frazee wouldn't be able to meet the mortgage on Fenway Park.

Fortunately he knew a couple of guys with pots of money—Colonel Jacob Ruppert and Colonel Til Huston, the owners of the New York Yankees. Frazee and the two colonels had been natural allies since their first days in baseball. They were all from the big town. They understood each other. Though to an outsider it might have seemed ingenuous to turn to a competitor for help, for Frazee it was perfectly natural to get in touch with the Yankee owners about his problem. Soon after the season ended they all sat down to see what could be done about getting him out of his fix.

For a price, of course. Ruppert and Huston were both millionaire businessmen, used to wheeling and dealing with both hands and both feet as well if it became necessary. Otherwise, though, they had very different backgrounds. Ruppert was the scion of the founders of Ruppert Breweries. A chunky bachelor in his mid-forties, he was aloof and patrician in manner and seldom addressed anyone by his or her first name. His circle included co-members of the elite New York National Guard "silk stocking" regiment, as well as the hoi polloi of the horsey set. A model of sartorial rectitude, at home at the opera, dog shows, and polo matches, Ruppert had served four terms in Congress as representative of the New York East Side gentility. When the primary system was instituted in 1908 he had voluntarily stepped down, preferring not to submit himself to the indignity of a primary fight.

Ruppert was no slouch as an entrepreneur, either. His rationale for the purchase of the Yankees in 1915 had been a plan to use the team for promotional purposes by changing its name to the Knickerbockers, after his best-selling beer—an idea that was discouraged by a consensus of editorial writers. (A similar unsuccessful *coup de nom* was attempted across the East River by a bread company, which tried to change the name of the Brooklyn Federal League team to the Tip-Tops.)

Colonel Tillinghast L'Hommedieu "Cap" Huston was an altogether different type, despite his aristocratic name. A one-time Army engineer, he was a self-made man who had made his fortune in the harbor-improvement business in Cuba. He had remained a gruff, disheveled, one-of-the-boys sort of fellow who liked drinking and playing cards with the sporting crowd. His greatest joy in life came from his private lodge on one of the Georgia Sea Islands, called Dover Hall, where he frequently brought parties of sportswriters and other cronies for drinking and hunting sprees. In his mind, owning a baseball team was pretty much of a lark, although that did not keep him from being as tough as leather when he chose to be.

Frazee, knowing these two as well as he did, must have expected them to drive a hard bargain. He had only one blue chip to play with, in any event. It was simply a question of determining how much they would pay for him—and of keeping the deal quiet so that the Boston fans and other American League club owners would be presented with a *fait accompli*.

Hints of a big deal in the works inevitably got out. On December 12, Davis J. Walsh of the *New York Evening Post,* in his baseball news roundup, quoted rumors that Babe Ruth might be coming to New York. When asked, Frazee got cagey and evaded the issue by announcing that he was so disgusted with Boston's sixth-place finish that he was ready to trade the entire team. Walsh reported his sentiments, then added, "We hope, however, that we have the privilege of doubting Mr. Frazee's well-known word in the matter of Babe Ruth. . . . The latter is too much of a popular hero with the Boston fans to be disposed of without precipitating a small-sized riot, with Mr. Frazee becoming the party of the second part." In Boston, equally threatening items began showing up on the sports pages.

But on January 6, 1920, across the front pages of their newspapers New Yorkers read about the newest

Bolshevik outrages, the Supreme Court's decision that the Volstead Act (prohibition) was constitutional, and the selling of Babe Ruth to the New York Yankees. The price was reported as $125,000, by far the most expensive baseball transaction ever consummated. (The actual contract sum was $100,000, but Ruppert also guaranteed the mortgage on Fenway Park for $350,000. That clause was not made public at the time, however.)

Yankee fans reacted with unrestrained joy. Various American League owners shouted charges of collusion. Giants' manager John McGraw gritted his teeth at the thought of competing with Ruth for New Yorkers' affections. New Englanders damned Frazee with the vehemence of Salem witch-hunters. Barrow fumed and publicly denounced the action, though Hooper and many others have always suspected that he helped arranged the deal and was paid off in one way or another. Ruppert and Huston looked forward to a rewarding season in 1920. Miller Huggins wondered if he would have any trouble with the slugger. And down at Billy LaHiff's, Runyon, Rice, McGeehan, and the rest of the Broadway sportswriters grinned at each other, drank a toast to the gods of good copy, and prepared to oil up their typewriters to meet the new challenge.

5

Into the Arms of the Mythmakers

ON THE AFTERNOON the Yankees announced the deal, Helen answered an insistent ring at the front door of the Ruths' Sudbury house. As she opened the door a dozen reporters, crowding up onto the stoop, shouted questions at her. For a moment she tried to think of something to say, then stammered that Babe was out of town and fled back into the house.

From Los Angeles, where he had been playing exhibition games, Ruth sent a telegram back to Boston. "I ain't going!" it declared, in effect. Out in California he proclaimed his love for the Boston area, his farm, and the great Red Sox fans, and his new business enterprises. (He had become part owner of a cigar factory the previous year.) They couldn't sell him like some lousy rookie. No, sir.

The reporters winked at each other, went back to their offices, and dutifully knocked out the required copy—one story expressing their genuine outrage at Ruth's departure, another extolling Babe's home-loving sentiments. "Ruth Won't Leave," exclaimed a headline over a *Globe* story. The public believed it, as always, and suffered along with their hero. But the sportswriters recognized a gambit when they saw one. They knew what he was after: Ruth wanted more money. (At first he held out for a percentage of the sales price. In the

102

end he settled for a hundred percent raise in salary, from ten to twenty thousand dollars.)

The New York baseball world could hardly wait for the start of the 1920 season. Finally, on March 1, the Yankees' spring training express pulled out of Penn Station, headed for Savannah, Georgia. Manager Miller Huggins was suffering from a severe cold, so he chose to remain in bed for a couple of days longer. But Babe Ruth, the greatest baseball bonanza since the invention of the curve ball, was on board—and the writers' mouths were watering at the thought of the stories awaiting them when they debarked in the south.

For the next six weeks a steady stream of headlines and features carried the preseason excitement to the fans of New York and America:

Babe Ruth Big Attraction at Way Stations in South; Home Run King Scatters Cigars with Lavish Hand

Ruth Complains of Indigestion

Ruth a Fizzle on Links; Home Run King Smashes Several Clubs

Ruth Twice a Strikeout Victim

Ruth's Big Bats Arrive in Camp

Ruth Begins Pounding Ball

Brooklyn Boys Indulge in Wild Pitching and Keep Babe Ruth Inactive

They Don't Dare Pass Babe Ruth (Because It Annoys the Big Boy)

Mr. Ruth, for the nonce, was very much to the fromage in a batting sense. He struck out twice . . .

Ruth's Error Defeats New York Squad

Ruth left the game with a lame ankle. It was no bluff. He really had one . . .

Ruth Strikes Out Twice

Ruth's Bludgeon Inactive

Ruth Turns on Blatant Fan Who Calls Him a "Piece of Cheese"

The fact that Ruth went into the stands Saturday with a fan shows that Babe is pretty much peeved at things in general. That he can larrup the ball as far as ever he had shown on many occasions. It is simply a matter of getting his sights adjusted.

Ruth Hits Ball into River

Babe Ruth Finally Recovers his Batting Eye and Pounds Ball out of Jacksonville Lot

Ruth Strikes Out Three Times

Along with their regular news stories, the writers also sent back a plentiful supply of extra features on the new sensation. One described an eating contest organized by Damon Runyon and author Irwin S. Cobb, who had wandered south for a few days of hunting and drinking at Cap Huston's lodge. Ruth and Cobb, a celebrated bottomless pit at the dinner table, were to take on any other pair of contenders. Bill Macbeth, writing in the *New York Tribune,* gave the fans a laugh with a blow-by-blow description of one of Babe's training meals: "Ruth polishes off a double sirloin and all the trimmings, plus a pint bottle of catsup. Just before he strikes dessert a waiter happens to appear with George Mo-gridge's dinner order. [Mogridge was a Yankee pitcher.] Ruth, who mistakes this for a side dish, cleans the platter and then nonchalantly orders a double portion of mince pie à la mode and a rice pudding"; whereupon all potential challengers withdrew, and Runyon declared Ruth and Cobb champions by default.

Reporters solicited opinions on the Ruth phenomenon from his acquaintances. When Ed Barrow was asked for a few words, he gave a thoughtful although somewhat tangential reply to Gene Fowler: "I would say that Ruth smokes altogether too much for a batsman who hoped to continue at the top for a number of years. . . . He smokes incessantly. He will start when he arises and will be found with a cigar between his teeth when he falls asleep."

Wally Pipp, the Yankees' leading slugger in years past, declined to speculate on how Ruth would do but was willing to forecast the number of home runs he (Pipp) would hit in the coming season as twenty.

George Sisler showed confidence in Babe's continued ability, stating in an *Evening Mail* interview that Ruth had no batting weaknesses, and that he might easily hit fifty home runs. "What about his mentality?" Sisler was asked. "Well, that is another proposition," allowed the St. Louis star.

Even baseball's rear guard felt impelled to get on record. Bill Hanna, one of Joe Vila's boys on the *Sun,* expressed his fear that high-scoring games might offend the sensibilities of fans used to *real* baseball. It is well known, he asserted, that "a profusion of runs is not wanted by the fans."

If Hanna was correct, the fans who watched the Yankees in their exhibition games must have enjoyed themselves, for the team couldn't seem to hit a ball out of the infield. Ruth in particular—as the headlines had reported—was having a terrible spring. The unusually large crowds that turned out to see him play (six thousand in Winston-Salem, ten thousand in Jacksonville, fifteen thousand in Brooklyn) frequently went home disappointed. At best he would rip a single or two, at worst strike out two or three times. His fielding was becoming a bigger threat to his own pitchers than his hitting was to the opposition. Not even the most optimistic report could disguise the fact that on the basis of his spring-training form, Ruth would be lucky to equal his 1918 totals, let alone threaten his 1919 record.

But Babe professed not to be worried. When the writers buttonholed him between deals of a poker game or on his way to meet some broad, he scoffed at their worries. "I'll hit fifty this year," he boasted. "Spring training don't mean nothing."

Ruth, of course, received most of the preseason attention, but the rest of the team also did its bit to provide good copy. The scrawny, wizened little manager, Miller Huggins, was widely admired as a shrewd baseball thinker. In his twelve years as a second baseman for Cincinnati and St. Louis of the National League he had hit as high as the .270s only four times. But in his quiet, thoughtful way he had picked up a vast amount of baseball technique and when he was named playing manager of St. Louis in 1913, at the age of thirty-three, no one had been surprised. He knew his stuff.

Huggins was a master of one-upsmanship. He studied opposing teams and players with great patience, evaluating their psychology, probing for their weaknesses. In a close game against the Philadelphia Phillies in 1917, Huggins, coaching at third base, launched a game-long series of complaints about the way in which the pitcher, a cocksure rookie, was allegedly doctoring the ball. Every complaint was rejected, to the rookie's delight and Huggins's apparent chagrin. Finally, in a late inning, with Cardinal runners on second and third, Huggins demanded to see the ball in a tone which implied that this time he had the kid dead to rights. Supremely confident, the rookie wheeled and immediately threw the ball toward Huggins in the third base coaching box. Hug casually stepped out of its way and, as the ball bounced against the grandstand and rolled out toward left field, he waved the runners home and treated himself to one of his rare smiles.

His most celebrated trick came after he had moved to the Yankees—during the pregame warm-up for the first game of the 1927 World Series with Pittsburgh. Aware that the fearsome reputation of that year's Yankee team was perhaps his strongest weapon, he instructed Urban Shocker, a pitcher with exquisite control, to pitch batting practice and throw nothing but half-speed pitches to precisely the spots where each of his big hitters liked them. Ruth, Gehrig, Lazzeri and Meusel responded by smashing drive after drive into the Forbes Field seats. With each one the spirits of the Pirate players, who were watching on the sidelines, sank further. By the time the game started they were feeling quite unnerved and never did regain their confidence. They lost the series in four straight games.

Important as his strategic maneuvers were, Huggins' largest contribution lay in his unusual ability to handle men. "He was a terrific manager," says Earle Combs. "He made a point of not bawling you out in front of everyone else. If he had something to say to you he'd take you into his office. I think everybody had a lot of respect for him except Ruth. He was a funny little guy, you know. He had a lot of superstitions. He was scared to death of taxis, for example. I don't know why. But he hated to get into a taxi. When he died, in the 1929 season, it was a tremendous shock to everyone. Just tremendous."

In purely baseball terms the 1920 Yankees were a team in transition. The nucleus of the club was a group of first-rate veterans: Wally Pipp at first base, Roger Peckinpaugh at shortstop, "Home Run" Frank Baker at third, Ping Bodie in the outfield, Bob Shawkey on the mound. Bob Meusel, a hard-hitting outfield prospect from the West Coast and Aaron Ward, a versatile young infielder, were the top newcomers. Muddy Ruel, another promising youngster, worked behind the plate. Duffy Lewis, obtained from Boston along with Ernie Shore, was attempting a comeback in the outfield. The pitching staff had also been bolstered by the addition of another ex-Boston star, Carl Mays. With Ruth added to the mix it became a very promising group, although not yet a great team.

But what a collection of hotheads and curfew-break-ers! Ruth was quite enough himself, but there were others just as troublesome. Mays' temper had grown worse, if anything, over the years. The way in which he had come to the Yankees typified the controversy that followed him around. In July of the previous year, beset by personal problems and disgusted with the ineptness of the Red Sox play, he had stalked off the mound in the middle of a game against Chicago and simply refused to pitch for Boston any longer. Frazee was willing to accommodate him with a trade to New York, but Ban Johnson, insisting that Mays follow baseball precedent and first return to the Red Sox, voided the trade by suspending the pitcher. Frazee, Ruppert, and Huston countered by revealing to the public Johnson's financial interest in Cleveland (which was then fighting New York and Chicago for the league lead) and accusing him of trying to prevent the Indians' rivals from helping themselves, and furthermore of having arranged the Speaker sale to Cleveland in 1915 for the same unethical reason. As if that weren't enough, the Boston and New York owners then took the unheard-of step of obtaining a court injunction forbidding the league president to interfere with the way they ran their clubs. The hubbub did not help the image of baseball in the eyes of the fans.

Ping Bodie, whom the sportswriters had nicknamed "The Wonderful Wop" (his real name was Franceto Pizzola), at one point packed his bags and stalked out of spring training in a huff over an imagined slight, vowing never to return. (He later did.) Frank Baker sat out the year because of illness in his family. The taciturn Li'l Abner of the team, Bob Meusel, seemed bent upon good-timing himself out of a job even before he had one. Under Ruth's benign guidance, he broke curfew, drank like a fish, staggered from party to party, and regularly fouled up in the field. A *Tribune* reporter, commenting on his disappointing start, mentioned that "during the spring training trip his utter disregard for training rules handicapped him," and warned him to shape up. As early as the third week of spring training the papers were speculating on whether Huggins would ever be able to control the team's penchant for high life. "Huggins read the riot act to his players this morning," reported the *Herald* on March 21. "There will be no more lack of system and discipline in the Yankee's training. Besides a curfew law, every player has been ordered to put in an appearance at the breakfast room before nine o'clock each morning."

The new regime helped restrain the partying, but it did not help calm the team's temper. No sooner had the season opened than Shawkey took exception to a call and got into a fistfight with an umpire. Pipp also tried to throw his weight around and got himself thrown out more than once for his trouble. And in May, Huggins himself assaulted another umpire and was suspended for a game.

Also in May, Ruppert and Huston received a notice of eviction from the Polo Grounds, where the Yankees had played as tenants of the Giants since 1913. (They were given a reasonable amount of time to find someplace else to play, of course.) Many observers thought the expulsion stemmed from Giants' manager, John McGraw and owner Charles Stoneham's resentment at their team being upstaged by Ruth and the Yankees. Baseball historian Harold Seymour suggests that the Giants were influenced by Ban Johnson, who was quietly launching a counterattack against the Yankee owners and hoping to use the stadium issue as a means to force them to sell out. In any case, the Yankees came out on top, as the two colonels were inspired to begin plans to build their own stadium on a piece of land they purchased just across the Harlem River from the Polo Grounds.

Another tempest blowing about the Yankees involved the Boston–New York relationship. Antagonism abounded around the league over Frazee's willingness to deal off stars of the caliber of Ruth and Mays to his pals in New York. In 1920 Wally Schang, one of the league's best catchers, was openly maneuvering to get himself sold to the Yankees. And there were even rumors that Ed Barrow was headed in that direction.

(It turned out that the other owners had good reason to be upset. At the end of the 1920 season Barrow did become the Yankees' general manager. And in the next four years, while the rest of the league fumed, a procession of Boston stars arrived in New York almost on a regular schedule. The haul included two future Hall of Fame pitchers [Herb Pennock and Waite Hoyt], two just slightly less valuable pitchers [Sam Jones and Joe Bush], the best third baseman in the league [Joe Dugan], a classy shortstop [Everett Scott], Schang, and several less important but handy players. Out of all the deals the Red Sox got only one player of value—catcher Muddy Ruel—and Huggins reportedly kicked himself afterward for letting him go when the Yankees could have sent cash instead, as they usually did.)

With Ruth adding his peculiar temperament and talents to this mixture, fans and writers expected an interesting year ahead in 1920. They didn't have to wait long. On a cloudy April 16, New York opened in Philadelphia before the largest Shibe Park crowd in several years. As Ruth strode to the plate for his first official time at bat as a Yankee, a delegation of fans emerged from the stands and held up the game while they presented him with an attractively wrapped token of their esteem. A pleased Ruth opened the box only to find a brown derby several sizes too small for his head—an indication of the Philadelphia fans' reaction to his boastful ways. Babe tried the hat on, letting it perch on top of his head like a vaudeville comedian. The crowd laughed and burst into applause. During the game he struck out twice and played poorly in the field, so maybe he wasn't all that amused.

The following day he fanned three more times and dropped a fly ball. He made another critical error in the next game to help the Yankees lose. As his average hovered around .230 he found new ways to gum up the works. On the twenty-third he lost an important run because of careless base running, then struck out twice with men on base.

The rest of the team was not doing much better. Macbeth registered his disgust after the team's home opener, despite the fact that they won the game: "The Yankees, after leading more or less of a life of shame on the road, made their bows for the season at the Polo Grounds yesterday. It is true that they won a game that was as loose as an eiderdown pillow with the cover off from Cornelius McGillicuddy's Apathetics . . ." began his lead paragraph.

But in the eleventh game of the season, after walking to the plate with a glowering frown on his face, as if he had finally decided to assert himself, Ruth blasted a ball over the roof of the right field pavilion at the Polo Grounds, duplicating his feat of five years earlier. As the big boy trotted around the bases, nodding to the wildly cheering fans, his smile of satisfaction could be seen from the furthest corner of the bleachers. The next day twenty-five thousand spectators swarmed into the park to see if he could do it again. Naturally, he could, and set off another ear-splitting celebration.

McGeehan rhapsodized about the event in his column that day:

> Home runs executed by Babe Ruth are not mere home runs. Each home run seems to possess an individuality and eccentricities of its own. After the game the multitude lingers in the lot to trace the path taken by the ball. . . . This one, according to Harry M. Stevens, crossed directly between the *E* and *R* of the Eveready sign and dented the outer wall of the grounds, from which spot it descended forcibly into a basket of peanuts, practically ruining three bags of the goobers.

On May 12 the Sultan of Swat smashed two home runs and a triple. He belted another stupendous homer on the thirteenth. Four days later more than thirty-eight thousand fans, the largest crowd in New York baseball history, jammed into the Polo Grounds, and more than fifteen thousand were turned away—only to have Ruth and the Yankees lose a wretchedly played game. But on the twenty-fourth a *Sun* headline proclaimed: "Mighty

Slugger Hits Ball over Grand Stand Flag Pole." And toward the end of the month, several New York papers
began to run "Truth about Ruth" boxes, in which they
charted and analyzed his home run statistics.

During late May and early June the Yankees, led by
Ruth, put together a ten-game winning streak and
moved into contention with Cleveland for the league
lead. On June 7 Ruth's average had risen to .328, and
his home run total was sixteen, nine more than the run-
ner-up slugger. By the eighteenth of that month he was
hitting .352 with nineteen homers, and fans around the
league were fighting to see him. A *Tribune* reporter
grandly proclaimed: "Babe Ruth is a bigger show
this year than baseball itself. . . . The infant heads
a procession whenever he walks abroad. They bring
their babies to the park and point him out. And
the hand that shook the hand of Babe Ruth is looked
upon with quite as much awe as the hand that shook the
hand of John L. Sullivan used to be."

In Washington in July Ruth drew the largest crowd on
record for that city. In Detroit he accepted a diamond-
studded watch fob presented by the local Knights of Columbus. He broke the record for the most strikeouts in
one day, with five. He led the Yankees, now being referred to as "Murderer's Row," to unbelievable 17–0,
19–3, and 20–5 victories, the latter two over the world
champion White Sox. He was reported killed in an auto
accident at Wawa, Pennsylvania, when he drove off the
highway and ended up in a ditch. (One New York paper
gave the tragedy an eight-column-wide headline.) And he
broke his 1919 home run record before the month was
half over. By the end of July his total had climbed to
thirty-six.

August began with "a crowd estimated at forty thousand, largest which ever witnessed an American League
game in Chicago . . . out in hope Ruth would put over
another home run." (He did not.) On following days he
skied an infield pop so high he was jogging into third
base by the time it came down, hit a home run with fatal
consequences to a fan in the nation's capital ("When

Ruth made the home run Theodore Sturm, a fan, suffered an attack of heart disease and died a few minutes after he was carried from the grandstand," according to the UPI), and drew the largest crowd in Cleveland history.

On August 17, as Cleveland and New York met in a critical series, an errant fastball thrown by a Yankee pitcher fractured Ray Chapman's skull. The popular Cleveland shortstop died that night, thus becoming the first known major league fatality. The pitcher, as one could almost have predicted, was Carl Mays.

All around the league, players professed the belief that the ornery sidearmer had probably tried to hit him. Word went out that the Boston and Detroit clubs were discussing petitions to ban Mays. Speaker, Cleveland's manager, publicly exonerated the pitcher, but later expressed a good deal of bitterness. (Although since Speaker, like his mentor, Bill Carrigan, fined his pitchers if they failed to throw at a hitter when he ordered them to do so, he was on shaky ground.) However, the Yankee management and New York sportswriters rallied to Mays' defense, as did the leaders of baseball—as always, worried about the game's image. Ban Johnson rushed out a statement containing the surprising news that "It is my honest belief that Mr. Mays will never pitch again. From what I have learned he is greatly affected . . . and may never be capable temperamentally of pitching again." The next day, when reporters managed to get to him, Johnson admitted to having gilded the lily quite a bit.

Throughout the ordeal Mays himself said nothing. To his teammates it looked as if he couldn't have cared less, though no one ever really knew what was in his mind. When his regular turn came around he was back on the mound, showing no ill effects. And after a while, as the pennant race heated up, the matter was forgotten.

As the end of the season approached, Ruth led a surge which sent the Yankees into the lead for the first time. But the sudden prosperity seemed too much for the team to handle, and it promptly folded. Ruth revived late in September to raise his home run total to an astounding fifty-four for the season, and his batting average to .376, but it was too late to pull the Yankees back into the race. The Indians hung on doggedly to win the pennant and, in view of the loss they had suffered when Chapman died, most fans felt they deserved to win.

From the beginning the major writers trained their big guns on Babe. McGeehan found his precarious physical state a treasure trove of good copy. He began what would develop into a year-round up-to-date health bulletin with a straightforward injury report in late April: "Babe Ruth strained a ligament in his back and will be out for an indefinite period." (Ruth was back on the field in two days.)

On May 19 McGeehan informed his readers that "The Babe is suffering from an eccentric knee which sometimes slips its moorings, causing his feet to point in different directions at times. The medicos are cranking up the joint and Babe may be able to resume his arduous labors tomorrow."

Within a week his optimism had declined: "The latest bulletin on that pale and interesting invalid, Babe Ruth, is a rather gloomy one. The Babe, having caught nearly everything else . . . is now reported to be tucked away in his little cot with a case of the flu."

But two days later McGeehan pried a favorable report out of the team doctor: "Ruth has now completely recovered from the attack of housemaid's knee which had laid him low. But later he picked up a slight attack of croup. . . . It seems the slugger grew so rapidly that he never had time to accumulate the usual infantile diseases and they are now all coming on him in a bunch."

During the next two months Ruth managed to stay off the sick list, except for one game in June when "the home run king was knocked unconscious when hit on the head by a thrown ball." But on August 12 he again dislocated his knee and had to be carried off the field. And on the twenty-ninth, he managed to contract a disease overlooked, until that time, by almost everyone in baseball. "Babe Ruth will be out of the Yankee lineup for perhaps ten days," wrote Dr. McGeehan. "Ruth was operated on yesterday at St. Luke's Hospital because of an infection in his left arm. . . . While the Babe was over in Nyack, he was nipped in the arm by one of the native mosquitoes. It was one of those man-eating insects that infest the vicinity. Ruth beat the mosquito off after a hard battle, but his arm was badly lacerated, and it soon began to swell."

What actually happened was simply another case of Ruth's misapplied home medicine. After an adverse reaction to the bite, he had attempted to drain the swelling himself and caused an infection. Despite McGeehan's pessimistic prognosis, however, he was back in the lineup almost immediately. McGeehan's readers may have been surprised when they saw Ruth back on the field so soon, but that was the Babe for you; he was nothing if not unpredictable.

Grantland Rice's earliest comments were occasional jokes during spring training, along the following lines:

FIRST SCHOLAR: What golf shot does a pitcher use when facing Babe Ruth?

SECOND SCHOLAR: I'm one down. Spill it.

FIRST SCHOLAR: The pitch and run.

One of the first mentions of Babe in verse linked him with Ping Bodie:

> Ruth and Ping—Ping and Ruth
> They can bing—and that's the truth.

As the season progressed and Ruth's accomplishments grew, so did Rice's inspiration. He made an attempt at wryness in this May 10 throwaway: "There is little truth in the rumor that Colonels Huston and Ruppert have requested 'Babe' Ruth to desist from knocking the ball out of the park until the cost of baseballs comes down a bit." And by midsummer an avalanche of verse on the subject of the Babe was falling on the faithful reader's head.

I know exactly how I felt that day when
    down and out
The doc informed me that I had the cholera
    and the gout.
But even as I spoke those words, before
    I hit the mat,
I wonder how the pitcher felt when Babe Ruth
    came to bat.
                    (Three additional verses)

Said W. H. Reuther to big "Babe" Ruth,
"My curve would cross you—and that's the truth."
"I'd murder that curve as sure as 'Luther,' "
Said big Babe Ruth to W. H. Reuther.

THE SCIENCE OF BATTING
by Babe Ruth

I grip my bat, I stand and wait,
I take a look at the right field wall,
I wait'll I get one over the plate
That's about all.
                    (Two additional verses)

How dear to this heart are the scenes of last summer
When fond recollections come back in a row.
When everyone whispered "This Ruth is a comer,"
He's certainly there when it comes to a blow.
            (Two additional verses—in the
            style of "The Old Oaken Bucket")

But after all—and who is there to doubt it—
When one takes up the darkness of despair,
I wonder how the baseball feels about it,
As Ruth's long bat comes swishing through the air.

                    (One preceding verse)
. . . But after all one thrill remains
As each wild echo grows,
When old Babe takes the home run trail
And hits one on the nose.

(Two preceding verses)
Howev'r it be it seems to me
If I was pitching to Babe Ruth
I'd figure twice
Or maybe thrice,
Before I'd cut the plate, forsooth.
(Two additional verses)

THE CRIME OF THE AGES

Why is the mad mob howling?
Hurling its curses out?
Why is the wild wind yelping?
What is it all about?

(Two intervening verses)

Maybe you've guessed the answer,
Hung to the bitter truth—
Only the rival pitcher,
Starting to walk Babe Ruth.

As the season ended, Rice rhymed a valedictory to the year of Ruth:

The Melancholy days are near when fans
    no longer thrill
When silence rules the roaring cheer and
    "Babe" Ruth's bat is still . . .
When winter's gray and sullen ghost
    comes on with phantom tread—
And bottles from no raging host can
    dent the umpire's head.
(Three additional verses)

Even from as dedicated a versemaker as Rice, that selection represented a good year's work. Or at least a long one.

McGeehan, like many others, also tickled his readers' fancy with dialect columns. His favorite character was an immigrant hustler named Izzy Kaplan. Early in the season Izzy took note of Ruth's hitting: "I chust been out to the Polish Grounds, looking at Baby Ruthstein when he is making run homes. All the time he is hitting the baseballs out of the lot instead of knocking them into the stands, where, maybe, you could get some of them back. . . ."

Later, Izzy commented on the rumors (which later proved true) that Ban Johnson had ordered the American League ball made livelier to help ensure a generous supply of home runs in the 1920 season. The league president categorically denied the charge, attributing the increased total of home runs to such new rules as the banning of the spitball and to the newly forged policy of bringing in a bright new ball when the one in use got dirty or scuffed. He also asserted that a better quality horsehide was being used in the ball's covering, which probably made a difference. But Izzy wondered if something wasn't being left out: "When all these fellows like Baby Ruthstein is hitting run homes at the Polish Grounds," he mused, "my brains is asking me what is the reason that baseballs should go further this year when a dollar wouldn't go a quarter as far. . . ."

Lardner also shared Izzy's skepticism, as he revealed in a column written some time later. "A couple yrs. ago a ball player named Baby Ruth that was a pitcher by birth was made into an outfielder on acct. of how he could bust them and he begins breaking records for long distance hits and etc. and he becomes a big drawing card and the master minds that controls baseball says to themselves that if it is home runs that the public wants to see, why leave us give them home runs, so they fixed up a ball that if you don't miss it entirely it will clear the fence, and the result is that ball players which use to specialize in hump back liners to the pitcher is now amongst our leading sluggers when by rights they couldn't take a ball in their hands and knock it past the base umpire."

In other papers, a torrent of similar columns, commentaries, and verse on the subject of Ruth overwhelmed the reader. " 'Here,' we remarked, 'is Babe Ruth. He is a well-known hitter. Possibly you have heard of him. He is married, and owns a new Packard car,' " wrote Runyon, gallantly attempting to explain the mysterious game of baseball to a young lady. (Unfortunately, Runyon had been assigned to cover politics all summer, and had had little chance to write about Ruth.) By the end of the season more words had been written about the King of Clout, the Behemoth of Biff, the Sultan of Swat, the Maharajah of Mash, the Infant Swatigy, the Big Bambino, the Colossus of Club, the Wizard of Whack, the Goliath of Grand Slam, and the Prince of Pounders than had ever been devoted to any other athlete in a single year. More people had watched him play than any other player. And more citizens of America, young and old, knew his name and could even recognize his homely round face than had ever heard of Ty Cobb or John J. McGraw.

Cash rewards poured in to Ruth almost as fast as stories about him poured out. "There was one time in St. Louis," Ernie Shore recalls. "We got into the locker room and someone handed Babe a pile of letters and he handed them to me to sort out. They were checks—one hundred and forty goddamned checks, anywhere from one dollar to five dollars. They were for his autograph, see. The fans figured he'd be sure to endorse something that meant money, and then they'd have his autograph."

On the other end of the scale was a movie contract from Baumann and Kessel Theatrical and Motion Picture Enterprises. Mr. Baumann called him one day in June with an intriguing offer. He and his partner wanted to star Babe in his own delightful baseball comedy. Their price was fifty thousand—fifteen up front and the remainder when shooting was completed. Ruth was agreeable. Why shouldn't he be a movie star? That thirty-five-thousand-dollar check would really be something to wave around. (Since the budget for the entire picture was well under that figure, Ruth's only chance of collecting payment was for the film to be a phenomenal success, but no one explained that fine point to him.)

Shooting began in and around Fort Lee, New Jersey, in July. (It was on location there that Ruth received the

semi-malarial mosquito bite described by McGeehan.)
Every morning a car arrived for Ruth, drove him to the
ferry, then delivered him to the location. After a hard
morning's work he was rushed back to the Polo
Grounds in time to play in that day's game. Often he
didn't even have time to wipe off his makeup and hurried into the locker room with heavily mascara-lined
eyes and sweaty no-shine pancake covering his cheeks,
chin, and forehead. "He really looked strange sometimes," laughs Bob Shawkey. Babe thought it was a riot,
and made horror faces at everyone he saw.

The film was entitled *Heading Home*. It opens in a
little baseball-crazy out-in-the-sticks town called Haverlock, where a George Ruth, his pious, hardworking
mother, Pigtails, his tomboyish little sister, and the family mutt struggle to eke out a hard living. George, a hulk-
ing lad of indeterminate age (Ruth himself was twenty-
five in 1920), can't seem to find a job—not surprising
since his only formal training has apparently been in
bat-whittling, an art he practices on a large chunk of
lumber which he drags around wherever he goes.

The citizens of Haverlock look upon George as the
village dummy. The girl of his dreams ignores him at a
church social. Finally the lad is called on to play in an
important game when the team from a rival town shows
up one man short, and he is chosen by the Haverlock
authorities to fill out their opponent's roster. He wins
the game for them in the fourteenth inning with a stupendous home run that unfortunately shatters the new
church window just as it is being dedicated.

Following that fiasco, Ruth leaves town in disgrace.
Word has gotten round of his potential, however, and he
catches on with another team. Meanwhile, the banker's
daughter, whom he still worships from afar, has become
entangled with a city slicker spitball pitcher, the new
star of the Haverlock team. Through a series of energetic complications, Ruth inadvertently saves her from a
fate worse than death, and she is restored to the good
graces of her family. Then, as the big game approaches,
Babe is all set to play the hero, but at the last second all

his bats vanish. To the rescue comes his little sister and his dog, bringing with them the old piece of whittling Ruth had left behind. Babe homers, the game and the girl are won, and we cut to a contemporary scene at the Polo Grounds. Ruth leads the Yankees out onto the field, and the film ends with a knowing wink from the narrator.

The world premier of *Heading Home* was held in October 1920 at the old Madison Square Garden Theater on Twenty-seventh Street in New York. Ruth and Helen were there, along with a smattering of minor celebrities, sports figures, the usual clique of Broadway freeloaders, and a mob of well-liquored sportswriters. Colonels Ruppert and Huston were out of town. Ed Barrow declined to attend, as did the few Yankees who lived in the New York area. They must have heard something, because *Heading Home* was a resounding flop. Even the hand-picked opening-night audience found the cliché-ridden story and the wooden acting of the star too much to take. By the time Ruth had found someone to ask for his overdue thirty-five grand, Baumann and Kessel had dissolved their partnership and vanished.

Even as Baumann and Kessel were shooting their comedy in New Jersey, Educational Pictures of New York, another small-time outfit, was making its attempt to capitalize on Ruth's popularity. In this case the filmmakers did not even make a pretense of handing out any checks. Halfway through the season they rushed into the theaters with a series of one-reel *Babe Ruth Instructional Films*. Put together from leftover newsreel footage, they bore titles such as "How Babe Ruth Hits a Home Run," and "Play Ball with Babe Ruth." Soon after they opened, an unknown lawyer tried to get into the act by convincing Ruth to file a $250,000 damage suit against Educational Pictures. When the case reached the courts the judge declared that Ruth was a public personage and could be photographed without his permission. Neither side actually prospered since the series proved to be a failure.

The year 1920 also saw the appearance of Pep Pindar, scourge of bullies and prep school all-rounder, in a stirring boys' adventure novel entitled *The Home Run King—Or How Pep Pindar Won his Title*. Pep is a poor boy who "in order to get a chance to play ball, seeks educational honors." He enrolls in Wingate Academy in the typical upstate New York town of East Wingate, alongside Pink Hooper, Tuck Wood, Clara Sweet, and the rest of his boyhood chums. There he develops his athletic prowess and leadership qualities, leads his school to a victory over its arch rival, and in the process wins a scholarship to Syracuse University. Pep's story was published by A. L. Burt, a subsidiary of the H. K. Fly Company. The author of the sports thriller was listed as none other than Babe Ruth.

Almost certainly Babe received only a token recompense for the use of his name, since "literary" rights to the signatures of semi-literate athletes were then worth very little. For the use of his byline over a three- or four-paragraph "personal analysis" of each home run he hit in the 1920 season, a New York news syndicate offered him the grand sum of five dollars a column. And Ruth accepted. Since Babe didn't bother much with reading the newspapers, he may have had no idea of the prominence with which his "analysis" was featured by various sports editors.

Occasionally there would be a sizable paycheck. "I remember Home Run Cigarettes paid him ten thousand dollars to endorse them that first year," Shore says. "I saw the check. That was an awful lot of money in those days." It was more, in fact, than Shore or any other Yankee was making for his entire year's work. "I got fifty dollars once for endorsing Nuxated Iron, which I think was some sort of patent medicine. That was when I was considered the most popular player ever to play with the Red Sox," Harry Hooper recalls. Shore and a couple of other fellows also once got fifty dollars to endorse Champion Sparkplugs. Joe Wood endorsed Coca Cola a year or two before that, and didn't get half as much.

For most players, even the great ones, half a dozen

minor endorsements was a good career's haul. But they wanted Ruth for everything—pipes, chewing tobacco, drinks, baseball equipment, golf clubs clothes, anything with which he could possibly be associated in the public mind. None of the proposals was as large as the one from Home Run Cigarettes, but some were sizable enough to draw envious sighs from his teammates. Half the time Ruth forgot to sign the contracts and the offers fell through.

After the 1920 season Ruth signed with John Mc-Graw, who was taking a group of major leaguers on a barnstorming tour of Cuba. The rest of the makeshift squad consisted mainly of Giants players, notably Frank Frisch, Jesse Barnes, Fred Toney, and Irish Meusel, Bob's brother. Helen also came along for the trip, as did a contingent of McGraw's bookkeeping and gambler friends. When the tour ended Ruth had taken in more than twenty grand. But he had spent a good percentage of his earnings on a series of dark-skinned señoritas and had been conned out of the rest by a couple of American hustlers. A famous Havana "adventuress," telling her story to a syndication outfit two years later, explained how the two sharpies set Ruth up by taking suites at the ostentatious Plaza Hotel, where the Ruths were staying, pretending to be millionaire horsemen. They baited the hook with a few winning tips, graciously allowed Babe to get his whole wad down with a friend of theirs on another sure thing, then set sail for the mainland with the proceeds. Since the author claimed Babe had lost the unlikely sum of $130,000, her word cannot be taken as gospel. But something like what she described probably did take place, since at the end of the tour the Ruths found themselves broke and stranded in Havana. Luckily Helen had put aside enough money to pay their passage home. They arrived in Boston not wealthier but apparently wiser than when they had left for Ruth made sure to stay clear of foreign entanglements for a few years following the 1920 debacle.

The con men and sob story artists had moved in long before the Cuba episode. "People took him for everything," Harry Hooper says. "Everybody had their hooks into him." (Hooper is a heavy, slow-moving man in his late eighties now, with a bad heart. He lives in a comfortable Santa Cruz, California, ranch-style house filled with his late wife's paintings. The Pacific Ocean comes almost to his back door and he spends a good deal of time looking out over the water from his picture window. He has trouble remembering day-to-day things, but his memory for the old days is crisp and sure. And when he talks about Ruth and the sharpies you can hear a distinct note of disgust in his voice.)

The baseball cardsharps, led by Everett Scott, cleaned up on him every time they sat down to play. (Ruth liked to play blackjack at twenty dollars a card with Scott.) Track touts followed him around with hot tips. Pimps palmed off fake virgins on him. He confided to Shawkey in Washington after a game that he was bringing a "real beaut of a showgirl" on the train with him that night. He'd given her a fifteen-hundred-dollar mink to make sure she showed. But the girl ran off to Chicago with her company and left him waiting in his drawing room, all ready in his dressing gown. Hangers-on followed him from bar to bar, hoping to scoop up some loose change. According to his companions on those tours, it was not unusual for him to forget a couple of hundred dollars in change in the course of an evening.

In Boston and occasionally in other cities around the league, Ruth had previously been tapped for public appearances by the Knights of Columbus and other Catholic groups, but once he became the home run king the fund-raising began in earnest. Nuns, priests, and brothers carrying balls and bats and requests for personal appearances waited for him in every American League city. Brother Gilbert of St. Mary's was all smiles as he took home a check for twenty-five hundred dollars to help the school's 1920 building fund. And on the last road trip of the season, Ruth played host to the St. Mary's band, which was trying to raise money to replace its instruments and bandroom, which had been destroyed in the 1919 fire. Some of Ruth's more freethinking colleagues felt that "the priests milked him for everything they could get," in the words of one of them. Sportswriter Westbrook Pegler disliked Ruth. ("The Babe was an unequaled exhibition, whose strength and accuracy with a baseball were of a pace with the madness for crazy pleasure, unheard-of speed, and aimless bigness convulsing the nation, but he also proved on close acquaintance to be unbelievably mean, foulmouthed, and violent," according to Oliver Pilat, Pegler's biographer.) But Pegler still delivered him to various private functions in need of a celebrity and then pocketed most of the fee, an off-the-record fact he revealed to Pilat. It was an easy enough trick. Many sportswriters arranged appearances for him, although Pegler is the only one who admitted to having cheated him.

When Ty Cobb endorsed Democrat James M. Cox after the presidential nominating conventions in July 1920, the Republicans wanted a baseball hero on their side as well. Operating through Bill Veeck, the owner of the Chicago Cubs, they approached Fred Lieb with an offer: four thousand dollars for the Babe, and another thousand for Lieb if he could deliver Ruth to Marion, Ohio, where Warren G. Harding was conducting his celebrated front-porch campaign. Lieb took the news of their windfall to Ruth. Babe had two reactions: first— "Hell, no, I'm a Democrat"; and second—"How much are they offering?" When he heard the size of the deal he allowed he could bend a principle a little (especially since he had never voted in his life, and wouldn't until 1944).

Lieb arranged a meeting to follow the conclusion of a Yankee series in Cleveland. But it turned out that the team had an exhibition game scheduled for that date and refused to let Babe out of it. Later in the season Lieb set up another date, but that, too, was canceled for some unremembered reason. Finally, as the season ended, the harried sportswriter felt certain that they were about to make connections. But before they could take the trip to Ohio the Black Sox scandal broke, revealing that the 1919 World Series had been fixed, and the market for endorsements by baseball players, even by Sultans of Swat, took a fatal nosedive. Lieb got nothing for his labors, Ruth's record as a lifelong Democrat remained unsullied, and Harding had to stagger home with only a twenty-six-percentage-point lead over his rival.

Since league rules forbade fraternizing between players on opposing teams, few of the Yankees had had much personal experience with Ruth before the national sensation appeared in their dugout. Shore, Lewis, and Mays, who had played with Babe in Boston, noticed that he was a little more self-important here in New York; at least back in Boston he had occasionally been willing to listen to advice, but no more.

He ignored required team meetings. He had no use for curfews. He had a payphone installed in the dugout, and when the phone rang he called to players willing to act as his secretary, "If it's a broad, get her number. If it ain't, screw 'em." He expected other guys to open his mail, read it, and sort it out for him. (Some guys did it once or twice out of curiosity, others were willing to toady to him every day.) On paydays he waved his check around for all the peons to see. When the Home Run Cigarettes check arrived he thrust it in his teammates' faces whether they wanted to see it or not. "Ever see ten thousand dollars, keed?" he chortled at them.

In the dugout and on road trips he took to indulging in practical jokes—a habit that would annoy people until the end of his playing days. "I remember once he grabbed a new hat off my head and threw it out the window as we went through a railway tunnel," says Mike Gazella, a utility infielder for the Yankees during the mid-twenties. "Another time he nailed my favorite pipes to the clubhouse wall. He was always doing things like that. There was nothing you could do about it. You know, he was—Babe Ruth."

Out on the field Ruth insisted that he never have to play the sun field. The sun, he said, bothered his eyes.

He also insisted on plotting his own strategy. Since signs from the bench were always "a black art to the Babe," (in Tom Meany's words), there was no point in anyone's trying to flash a signal to him once he had left the dugout. Miller Huggins did manage to convince him to cut down on his attempts at stolen bases, a skill on which Ruth prided himself, but that was probably the closest anyone ever came to actually tempering his method of play. (Ruth was actually a pretty good baserunner in normal circumstances. What probably worried Huggins was the fear that Ruth would throw away an important game by trying to execute some daring surprise maneuver on the basepaths. His anxiety was well-founded, as Ruth proved in the seventh game of the 1926 World Series. In the ninth inning of that game, with two outs, the Yankees trailing St. Louis by one run, Ruth on first, and power-hitting Bob Meusel at bat, Babe took it into his head to try to steal second. He was thrown out by ten feet, ending the inning and the Series. "I knew they wouldn't be expecting it," was his explanation.)

The Yankees also soon discovered that, though Ruth rarely tried anything with men his own size, he often pushed smaller men around. Mark Koenig, a man considerably smaller than Ruth, remembers an exhibition game in which he and Tony Lazerri messed up a double-play ball, causing the game to go into extra innings. Ruth, who had a girl friend waiting for him, was exceedingly put out. After calling Koenig every name he could think of, he knocked him down the dugout steps as soon as his back was turned. But when the latter challenged him to fight, Ruth, as usual, backed away.

The man who received the worst treatment was manager Miller Huggins. Huggins was a scrawny, weather-beaten five-feet-seven and weighed little more than half of what Ruth did. Whether because his size made him a natural target, or because his quiet strength of character seemed to command great respect from the other players (something that Ruth could never fathom), or because he was the man who had the job of telling Ruth what to do, Babe disliked him from the first day of their acquaintanceship. He called him a "little squirt" to his face, shoved him out of the way in the clubhouse, and lost no opportunity to explain to reporters what a lousy manager he was, and why if Ruppert and Huston had any sense they would get rid of him.

But most of the players seemed to feel that somehow Babe could not be judged by ordinary standards. Any other ballplayer could be considered in two lights: his character in the clubhouse and his abilities on the field. But with Ruth a third element interposed itself. Ruth had a public image so overpowering that no one who knew him could help but be influenced by it. Ruth had become the nation's greatest hero. If fifty million Frenchmen couldn't be wrong, how could fifty million fans? The way they adored him, the players reasoned, there had to be a lot of good in him. ". . . Sometimes I still can't believe what I saw," reflected Hooper in *The Glory of Their Times.* "This nineteen-year-old kid, crude, poorly educated . . . transformed into the idol of American youth and the symbol of baseball the world over—a man loved by more people and with an intensity of feeling that perhaps has never been equaled before or since." It is not surprising that the men who played with him were carried along, to some degree, by such a strong swell of adulation.

Besides, to walk down the street with Ruth, to sit at a table with him, to have your picture taken with him, or to be invited to share a card game or whorehouse excursion with him set you apart from the rest of mankind. Again not surprisingly, most of the players, not to mention most of the sportswriters, priests, pimps, bootleggers, promoters, touts, grand lodge poobahs, prostitutes, and delivery men who had occasion to deal with Ruth, wanted to consider themselves his friend. To transform his often unpalatable behavior into boyish pranksterism was an easy trick.

With Babe on the roster, the pennant and the World Series became a distinct possibility. As his salary shot upward, it would inevitably provide some upward drag for the other players'. More fans in the parks meant more profit for the club, and a little of that profit could be expected to be reflected in their paychecks. They might not be worth half of what Ruth was getting in 1920 ($20,000) but maybe they could argue for a third in 1921 (when Ruth received $30,000), or a fifth in 1922 (when Ruth received $52,000).

Anyway, how could you dislike a guy who invariably picked up the tab when you were with him. "Keep your money in your pocket," Babe would roar, and there was no disputing him. Or a guy who invited you to the perpetual open house at his apartment, where he supplied the finest booze and the classiest women money could buy (at least when Helen had retreated to Boston, as she often did). Or who on impulse would give away some expensive item he had just bought, or who was an easy touch for a loan if you happened to get caught short (although he could be expected to remember to ask for the money back at payday), or who threw away huge sums at cards and took his losses without complaining. (Usually, that is. Koenig remembers one game where Dutch Reuther, one of the Yankee pitchers, bluffed Ruth out of a large pot with a pair of deuces. When Reuther showed his hand, Ruth flew into one of his rages and stormed out of the room, ending the game.)

He also allowed himself to be taken to a large number of charity benefits, hospitals, orphanages, and the like. It didn't happen as often as some sportswriters have indicated, and Ruth himself rarely initiated such visits, but he often seemed willing to interrupt his day to let a bunch of wildly excited orphans, cripples, or delinquents pummel him to their hearts' content. Most of the other baseball stars put stringent limits on such appearances. But if you could catch Ruth between parties, he usually was game.

So what could you say? Babe was a character, that's all. Something apart from every other human being you had ever met. And whatever your feelings about him, you could never forget that he was the great, the incomparable, the idolized Babe Ruth. After 1920 only a Solomon could have looked at Ruth and separated the real man from the mythological hero.

Being the wife of the superstar of the year, as another generation would have phrased it, was becoming an ordeal for Helen. The ever-present reporters, to whom she could never think of anything to say, overwhelmed her. Photographers were always demanding pictures. The masses of autograph-seeking strangers who appeared the moment she and Babe stepped out of doors, pinning them against the walls of buildings and beating on the windows of their taxis, gave her nightmares. After an evening out she sometimes found her hands shaking uncontrollably, and then it would take a heavy dose of sedatives to put her to sleep.

She and Babe had taken a lavish apartment in a building in the West 150s, not far from the Polo Grounds, but the cavernous rooms were as much a prison as a home. The Babe's increasing popularity necessitated elaborate security precautions to keep out not only the ardent fans, but also business agents, promoters, and various other would-be visitors. As simple an event as eating in the coffee shop down the street became a sideshow for the benefit of other diners, who crowded around their table in swarms. The only escape from the fans seemed to be to keep a pace so swift that no one had a chance to bother them. That procedure suited Babe fine, but Helen couldn't manage it. As a result they almost never went out together. Their rare moments of domesticity during the season took place in their apartment and on occasional road trips. She still managed to attend most of the games, but for the rest of the time she was on her own even more than before.

Even back in Boston it had been a strain to live up to Babe's style of life, and very early on she had looked to the bottle for help. In the first years of her marriage she had often passed out at the end of an evening, but by 1920 she had developed a tolerance almost as great as her husband's. "I'd never seen a woman in her early twenties drink that much," Grace Monroe recalls. "Whiskey, beer, anything. She could practically out-drink him." But Helen did not have Babe's constitution. The booze that filled up her time also gave her chronic stomach and intestinal problems, left her sunken-eyed and listless, and provided only temporary emotional relief.

But Helen in 1920 was no longer willing to sit home waiting for her husband. She had had enough of that. Now when she felt well enough she sought out the company of men who would treat her with at least a show of respect and had brief affairs with some of them. Most people who saw what was going on figured she was just getting back at Ruth. The players felt sympathy for her, and in fact she seems to have grown in their estimation, especially since she continued to display a certain ability to remain cheerful and friendly in the face of what they knew were great difficulties. Spending even a few hours a day with the idol of American youth, as sportswriter Dan Daniel had labeled him, taxed their patience; they shuddered to think of what Helen must go through at home with him. And wondered how much longer she would put up with it.

6

Riding the Whirlwind

ON SEPTEMBER 27, 1920, Eddie Cicotte gave testimony before a Chicago grand jury that knocked the baseball world for a loop; he and seven other White Sox players had conspired with gamblers to fix the 1919 World Series. Young boys in Chicago burst into tears at the news. If they didn't actually trail after Joe Jackson, one of the leading culprits, pleading, "Say it ain't so, Joe," they could have. The club owners' hearts sank as they contemplated the possible collapse of the game. Some fans, Ring Lardner among them, soured on the game permanently. The sportswriters, who for the past year had resolutely ignored rumors of the fix, now demanded justice. "Let the guilty be punished," intoned McGeehan, and he was echoed in a thousand other columns. Only veteran writer Hugh Fullerton, who in the face of strong hostility from his fellow journalists and from the baseball establishment had broken the story, emerged from the mess with his honor intact. (Fullerton was actually on the staff of the *Chicago Herald and Examiner,* but that paper refused to print his accusations. His articles exposing the scandal appeared in the *New York Evening World,* the only paper in the country that would touch the material.)

The distraught owners knew that it was up to them to take whatever drastic steps were necessary to rescue the game from the morass it had fallen in to. Ban Johnson

—aging, increasingly erratic, often drunk, embroiled in disputes with various club owners—was clearly not up to handling the situation. They decided to replace the National Commission with a Commissioner of Baseball who would exercise a power amounting to dictatorship to shape the future of the game. Johnson could remain American League president, with jurisdiction over internal league affairs, but the new commissioner would decide all matters affecting the game as a whole.

A committee of owners went to work on a candidate list, which included such eminent figures as General John J. Pershing, Senator Hiram Johnson, and former Secretary of the Treasury William McAdoo. Ban Johnson, not surprisingly, fought the whole idea, and there were weeks of acrimony between the American League president and his enemies among the owners. "If you [Johnson] had any sense of justice or realization of the harm you have caused baseball, or one spark of manhood, or any regard for the game which has made you possible, you would tender your resignation," wrote Harry Frazee from his Barrymore-bound office on the Great White Way. In November Johnson finally capitulated and the owners made public their choice for Commissioner—Federal Judge Kenesaw Mountain Landis.

They could not have found a more appropriate figure to absorb the lightning that was striking baseball from all sides. A courtly, colorful, small-town southern puritan with a thin, angular figure, white hair, and a Lincolnesque chin beard, Landis was one of those American Gothic characters who appeared so inherently representative of traditional American virtues that failure to praise his selection would seem an affront to the memory of the founding fathers. He had been appointed to the federal bench by Teddy Roosevelt. As a judge in the Chicago district he had presided over a large number of highly publicized cases, ranging from the government's anti-trust suit against Standard Oil to the sedition trial of IWW organizer Big Bill Haywood. His handling of those trials (he fined Standard Oil twenty-nine million dollars, and gave Haywood twenty years—both decisions that

were overturned in higher courts) convinced many
Americans that he represented everything good and true
about their country.

There were a few who did not salute the selection,
who argued that Landis was one of the least responsible
jurists ever to sit on the United States bench—a harsh,
arbitrary grandstander, openly biased against immi-
grants, unionists, nonwhites, and "sissies," a category in
which he included anyone interested in cultural matters.
Critics could also point out that over the years he had
achieved a rate of reversal by superior courts unparal-
leled in the history of American jurisprudence and that
several times cases had been taken out of his hands even
before the trials started because of prejudicial opinions
he had uttered in public. "Few men have been as zeal-
ous in the suppression of minorities, and his charges to
juries were dangerously similar to patriotic addresses,"
comments baseball historian Harold Seymour. John
Dos Passos put it more pointedly in *Mid-Century:*
". . . The Judge could hand out twenty-five-year sen-
tences as lightheartedly as he'd fine some Joe five bucks
for speeding. . . . Underneath he was a butcher."

But Landis had a national reputation as an incorrup-
tible, hundred percent American, and that was what the
owners needed. They could also be reasonably confident
that the judge, both by inclination and by contract,
would be on their side in any case involving the rights of
a player against those of an owner. There was a slightly
embarrassing episode when Landis at first insisted upon
retaining his seat on the federal bench to make sure of
drawing a salary from both jobs. But after several
months of pressure from both the government and the
baseball establishment, he was persuaded to resign the
judgeship.

With Landis installed as Commissioner and the White
Sox fixers headed for trial (though they were eventually
acquitted for lack of evidence, their professional gambling associates having denied everything), the baseball
hierarchy held its breath and waited to see how the public would react. Would the appointment of a czar and

the assurances of rigorous policing in the future carry the game over this roughest of all patches in its history, or would the fans turn away from baseball?

The owners did not have to wait very long to learn that the fans were more interested in speculating about what the Babe would do for an encore in 1921 than they were in rehashing the delinquencies of the White Sox. Would Babe equal the miraculous year of 1920? Could he lead the Yankees, now augmented by the return of Frank Baker and the addition of Wally Schang, Waite Hoyt, and Ed Barrow from the Red Sox, to their first pennant? Was Ruth for real?

He was. In 1921 Babe hit .378, with 59 home runs, 44 doubles, 16 triples, 170 runs batted in, and 177 runs scored. In home runs, RBIs, bases on balls, runs scored, total bases, and extra base hits he set all-time major league records (the last three of which still stand). Nearly sixty percent of his 204 hits went for extra bases, a figure that even people who watched every game found hard to comprehend. He didn't equal his 1920 record; he surpassed it. There had simply never been anything in baseball like Babe Ruth in 1921.

"I was about eleven years old, going on twelve that summer, and our Uncle Morris took us to see a game," recalls a Cleveland woman. "My parents thought he was crazy. My father never heard of such a thing—girls going to baseball games. You know, back in Russia . . . anyway, the Yankees were playing and everybody was screaming for Babe Ruth. Even I knew about Babe Ruth, that's how famous he was. You could tell who he was as soon as the players came out to warm up, he was so much bigger than anybody else. My God, the excitement. The screaming and yelling. My sisters and I were screaming and yelling and we didn't even know what for. He hit a home run that day. You couldn't believe the commotion. The stands were shaking."

The Yankees won the pennant by four games over Cleveland. Ruth's hitting was a major factor, of course, but since the Indians had no less than seven regulars hitting .310 or higher, it didn't tell the whole story. The

Yankee pitching staff, with Mays at 27–9, Hoyt 19–13, and Shawkey 18–12, deserved almost as much credit as the King of Clout.

The Giants had taken the National League pennant and the clash between McGraw's charges, who still played scrappy, old-fashioned, scientific baseball, and the sluggers of Murderers' Row looked like the best baseball show in years. Along Broadway the various celebrities were quick to choose sides. The sportswriters made the most of the opportunity to dramatize the Series as a confrontation between the two totems of baseball. It was the old against the new, brains against brawn, McGraw against Ruth.

The vaunted battle turned out to be a sorry defeat for Babe and the Yankees. Although Ruth singled in the first run of the Series and hit one homer in the fourth game, he also struck out eight times in the first five games. An abscess on his elbow then forced him to watch the rest of the best-of-nine-game series from the bench, except for a futile pinch-hitting attempt. The Giants won going away, five games to three, and McGraw crowed, ". . . I signaled every pitch to Ruth. . . . We pitched only nine curves and three fastballs to Ruth during the entire Series. All the rest were slowballs, and of twelve of those, eleven set him on his ear."

Ruth's ears were already burning from Joe Vila's suggestions in the *Sun* that he was afraid of McGraw and had been dogging it, using the abscess as an excuse not to play. He never bothered to read the papers, but word had reached him of this new, frank criticism, and his outrage was all the greater because it seems to have been the first time he ever realized that people might be writing uncomplimentary things about him. Waiting for a game to get underway, Ruth spotted Vila in the Polo Grounds' press box, then located at ground level behind the plate, strode over and threatened to beat the crap out of the sportswriter. Nearby fans watching the scene hissed their disapproval. Vila, a man forty years Ruth's senior, picked up his typewriter and held it up in front of him to ward off the blow that Ruth looked ready to throw, while the other sportswriters tried to remonstrate. Eventually Babe seemed to come to his senses and allowed himself to be escorted back to the Yankee dugout.

Near the end of the season a promoter had talked Ruth into signing for a post-season barnstorming tour of upstate New York, Pennsylvania, and Ohio. Baseball regulations forbade World Series' participants to take part in such tours—a rule promulgated ten years earlier out of fear that they might detract from the importance of the Series. When Babe was reminded of the rule, he boasted he was going anyway. Bob Meusel and Bill Piercy, a Yankee relief pitcher, declared their intentions to go along. Carl Mays and Wally Schang had also signed for the trip but said they would think it over.

Judge Landis, warming to the first serious challenge of his authority, paid a personal visit to the Yankee clubhouse during the Series. He pointed a bony finger at the players and warned them not to set themselves above the law. Mays and Schang quickly decided to stay home, but Ruth and the others persisted in their plans. Landis declared that "This case resolves itself into a question of who is the biggest man in baseball, the Commissioner or the player who makes the most home runs." Everyone with an interest in the affair—Barrow, Ruppert, Huston, and the sportswriters—advised Babe to forget about it. But the Wizard of Whack felt that he had taken enough—they could keep their advice. When the first exhibition game of the tour got underway on a rainy October day in Buffalo, Babe stood defiantly at first base. A few days later Cap Huston caught up with the tour at Scranton, Pennsylvania. Since it had been raining every day and fields in the towns in which games were scheduled had turned into virtual swamps, the promoter was only too happy to let the colonel buy him out at a nice profit. Things seemed settled in a reasonably satisfactory way for all concerned.

Judge Landis had not yet been heard from, however. He threw the book at the miscreants. Ruth, Meusel, and Piercy were fined a month's salary each and suspended from league games until May 20 of the following season. To make certain that they paid up, the judge confiscated their World Series' shares. He knew that the idea of doing without Ruth for the first thirty-nine days of the season would cause Huston and Ruppert considerable anguish, but he refused to discuss the matter. Nor did he heed the cries from the sportswriters that he was depriving the boys of America of their hero.

Babe said he didn't care. He was still more important to baseball than some old goat sitting in an office in Chicago. He could console himself thinking about the substantial new contract he would soon be negotiating with the Yankees. Besides, he had a business manager now; Christy Walsh would take care of him.

Early in 1921, Babe had ordered a new keg of beer from the bootlegger around the corner from his apartment. The thin, wiry young-looking guy who brought it over was wearing a neat business suit instead of a deliveryman's outfit. Before Babe could even give him a tip he had focused his guileless blue eyes on Ruth, stuck out his hand, opened his mouth, and started talking a mile a minute. It turned out that he was some sort of agent or something who had had the nerve to bribe the bootlegger to let him bring the booze. He really seemed interested in Babe—said he was getting robbed blind by the newspaper guys who were using his byline. Said he ran some kind of syndication business and if Babe would let him handle his writing stuff, he'd make a hell of a lot more money for him. What could Babe lose—the five dollars a home run that he was now getting from the papers? It was a disgrace, the guy said. Babe was the most exciting ballplayer of all time and here he was getting peanuts while the papers were raising their circulations like crazy just by using his name.

Babe didn't know quite what to say. Neither did Helen. They'd never heard of a baseball player with an agent and they weren't quite sure what an agent did, but when you thought about it, why not? This guy said he had other guys signed up, like that flier, whatever his name was, and it looked like he'd gotten a lot of his stuff in the papers. At least he had a lot of stuff to show. He said they could ask Lieb or Runyon or any of those guys about him. What the hell, the guy looked honest. Babe might as well try it. The guy pulled a contract out of his pocket and handed Babe a pen. The Sultan of Swat signed, shook hands with his new "literary" agent, and saw him to the door. Then he promptly forgot all about him.

Out in the hall Christy Walsh took a deep breath. He'd made it—he'd signed up Babe Ruth. Now he could get started on his grand design. For three years—ever since he'd given up his job as a sports cartoonist back in Los Angeles and come to New York at the age of twenty-seven—he'd been waiting for a chance to make his mark in the wide-open communications field. He had one simple, original idea on which to build; it could be expressed in a single word—ghostwriting. The practice of buying a famous name for its jacket value had probably been around as long as the printed word, and the use of ballplayers' bylines had been popular since Sid Mercer of the *New York Globe* had put together a package of Giants' players to cover the 1911 World Series. But Walsh proposed to turn it into an organized business—if he could convince the right celebrities to go along with his ideas.

Walsh was very nearly broke when he landed his first client in 1919. He was "that flier," the toast of the skies, Eddie Rickenbacker. A series of exciting war memoirs and commentaries about the air races promptly appeared under his byline in the *Evening Mail*. With those as a calling card, Walsh sold the notion to other big names—Jack Kearns, Florenz Ziegfeld, John McGraw —and by mid-1920 he was in business. Eventually Walsh built up an immense ghostwriting syndicate which counted a substantial percentage of the nation's newspapers as its customers. At its height, in the late twenties, it owned the byline rights to the names of almost every major sports figure, and a large number of well-known nonsports celebrities. The latter group ranged from

Shipwreck Kelly, the flagpole sitter, to Hendrik Willem Van Loon, the eminent historian. He concomitantly developed a large stable of ghostwriters, which on occasion included such top names as Lardner, Runyon, and Fowler, as well as many of the other ranking sportswriters of the day. And during various periods he also served as business representative to such sports figure as Huggins, Gehrig, Shawkey, Pop Warner, Knute Rockne, and Alonzo Stagg.

Walsh's greatest ghostwriting gimmick was instant analysis. Participants in a major event would ostensibly be writing their inside reports even as the events were taking place. During the World Series, for example, it was not uncommon for the ghostwritten thoughts of the opposing managers, the leading players of both teams, and sometimes even the trainers and batboys to appear in competition with each other in different newspapers, all under Walsh's aegis. The value of an individual's name depended upon his popularity, of course, but Walsh always struck a hard bargain for himself and his charges. (Walter Johnson received more—$7,000—for his "in-depth analysis" of the 1924 World Series than he got as his winner's share—$5,969.64. And Johnson was only one of eight baseball greats Walsh had working on that Series.)

But that was all in the future. In 1921 Walsh was still on shaky ground. The clients he represented were valuable, but they weren't quite what he needed. He was missing a real blue chip, a truly major figure who could give his enterprise the impetus to really get off the ground.

And now he had him. Walsh went to work with his customary energy. He quickly lined up twenty-five papers across the country to receive Babe's personal analysis of each home run he would hit during the 1921 season. And they were paying for the privilege, too. Before the season started Walsh knocked on Babe's apartment door and presented him with a check for one thousand dollars as an advance. Babe clapped him on the back and looked at him with new respect. This guy really knew

what the hell he was doing, he told acquaintances. By
the end of the season Walsh had increased Babe's "literary" earnings from the meager five hundred dollars of
1920 to fifteen thousand, a sum that represented not
only newspaper syndication but royalties from instructional manuals as well, and Ruth was ready to go along
with anything Christy said. (Except when he talked
about saving some of his money.)

So after Babe's abortive 1921 barnstorming tour ended, Walsh quickly stepped into the breach and signed his
new meal ticket with the Keith Organization for a vaudeville tour. That in itself was nothing new for baseball
players. As far back as 1888 Cap Anson, star of the
Chicago White Stockings, had toured the outback in a
popular melodrama, and in succeeding years Ty Cobb,
Christy Mathewson, John McGraw, Hughie Jennings,
Rube Marquard, and scores of other diamond stars had
sung, danced, joked, and emoted for audiences all over
the nation. In fact, as Joe Laurie, Jr., points out in *Vaudeville,* there were very few vaudeville shows that did
not have a sports celebrity of some kind as box-office
bait. Champion boxers, golfers, marathon runners,
pole vaulters, six-day bicycle racers, jockeys, billiard
and pool players, channel swimmers, and everyone else
who had ever won anything played the two-a-day circuit
in the course of the teens and twenties, right alongside
the Hungarian acrobats, baggy-pants comics, and croon-
ers—not to mention accused murderers and particularly
hideous sideshow freaks whom the public had expressed
a desire to see in person.

At three thousand dollars a week for a twenty-week
tour, Babe's contract was one of the most lucrative ever
offered an athlete, and also one of the longest. Under
normal circumstances, twenty weeks starting in mid-
November would have required Ruth to miss all of
spring training. But Judge Landis had decreed that 1922
would not be a normal year, so Walsh saw no reason not
to turn the suspension to their advantage and pick up
some extra change.

The tour opened at Proctor's Theatre in Mt. Vernon,

New York, in the third week of November. From there
Ruth went to the Palace in New York, where those of
the Broadway crowd whose curiosity got the better of
them came to watch his act on opening night.

As the curtain rose the orchestra played "Take me
out to the Ball Game." On stage a phone began to ring,
and Babe, wearing his Yankee uniform and carrying a
set of golf clubs, lumbered out to answer it. (He
wore a thick bandage on his left wrist, which most
of the audience expected to play some part in the show,
but actually covered a severe skin infection.) At first
Babe seemed nervous and took up a station facing the
back of the stage. But as the overflow crowd cheered
and applauded he jerked his head around, squinted out
over the footlight, and stiffly saluted his eager fans.

Wellington Cross, a veteran song-and-dance man who
had been recruited for the act, brought Babe's attention
back to the phone call, and Babe managed to croak out
that it was Bob Meusel on the line, all the way from
California. But that was all the audience could make out
of that exchange. "We were no nearer than the first row
in the orchestra, and so were unable to hear clearly,"
wrote one critic the next day.

Cross, sensing the pace slowing, abandoned the phone
and launched into the next bit of dialogue. Things went
smoothly for a while:

CROSS: What can you do, Babe? Can you sing, dance,
        or act?
RUTH: No.
CROSS: That's good. You surely belong in vaudeville.
        Tell me, Babe, what made you think you could
        act?
RUTH: I saw you.
CROSS: What does a pitcher say when he whispers in
        the catcher's ear at a critical moment in the
        game?
RUTH: Fix it up for two and make mine a blond.

That exchange ended when Babe forgot the answer to
the next question.

Cross, seeing his partner floundering, signaled the

piano player to begin a snappy rendition of "Little by Little and Bit by Bit," a slightly risqué popular song. Ruth recovered enough to join in on alternate verses, and with the conclusion of the tune the first half of the act ended.

A few moments later Ruth, dressed in a business suit, returned to the stage to be blindfolded in preparation for a mindreading act. Cross stepped down into the audience. Taking various items from the spectators, he held them up and asked Babe, now standing alone in the middle of the stage in an attitude of intense concentration, to focus all his mental powers in identifying them. This time Babe managed to carry it off:

CROSS: See if you can *strike* this.
RUTH: A match.
CROSS: What is this? Now *watch* out.
RUTH: A hat.
CROSS: What is this I hold in my hand? You could tell me if you *felt* like it.
RUTH: A hat.
CROSS: What is this a *piece* of? (Tears a sheet of paper)
RUTH: Paper.
CROSS: How many articles do I have in my hand?
RUTH: Uh . . . um . . .
CROSS [*To a woman*]:Stop it madame. You make me *sick—sick—sick.*
RUTH: Oh, yeah. Six.

Finally Cross vaulted back up to the stage, Babe removed his blindfold, the two men bowed and headed for the wings—Cross waving his hat and high stepping, Babe half strutting, half running. The audience gave the pair a loud ovation. And *Variety* said it wasn't nearly as bad as it could have been.

With that moderate success under their belts, the tour moved on: Newark, Boston, Providence, Philadelphia, Baltimore, Washington, Pittsburgh, Cincinnati, Cleveland, Detroit, Grand Rapids, Chicago, St. Louis, San Francisco. Babe's stage presence actually improved as the tour moved on, although his timing remained hopelessly off and he continued his habit of speaking through the laughs so that people had trouble hearing.

"It's a funny thing about the Babe in vaudeville," wrote Laurie. "When he was at his height in baseball and was getting a big salary in vaudeville, he didn't prove to be a drawing card, while Jack Dempsey was breaking all records. Showmen explained this by saying that people could see Babe Ruth any time for a quarter or fifty cents, while it took at least three bucks to see Dempsey when he was fighting." But in many of the tour cities the fans had never had a chance to see him at all. Possibly the public was reacting to the emptiness that always seemed to characterize Ruth when he stepped out of uniform. Dempsey projected a thrilling aura of power and determination, but Ruth projected not much of anything.

Still, the tour was a financial and publicity success for Babe and Walsh. On opening night flowers ordered by the Keith organization filled his dressing room. Stagehands brought in buckets of champagne for Babe, Walsh, Helen, Cross, and the dozens of booking agents, promoters, gladhanders, chorus girls, and columnists who crowded around the new star. If he didn't set the audience afire, the other side of the curtain came through. Telegrams of congratulations from Julian Eltinge, the noted female impersonator, Norman Karyl, the Creole Fashion Plate. Hollywood agent Lou Anger, Eva Tanguey, Buster Keaton, Francis X. Bushman, Joe Weber of Weber and Fields, Eddie Foy, Eddie Rickenbacker, Billie Burke, Colonel Huston, John D. Reese, bonesetter to the stars, and dozens of other luminaries lay in a pile on his dressing table. (Walsh saved them all for his scrapbooks and they are now in the National Baseball Library at Cooperstown.) Some unknown wise guy, probably one of the sportswriters, wired, "If I had your agent, your author, and your partner, I could do the act myself," and signed it "Helen Keller." But Lady Duff Gordon, European social correspondent for the *Tribune,* spoke for the more traditionally inclined when she telegraphed, "Through absence missed your date

Babe, in a stepping-out mood, a
few years after his retirement.

Babe and Helen's wedding photo, taken just after their marriage in October 1914. It has
been "augmented" with colored
inks, a popular process of the
time. Babe was nineteen years
old and Helen sixteen.

Babe pitching for the Red Sox,
c. 1915.

A 1921 newspaper ad.

Babe and Helen on the Sudbury Farm, *c.* 1922-23. This was one of many such poses designed to halt rumors of marital discord between the Ruths.

Miller Huggins and Jacob Ruppert at Yankee Stadium.

Miller Huggins and John J. McGraw before the 1923 World Series.

THIS STORE CLOSED
Friday Afternoon
October 31, 1924, on Account of
WALTER   BABE
JOHNSON-RUTH
BALL GAME
Brea Bowl, Brea, California   Auspices Anaheim Elk's 1345

Helen at Yankee
Stadium, 1923.

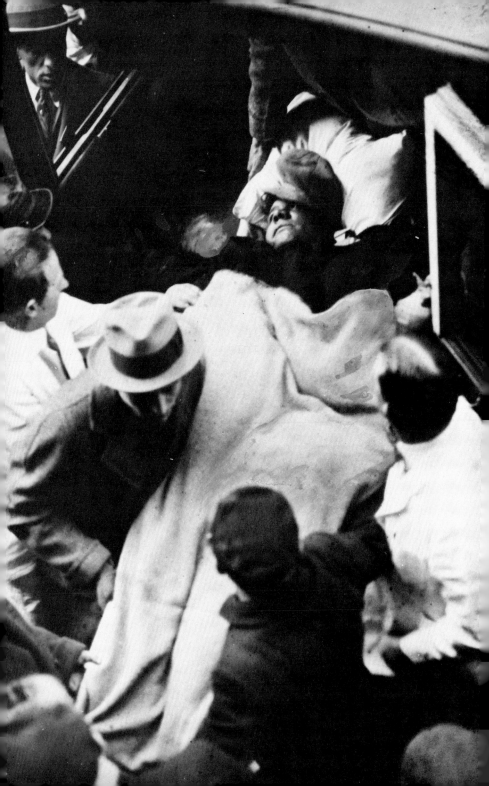

SEE "THE BABE" IN ACTION!

Don't Wait Till the Crowds Are So Big That You Can't Get in

SEE HIM TODAY!

THE IDOL OF MILLIONS!

THE KING OF SWAT!

He Broke Ten Records in the World's Series!

Three Home Runs in One Game!

He's Come to Those Who Cannot Go to Him!

AND ON THE SAME BILL: THE EMINENT STAGE AND SCREEN STAR

| IN PERSON | WILLIAM DESMOND | IN PERSON |

And Other Big Acts and Pictures

Ad for 1926 vaudeville tour.

Opposite:
Babe is lifted into an ambulance
after his collapse during spring
training in 1925.

Babe entertaining a baby
for photographers — 1927
barnstorming tour.

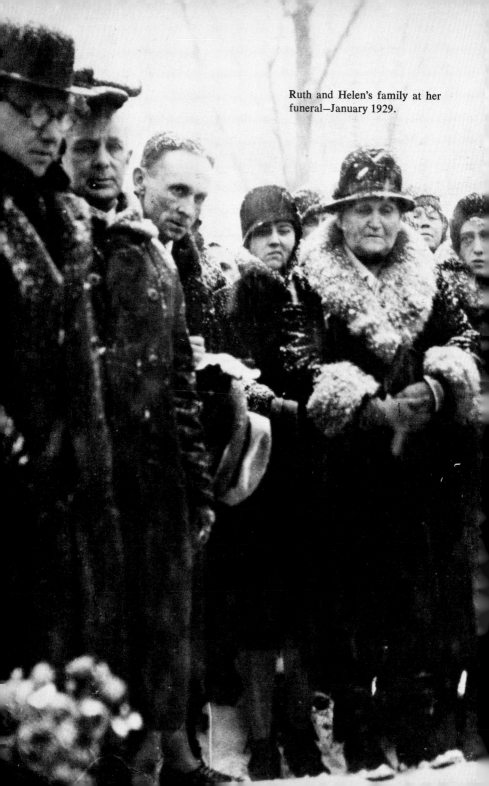

Ruth and Helen's family at her funeral—January 1929.

1

2

1/Mark Koenig
2/Miller Huggins
3/Lou Gehrig
4/Bob Shawkey
5/Earle Combs
   "the handsomest
   man in baseball"

3

4

5

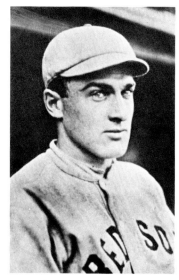 

Larry Gardner   Harry Hooper

The Red Sox starters in 1916.

Shore   Leonard   Foster   Ruth

SCENES FROM "HEADING HOME," 1920.

1/A priest protects Babe from
irate mob after his home run
wins the game for the rival team.
2/ Leaving home.

3/Babe on the Haverlock diamond.
4/Ruth signing autographs (a
documentary shot).

1

2

3

4

Babe and Claire leaving for theater on the night they announced their impending marriage—4/16/29.

Claire at Yankee Stadium—
Opening Day, 1929.

Babe and Claire at the beach
in the early thirties.

Babe being carried off the field after an injury—1931.

Babe Ruth Day—April 27, 1947.

The Colossus
of Clout
at the plate.

though late send heartiest congratulations for your act." Few, if any, of these celebrities had ever met Ruth, and he had certainly never heard of any of them, but they were all part of show biz, the fraternity that always recognizes one of its own. Anyone who could get the kind of contract Ruth had received was a trouper from the word go.

The lively diversions and extra cash provided by the vaudeville circuit helped make up for Babe's recent troubles with baseball authorities. But some observers wondered if he weren't still smarting from the punishment he had received from Judge Landis. They noticed he drove himself along the primrose path at a faster clip than ever before. A teammate passing through Chicago while Ruth was performing in that city recalls that he took twelve chorus girls and a case of whiskey into his hotel room and holed up for the week, coming out only for the shows at night. In interviews he became increasingly testy: "arrogant, unpleasant, and grouchy" were the adjectives a critic used to describe Ruth's behavior during an interview for the *Philadelphia Public Ledger*.

The Yankee management didn't like the reports filtering back to New York. They were relieved when the tour, instead of lasting the full twenty weeks, was terminated in mid-February by mutual consent of Ruth and the Keith officials. Ruth headed for Hot Springs to try to shed some weight, and Colonel Huston met him there, partly to talk contract but also to try to drill some sense into his head. When Babe took a look at his new contract, he found that besides formalizing their agreement to pay him fifty-two thousand dollars a year for the next five years, the Yankees had inserted several new and unique clauses. Among them were pledges to "refrain and abstain entirely from the use of intoxicating liquors," and "[Ruth] shall not during the training and playing season . . . stay up later than one o'clock A.M. . . . without the permission and consent of the club's manager." In effect a morals clause similar to those found in Hollywood contracts, it even allowed the club to terminate his employment for extreme infractions, as well as giving management the option of withholding up to half of his salary should unforeseen complications with the authorities arise.

With the contract Babe also had to swallow a stern lecture from Colonel Huston on the subject of his behavior; a man in his position, making his kind of money, with his future, ought to exercise more care in the way he lived, the Yankee owner pointed out. There was just too much at stake to keep up drinking and fooling around with women the way he did. Ruth seemed to listen this time and take in Huston's import. "I'll promise to go easy on the drinking," he replied seriously when his employer had finished. "But I won't stop fucking for nothing." Since Huston was an extremely heavy drinker himself, he may have felt that Ruth had his priorities mixed, but there wasn't much he could do about it.

The sportswriters cracked up when they heard the story, but the Yankee management had ceased to find any amusement in Ruth's lifestyle. As the opening of the 1922 season approached and their leading player, the attraction around whom they were building their huge new stadium in the Bronx, continued to spend night after night carousing until dawn, disturbing possibilities began to cross their minds. There was no telling what kind of trouble he might get himself into. Landis had not explicitly forbidden him to work out with the team, so they hustled him off to spring training, hoping that a return to the diamond would straighten him out.

The team had moved its spring training camp from Savannah to New Orleans the year before, and Ruth had managed then to make the acquaintance of all the whores in the area. He quickly renewed last year's relationships, and added a few more, letting the girls compete for his favors. Occasionally the management's worst fears almost came true. "Once down there, on a trip somewhere, I was playing cards in the writer's car with some fellows when Babe came rushing through the car, in one door and out the other," recalls Lieb. "He was being chased by some woman with a knife in her hand. We just kept on playing. I heard later that she was the wife of a state legislator."

The rest of the Yankee team also seemed bent on using spring training to celebrate their victory of the previous year. "Yankees Training on Scotch," ran a headline in the *American*. Meusel, temporarily chastened by his suspension, ran and did endless calisthenics to get in shape, but most of the others found the temptations of Bourbon Street too much to resist. The team's four newly acquired regulars—Everett Scott, Joe Bush, and Sam Jones from the Red Sox, and center fielder Whitey Witt from the Athletics—were not only all top-rate men on the field, but accomplished playboys as well. When they were added to the already high quotient of gamblers and partygoers on the team, every night became New Year's Eve at the Yankees' camp.

Hoping that Ruth might at least calm down if he were given some extra responsibility, Barrow convinced Huggins to appoint Babe captain of the team, a position formerly occupied by Roger Peckinpaugh. (Peck, a popular Yankee veteran, still at the top of his game, had been traded to Washington after the 1921 season to the surprise of almost everyone. Fifty years later, sitting on the grassy back terrace of his house in suburban Cleveland Heights, an old man still shaken by the death of his wife six months earlier, he can talk about the circumstances philosophically. Ruth had done it to him. During the 1921 season Babe's dislike for Huggins had grown; he'd taken it into his head to promote Peckinpaugh as a candidate to replace the mite manager. Huggins had no way to shut Ruth up, but he sure could get rid of Peck, and did.)

Ruth was undaunted; he interpreted his new position as captain, which was supposed to involve nothing more than making sure that the umpires at home plate had a lineup card before the game, to mean that he now shared the managerial responsibilities with Huggins. He now began positioning players according to his notion of where they should play, bawled them out when they made errors, and gave advice which often contradicted the instructions of Huggins and the coaches. "The coaches were trying to change my style of batting," recalls utility outfielder Ben Paschal. "I used to hold the bat down at the very end. Ruth came up to me and asked if I'd always hit good with it that way. I said I did, and he said to stay the way I was and not let them change anything."

When the season started, the effects of the team's desultory approach to spring training began to tell. Only the continued fine work of the "five-star pitching staff" (Shawkey, Mays, Hoyt, Bush, and Jones), plus the fact that no single American League team seemed strong enough to establish a commanding position, kept them in contention. But Huggins was worried. He had Ruth and Meusel sitting on the bench and under normal circumstances the team could be expected to make its move when they returned to the line-up. But this year Ruth was just not in good shape, mentally or physically.

In the days preceding his return from the suspension there was extensive speculation and excitement about the Babe's attitude and condition. A *Tribune* headline on May 18 read: "Fans Storm Yankee Offices for Tickets to Babe Ruth's Debut at Polo Grounds Saturday." Grantland Rice took the occasion to compose a forty-two-line ode which began:

> The Long Sleep is over—the Nation is waking—
> The Dead Epoch fades and the Live one is back.
> The old earth rebounds with a quiver and quaking,
> And high flies the dust as he thuds on the track.

On a warm, humid May 20 a lively crowd of thirty-six thousand fans jammed the Polo Grounds to see how the King of Clout would do. But for the first time since he had come to New York, really for the first time in his baseball career, Ruth heard a sprinkling of boos mixed with the cheers from the home folks as he trotted out onto the field. Taken aback, he tried to show his disdain for the crowd by raising his cap and bowing in all directions, but the boos only grew louder. Growing angrier as the day went on, he lunged at every pitch near the plate, but the best he could do all day was a feeble pop-up to George Sisler at first base. The Yankees lost the game to St. Louis, 8–2.

Five days later, in a game against Washington, he tried for an extra base when center fielder Sam Rice fumbled his base hit. Umpire George Hildebrand called him out when he overslid the bag. Covered with dirt, Ruth leaped to his feet and charged the offending ump. Hildebrand pointed to the dugout. Babe bent down, scooped up a handful of dirt, and flung it in the umpire's face. As he stalked off the field the fans let him have it. Ruth spotted one man behind first base making what the following day's papers referred to as an "indecent gesture." He leaped over the low wall into the stands and chased the offender up the aisle. Women screamed; some fans dived out of the way and others rushed forward to get a better look. Finally Huggins and some of the players dragged Ruth off the clubhouse roof, where he stood swearing his defiance at the booing fans. In the dugout the players just stepped out of his way as he continued to rage and rant until he finally headed for the showers. Then they looked at each other and shook their heads.

Ray Kelly in the *Times* began his story, "Babe Ruth, noted Sultan of Swat, gave an exhibition of childish anger and generally ungentlemanly behavior today . . ." Hugh Fullerton revealed, "Ruth was supposed to have just received word before the game that he had lost a large bet on the horses," and gave his opinion that Babe was unfortunately easily led and influenced by bad companions. Many papers even devoted space to the affair on their editorial pages: ". . . [Ruth] may . . . reflect that the paths of glory, on their inevitable way to the grave, sometimes detour to vanity and self-esteem," chastised the *Tribune*.

Ban Johnson had to find an appropriate punishment. After thinking it over, he allowed himself to be convinced by Huston and Ruppert to show some mercy, since Ruth had been so severely penalized by Landis. He let Babe off with a two-hundred-dollar fine, a one-day suspension, and the forfeiture of his captaincy. (The last action was greeted with sighs of relief by everyone on the team, especially Huggins, who quickly named Frank Baker to take his place.) But Johnson released a statement to reporters that made no attempt to whitewash the incident; in his view Ruth's outburst had stemmed from the fans turning against him, because "Ruth plainly did not possess the mental strength and stability to brave this sudden reversal of public adoration."

Returning to the team, Ruth sat brooding on the bench. He was mad at everyone. Even at home things were going badly. Helen's health had deteriorated over the past winter. In early May she entered St. Vincent's Hospital for a major operation, so serious that no details were released to the press, although people close to the situation thought she had cancer. The doctors seemed to think they had caught it in time, but her recovery would be slow and painful. And Babe had little patience with the role of nursemaid.

His batting average hovered around .260, the home runs came slowly, and his fielding fell to the standard of a minor leaguer. "We saw Ruth throwing to the wrong bags," wrote Frank O'Neill in the *Sun*. "The big fellow is prone to stand on a dime, and while he makes his share of brilliant and sensational plays, he misses a good many balls, too."

"It is said he is not in good physical condition, that he is worrying over matters foreign to baseball—maybe bets on the horses—that the opposition pitchers no longer fear him and are killing him with slow balls and low curves," wrote Joe Vila. "It's barely possible that Ruth had lost his nerve as a result of the panning he received when he climbed into the stands in search of a loud-mouthed tormentor. At any rate, Ruth has ceased to dominate baseball, which, after all, is bigger than all of the stars put together." In another story Vila affirmed, "If the eminent Babe Ruth had obeyed the rules which have made baseball the national game, he wouldn't have lost his batting eye and his wonderful popularity."

On June 19, at Dunn Park in Cleveland, umpire Bill Dinneen outraged the Yankees by ruling an Indian runner safe at second in a close play. Ruth hurried in from the outfield to take up the argument, brushing aside Huggins' attempts to shoo him away. Babe shoved his big face up against Dinneen's and told him what he thought of him. Dinneen backed away, warning Ruth to go back to left field. Babe followed after him, kicked him in the shins, and was ejected from the game. He cursed out the umpire all evening to anyone who would listen. Before the start of the next day's game he spotted the umpire in the Indians' dugout and rushed in after him. The Cleveland players watched wide-eyed as he challenged the surprised ump to come under the stands for a fight. When Dinneen refused, Babe called him a "yellow bastard" and started to go for him, but the Indian players got between them and sent Babe packing.

This time Ban Johnson wasn't so tolerant. He suspended Ruth for five days (three for the kicking offense and two for the insults). He also composed a stinging letter to Babe, in which he defended Dinneen: ". . . If you [Ruth] could match up to his [Dinneen's] standard you would not be in the trough you occupy today. A man of your stamp bodes no good in the profession." After additional castigation of Ruth's general behavior and lack of team effort, Johnson finished off with a cold warning: ". . . It seems the period has arrived when you should allow some intelligence to creep into a mind that has plainly been warped. . . ."

For once baseball opinion seemed to be united behind the league president. Lieb was one of several who denounced Ruth for being unable to take criticism. Rice, while staying above the battle, ran several items on the necessity for players to respect umpires. Other reporters wondered in print why Ruth still seemed to be making no effort to get in shape. It was McGeehan, normally Babe's biggest booster, who asked: "Can Babe Ruth be through?" (McGeehan was not capable of staying serious for long, however, even in this matter. Reporting on a Yankee game in July in which both Dinneen and Hildebrand were umpiring, he wrote, "Much more impressive than [Ruth's] home run was the noble and forgiving

figure of the Babe, who was heard to say to Bill Dinneen, 'Hello, Bill,' and to umpire Hildebrand, 'Hello,
Hildy.' The Babe has forgiven Hildebrand for having his
face in the way when he was throwing sand, and has
shown that he was willing to forget that Dinneen got his
shins caught in his spikes.")

Babe continued to look bad at the plate (on July 1 he
was hitting .267, with eight home runs). Surprisingly,
the Yankees still remained within striking distance of
the league lead, mainly because their competitors were
playing as inconsistently as they. Cleveland, the team
that had given them the most trouble over the past few
years, had aged, and St. Louis, the league leader during
most of the summer, was really a two-man team, the two
being Ken Williams, who was setting the pace in home
runs, and George Sisler, hitting well over .400 and leading in every other category.

Sportswriters commented that the Yankees, given the
talent on their roster, should have been well ahead by
that time. "There is a reason for the Yankees' flop,"
wrote a *World* reporter. "The boys have been betting on
the races and playing poker and enjoying parties in hotel
rooms. . . . Scores of empty bottles o'mornings in St.
Louis and Detroit bore mute witness to that." Frank
O'Neill summed up the writers' prescription for recovery
when he stated on July 21 in the *Sun* that "time has
come for the mite manager to enforce rigid discipline in
managing the Yankees."

On July 23 Babe returned to the dugout steaming
after dropping a fly ball. Looking around for someone
on whom to vent his anger, he made the mistake of
dressing down Wally Pipp for a baserunning error he
had committed earlier. Pipp, already hot under the col-
lar, was primed and waiting. As Vila tells it, "Wally replied that Huggins was the manager. Babe flew into a
rage and vilified Pipp to the highest. Wally did not de-
mean himself by profanity, but flashed a smashing hook
to the chin and went in to clean up—Ruth telling anyone how to run the bases is funny." Vila went on to add,
"Babe . . . is lucky he escaped so lightly, for Pipp was

blind with rage and ready to battle the world. He probably could whip all the Ruth's between wherever you are standing and the North Pole."

McGeehan treated the affair with typical lightheartedness: "Like all of the Pipps," he wrote, "Walter was slow to lash himself into a resentful wrath. When the climax came he took a most earnest sock at the Babe, wrecked a lot of clubhouse furniture, and then resumed playing baseball at top speed."

"Actually," says Bob Shawkey, "it wasn't as big a fight as some of the papers made out. Pipp was, you know, very strong and fast with his hands. What happened was he just slapped Ruth around with his open hands."

Possibly that fight, in which Ruth actually got kicked around, had some cathartic effect, for the Yankees began to play better baseball soon afterward. Huggins was relieved, as was Walsh. For when Babe's playing improved, so did his disposition. By August 19 he had brought his batting average up to .318, and his home run total to twenty-two. It was not up to his previous showing, but he was playing better, and so were his teammates.

Third baseman Frank Baker's skills had been declining rapidly, making that position the Achilles' heel of the team. Barrow knew that Frazee was, as usual, hard-pressed for money, and engineered a deal which brought down from Boston Joe Dugan, the league's best third baseman, and Elmer Smith, a hard hitting utility outfielder. Having Dugan at third made all the difference, transforming the leaky Yankee infield into a first-rate defensive unit. It didn't hurt that at the plate Dugan hit .294 in his sixty games as a Yankee, a considerable improvement over Baker. The rest of the league cried foul, as usual, but neither Frazee nor Barrow paid any attention.

At the end of August it was nip and tuck for the lead between the Yankees and the Browns. Sisler gave no indication of slowing up. (His final record for the season, .420, still stands as the highest in American League history.) And with Ruth almost himself it looked like an exciting month ahead.

But on the last day of August Ruth blew up and cussed out umpire Tom Connolly after being called out on strikes. One of Babe's pungent remarks enraged the umpire. His craggy Irish mug turned a smoldering red. Ruth repeated the phrase. "You're out!" Connolly shouted, and then turned his back and walked quickly away to try to regain control of himself. The incident was observed by two thousand boys and girls from New York orphanages, who had been brought to the game specifically to see their hero, and the papers had their say on the boorishness of setting such an example. Johnson, who must have wondered if this would ever end, suspended the Maharajah of Mash for another three days, citing his "vicious and vulgar" remarks to Connolly. "Ruth has the mind of a fifteen year-old," the league president later remarked privately to associates.

Ruth's play continued at a fairly decent level when he returned, though he rarely came through in the clutch. In early September Sisler injured his right shoulder and was forced out of the St. Louis lineup for several games. He returned for a critical three-game series against the Yankees starting on the sixteenth, but the pain in his shoulder proved so intense that he had to sit down again. That was the break the Yankees needed. New York took the series, built up a lead of four games within the week, and hung on by the skin of their teeth to finish the year one game ahead of the Browns. Once again pitching had been the deciding factor—with Bush at 26–7, Shawkey, 20–12, and Hoyt, 19–12, leading the way.

Ruth ended the year with a .315 average, thirty-five home runs, and ninety-six runs batted in. It could have been worse in view of the way the season had begun, but it sure wasn't what the public had expected of the Babe, or he of himself. And even those respectable-sounding statistics were misleading, for he had seldom come through when it really counted.

The 1922 World Series was a replay of the previous

year's, except that this time McGraw's Giants utterly humiliated their crosstown rivals. The series had been reduced to the now traditional best-of-seven format, and of the five games played, all the Yankees could manage was one tie in a game called because of darkness. And Ruth put on his worst Series performance ever. In seventeen times at bat he hit one single and one double, for an average of .118.

The Giants started riding him from the bench from the first inning on. ("Hey, Ruth, your mother was a nigger," was one taunt that they knew would get him.) After the finish of the first game he and Meusel invaded the Giants' dugout to challenge the whole team to a fight. McGraw and his men just turned their backs on them. In the third game, Babe was freely booed by the crowd when, as Bill Macbeth described it, "Ruth deliberately bumped Groh [the Giants' third baseman] with such force as to flatten him. Ruth's 'charge' seemed deliberate unsportsmanship." Groh was the smallest man on the field.

After the Yankees had been humbled for the fourth and final time in the Series, with evident satisfaction Vila announced to his readers that "Babe Ruth is an exploded phenomenon." McGraw, gleeful over what he viewed as a triumph of thinking-man's baseball over mere slugging, was quoted to the effect that "The fading Bambino proved conclusively during the late engagement that he had been tremendously overrated."

Rice put it this way:

> "The only tune I used to play
> Was Over the Fence and Far Away,"
> Says Mr. Ruth. "But now alas,
> I often fan, pop out or pass,"
> But in the world of sin and woe
> Harsh events oft happen so.

Walsh advised Babe to grab up an offer of a thousand dollars a game to barnstorm the upper Midwest, where his name was still revered. John Kieran of the *Tribune* commented, "The idea seems to be to get him somewhere beyond the reach of the echoes of the recent strife at the Polo Grounds."

The pessimism over Ruth's future had little to do with his physical abilities. The man was only twenty-seven years old, and even at the rate he abused his body he should have had the physical potential to continue as a star for some years to come. But a baseball player had to have some degree of common sense, some self-control, and it was hard to find any of either in Ruth. Early in the year Barrow had even gone to the extent of hiring a private detective to keep an eye on Babe, setting a precedent that he was to return to many times over the years.

But not even a detective could oversee Ruth all the time, as Barrow well knew. It was not difficult to imagine him knocking down a child as he ran a red light in his latest roadster, or beating up an innocent bystander in one of his frequent temper outbursts, or misreading the expectations of a young girl eager to shake his hand and letting his lusts run away with him. The circumstances of one unsavory rape in which he had been involved were already known to several sportswriters. The writers had also seen him fleeing from a gun-toting citizen in Detroit. (He escaped by hiding in a parked taxi, slipping out the street-side door, and racing away around a corner.) The time might come when fast footwork and/or a handy bankroll would not be enough to keep Ruth out of trouble.

Sometimes untidy items about the Big Bambino's private life did slip out in spite of the precautions. In September 1922 a picture of Babe holding a baby in his arms appeared in many of the New York papers. The caption under the *Sun's* photo read: "The Secret Is Out —Babe Ruth Is Father. The home run slugger and his wife, who for sixteen months kept quiet about the fact that they had a child because the infant weighed only two and a half pounds at birth and Babe feared kidding."

"When was she born?" asked reporters. "February 2, 1921," replied Babe. "June 7, 1921," said Helen.

"Where?" asked the reporters. "Columbia Hospital," replied Babe. "St. Vincent's," said Helen. "I don't get it, Babe," said a reporter. Ruth went back to check signals with Helen and returned to explain with a red face that he had mixed up his own birthday with that of the baby's. "Now I've heard everything," one of the reporters muttered.

Many of the writers already knew about the presence of the baby girl, whose name was Dorothy, in the Ruth household. Helen had showed up at spring training in 1922 with the then nine- or ten-month-old child in tow. Since no one had noticed any signs of pregnancy during the previous year, the players and writers found this sudden manifestation of progeny slightly surprising. The perfunctory manner with which Helen treated the baby contributed to speculation that Dorothy was Ruth's child by another woman, and that Ruth had probably agreed to take her in to avoid a paternity suit. As a bizarre footnote to the incident, Hugh Fullerton reported in the *World* that Helen and Ruth had had two children born dead, and their fear that this one might not survive either accounted for the lack of notice given her birth. There seems to be no corroboration for this assertion, however.

In the course of a single year Ruth's situation had changed more drastically then anyone could have imagined. During the regular season he had played unimpressively, and he had failed miserably in the Series. He had been suspended four times (for a total of forty-four games). At home he had a sickly, resentful wife and an unplanned daughter. All around him his enemies were gathering to dance on his grave, should he fulfill their predictions and continue his decline. It was enough to give pause to even the Sultan of Swat.

The lack of imagination that so many had noticed in Babe actually proved an asset, however. He could take offense at an imagined slight and complain for months, but he appeared incapable of fathoming the extent to which other people might be upset by his actions. Since he never read the newspapers, he missed most of the reporters' criticism. When he was out chasing other men's wives it never occurred to him that Helen might be reacting by stepping out on her own. Besides, if he did lose his temper sometimes, he always apologized the next day. What else did anyone want?

And the fans still loved him. A few boos didn't matter when the money still flowed in at the box office. When he was out on suspension attendance dropped by a good fifty percent. It would take more than a few fights with umpires to make the fans of America cast off their hero. He could see that as well as anyone else.

Still, the doubts remained. In November, prompted by a plea from Walsh, the New York chapter of the Baseball Writers Association invited Ruth to be the guest of honor at their annual dinner. Held at the Elks Club, it was called the "Back to the Farm" dinner because its theme was to be convincing Ruth to spend the winter getting in shape in Sudbury. A huge papier-mâché cow stood in a pile of hay on the head table, and as the evening progressed the skits and songs of the writers abounded in references to country life and how happy Babe would be amid his pigs and chickens. Babe roared with delight at the jokes. Finally the featured speaker, then state senator Jimmy Walker, rose and called for attention. The most detailed version of what happened next occurs in *Beau James,* Gene Fowler's biography of Walker:

> [He] opened his speech with the words, "Babe Ruth is not only a great athlete, but also a great fool. . . ."
> Senator Walker pointed a finger at Ruth. "You are making a bigger salary than anyone ever received as a ballplayer. But the bigger the salary, the bigger the fool you have become. . . .
> "But worst of all, you have let down the kids of America. Everywhere in America, on every vacant lot where the kids play baseball, and in the hospitals, too, where crippled children dream of the movement forever denied their thin and warped little bodies, they think of you, their hero. They look up to you, worship you. And then what happens? You carouse and abuse your great body, and it is exactly as though Santa Claus himself suddenly were to

take off his beard to reveal the features of a villain. The
kids have seen their idol shattered and their dreams broken."

At first Ruth's face had shown anger and resentment.
But now he was sobbing. His sobs shook not only his massive chest, but the table and the chairs. . . .

"If we did not love you, Babe, I would not tell you
these things." More sobs from Ruth. . . . "Will you not,
for the kids of America, solemnly promise to mend your
ways? Will you not give back to those kids their great
idol?"

With a gargantuan cry Ruth exclaimed, "So help me,
Jim, I will! I'll go to my farm in Sudbury and get in
shape."

The episode went down in baseball history as the
"dirty-faced kids of America" speech, but how much of
Fowler's version is actual history, and how much is pure
fantasy, is hard to say. Fowler was notorious even in his
own day for his tendency to embroider. And since he
wrote his account some twenty-five years after the event,
it is certainly possible that his version of Walker's
speech owes as much to his own histrionic talents as it
does to his memory of what actually transpired.

There is evidence, in fact, that the whole celebrated
affair was something of a put-on. "Jimmy Walker, of all
people," snorts Lieb, who was then president of the
Baseball Writers Association of America and prominent
at the dinner. "He was the last person in the world to be
giving a Boy Scout speech. I remember the dinner, but I
certainly don't remember Ruth crying." (Although he
included the by-then famous incident in *The Babe Ruth
Story*.) It strains the imagination to picture such cynics
as McGeehan, Runyon, Baer, Pegler, and the rest taking
such a performance by Walker seriously, or to conceive
of Ruth being diverted from the paths of sin in a single
evening. Which did not prevent the writers from making
it into a story that wrenched the hearts of their readers
for years to come.

Ruth did return to the Sudbury farm, however, and
from all evidence did make some effort at getting into
shape by working around the place sawing wood, chop-

ping down trees, and moving boulders. But a new problem was coming to a head that winter: Helen had informed him that she was ready to call it quits. Plagued
by loneliness, still weak from her spring surgery, burdened with someone else's baby, she was at the point
where the easiest course would be to dispense with the
sham of her marriage and try to make a new life for herself. But a headline-making divorce was the last thing
Ruth could afford at that moment. A priest (more than
likely sponsored by Walsh) was brought on the scene to
attempt a reconciliation. His influence was added to the
pleas of the Ruths' other advisors, and somehow he convinced Babe and Helen to try to patch things up.

Over the years the combination of physical discomfort
and loneliness had led Helen to narcotics for relief. She
was well on her way to becoming a full-fledged morphine
addict. Since she always had adequate funds and sources
of supply, her habit didn't affect her ability to function so-
cially; she continued to attend spring training with Babe
and made some public appearances with him, as in the
past. But the fact that the wife of baseball's greatest hero
was a drug addict could not have made those concerned
with keeping up his image rest any easier.

7

Making it Pay

WHILE BABE SPENT the winter of 1922–23 sequestered in his Massachusetts farmhouse, back in New York Colonel Ruppert and Colonel Huston were at war with each other. Miller Huggins was the bone of contention. The "mite manager" had been hired by Ruppert while his partner was serving in the Army in France during the war and Huston had never really approved of the choice. Now, disappointed at his team's second straight World Series collapse, Huston vowed that "Miller Huggins had managed his last game for the Yankees." Ruppert defended him on the basis of the team's success in the pennant races. In the end the dispute proved unresolvable. Ruppert bought out Huston's share of the team for one and a half million dollars, thereby becoming for all practical purposes the sole owner of the Yankees.

Barrow took advantage of the opportunity to purchase ten percent of the Yankees' stock. Perhaps motivated by this new involvement, the general manager went back up to Boston to try his luck at prying loose some more talent from Harry Frazee. Knowing that the Red Sox owner was thinking about selling out (he did in July), his former employee was eager to pluck the last fruits remaining on what had once been a heavily laden tree. The trip was a productive one. Barrow came back

161

with two new pitchers, veteran Herb Pennock and George Pipgras, a promising youngster.

Pennock was the major acquisition; the epitome of the thoughtful craftsman on the mound, he had been in the league for ten years, first sitting on the bench for the great Philadelphia and Boston teams of the teens, then becoming a regular for the Red Sox after they had dropped into the second division. But even with the lack of support of his fellow Red Sox, he had developed a solid reputation; with the Yankees behind him no one doubted that he would become a big winner.

In Pennock the Yankees had bought more than just another pitcher. An intelligent, understanding man, he quickly became the most respected individual on the team, looked up to both by the other players and by the press. Like Christy Mathewson of the Giants and Harry Hooper of the Red Sox, he gave the team a certain dimension of dignity that had been missing before. Even Ruth was won over by Pennock's graciousness and expressed nothing but admiration for the pitcher and his wife.

There was a third significant addition to the Yankee system in the off-season—a shy, clumsy, muscular twenty-year-old dropout from Columbia University by the name of Lou Gehrig, who could already hit like a major leaguer. Barrow had the boy in mind as an eventual replacement for Pipp at first base, provided he could ever learn to field his position. In the next two years Gehrig would spend most of his time in the minors, but Barrow intended to keep a close eye on him.

But the biggest change for the Yankees before the 1923 season was the completion of their new ball park, which had been under construction for over a year on that piece of land in the Bronx across the Harlem River from the Polo Grounds. To go along with their extraordinary slugger, the team now had an extraordinary place for him to play. The huge, three-tiered concrete and steel stadium represented a new era in the economics of sports in America. Built at the cost of 2.5 million dollars, Yankee Stadium could hold over seventy-

five thousand spectators for baseball and more for boxing and other sports, a capacity exceeding that of any
other major league park by a good twenty thousand.
Some of its dimensions also raised eyebrows. Its
right-field fence was both the closest to the plate (296
feet along the foul line, extending to 367 in dead right
field) and the lowest (43 inches high) of any field in the
majors. Though no one would ever accuse the Babe of
needing to profit by cheap home runs, it was clear that
an occasional flyball that would have been an easy out
in another field might drift into the invitingly close
right-field seats at Yankee Stadium. And that the Yankees would be in the market for left-handed sluggers for
the foreseeable future.

Was Ruth in shape for the 1923 season? The answer
seemed to be yes. The "Battering Bam" had indeed
tended to his knitting in the off-season. At spring training his morale and his batting eye seemed back to normal, as was testified to by a succession of record-setting
home runs in various minor league parks. With Pennock
replacing Mays, who at the age of thirty had started to
slip badly, in the five-star rotation, the Yankees were
automatically considered heavy favorites to take the
pennant. The St. Louis Browns were given up for dead
when George Sisler's severe chronic sinus condition
forced him to drop out for the entire year. Detroit and
Cleveland, both strong teams at the plate, might give
some challenge, but their lack of pitching depth would
surely do them in over the long haul. In most observers'
opinions only an act of God could dethrone the Yankees. There were only two questions left: how well
would Ruth do, and whom would they meet in the World
Series?

That prediction assumed that nothing would happen
during the season to upset Ruth's precariously balanced
equilibrium, of course. A disastrous new blowup by
Babe was always a possibility, as was demonstrated all
too clearly by an incident during the preseason exhibition schedule. Frederick Fried, today a well-known art

historian and collector of local artifacts (he initiated the famous sculpture garden at the Brooklyn Museum) but then one of a gang of young kids who lived opposite Ebbets Field in Brooklyn, was at the center of it.

"We [the kids] used to help out in the clubhouse, run errands for the Dodger players, watch their cars during games, and so on. They'd usually tip us a nickel or a dime. Some of them would come out after games and play ball with us, too. I remember Zack Wheat and Dazzy Vance and Jack Fournier particularly. Of course they were the big stars.

"The Yankees used to play exhibitions at Ebbets Field before the season started. Before one of those games, this was in 1923, I was in the visitors' locker room and Ruth was in there. I remember noticing that he was spitting tobacco juice all over the place. He was having some kind of trouble with his shoulder and asked if anyone had any rubbing alcohol. My brother was an Olympic bike racer, so I knew about such things. Ruth gave me a dollar and ordered me to go get him an alcohol preparation. It was Sunday, and the nearest open drugstore was nine blocks away at President and Empire. I ran like hell. I was really excited. I ran up to the druggist shouting, 'It's for Babe Ruth! Hurry!' The druggist made me wait until he served another customer, and then I dashed back with the preparation. When I got back Ruth was furious because I had taken so long and he thought I was cheating him or something like that. I can still hear him screaming at me. 'Thirty cents! fucking sons of bitches, I can get it for fifteen cents at Yankee Stadium!' He grabbed the change out of my hand. I didn't know what to do. I thought maybe he would give me a tip. Instead of that he shouted, 'I told you to get the hell out of here,' and when I didn't move he spit at me. *Spit right at me.* Hit me on the leg. I was in shock, I guess you could say. But you know me— what did I know—I still took out a baseball and asked him to autograph it. He knocked it out of my hand and walked out. Another player, a young guy—I always thought it was Gehrig but maybe not, I was practically hysterical by then—put his arm around my shoulder and gave me a half dollar." As Fried tells the story today his voice begins to shake with emotion before he is half through. The memory still upsets him so much he can hardly finish it.

On April 18, 1923, Yankee Stadium opened its doors to the public for the first time. The largest crowd ever to attend a baseball game—76,217 fans—puffed its way up the ramps and jostled down the aisles into the freshly painted steel seats. They wore winter jackets, hats, and heavy sweaters to shield them against the chilly forty-nine-degree temperature and waved Yankee pennants in the brisk breeze. Governor Al Smith, Commissioner Landis, and Bronx Borough President Bruckner and their wives sat with Colonel Ruppert in the celebrity box by first base. (Mayor Hylan was invited, too, but his popularity had fallen so low in New York that he did not choose to risk exposing himself unnecessarily to the citizens.) Scattered around the huge, high-pillared park were a thousand Bronx Elks, delegations from the Lions, Moose, Rotary, Kiwanis, and a dozen other organizations, an array of resplendent military brass, and thousands of ordinary men, women, and children eager to get a glance at the engineering marvel of the age, or at least of the West Bronx. The Seventh Regiment band, conducted by sixty-nine-year-old John Phillip Sousa, kept up a steady march beat over the hubbub. Outside the gates twenty-five thousand latercomers, unable to gain entrance, milled about on the dirt roads surrounding the stadium, sending up great clouds of dust into the atmosphere. When they heard a tremendous roar shake the rafters of the park, signifying that Babe Ruth and the Yankees had taken the field, some of them burst into tears of frustration.

Nothing much happened in the first two innings. Both the Yankees and the Athletics, their opponents on the big day, seemed slightly awed by their new surroundings. But in the bottom of the third Aaron Ward punched a single to left to lead off for the home team.

Everett Scott sacrificed him to second. Bob Shawkey, who had drawn the honor of pitching the opening game in the new park, tapped a roller to A's veteran slowballer, Howard Ehmke. Ward was trapped between second and third, but managed to elude a tag until Shawkey had chugged into second. Whitey Witt, next up at bat, drew a walk. Joe Dugan blooped a single into right field, scoring Shawkey and sending Witt to third. And that brought up Babe Ruth.

The fans moved to the edges of their seats. They were familiar with Ehmke's leisurely contortions as he prepared to deliver a pitch, but now the lanky hurler seemed to slow down almost to a state of yogic transcendance. Eventually he wound up and threw. Ruth, overanxious, missed the slow curve by a foot. The next ball, another curve, hung outside. A third slow curve followed, fooled Ruth again, and he foul-tipped it into the dirt. Another off-speed pitch drifted outside. Ehmke, taking all the time in the world, his mind seemingly occupied by other things, calmly glanced at the baserunners, gradually folded himself up in sections, reached a point of resistance, unfolded himself, and finally let go of the pitch. The inevitable slow curve meandered toward the plate. Ruth waited, his bat waving menacingly in the cool, clear April air. Suddenly his right foot lunged forward, he whipped his body around, connected right on the button, and drove the ball on a straight line toward the seats in right field. A fan ducked and the ball smacked into the back of a seat with a loud crack. As he circled the bases the cheers of the vast crowd rolled over the field like successive thunderclaps. When he reached home plate he raised his hat and bowed twice, once to the right, once to the left, before disappearing into the dugout.

Ruth continued playing at top speed and made an effort to stay out of trouble, and as the writers had predicted, all that remained for the rest of the league was a battle for second place. Curiously, for some reason, Babe did not approach his past home run accomplishments. His total of forty-one was still good enough to lead the league, however, and he made up for the slight decline in four-baggers by bringing his batting average up to .393, the highest of his career. Along with it he hit 45 doubles, 13 triples, and drove in 130 runs. At the end of the season he was unanimously chosen the league's most valuable player by the baseball writers, an honor he considered greater than any other he had yet received. (The award had been instituted only a year earlier, when George Sisler had won it.)

Witt, Pipp, and Meusel also hit over .300. Jones won twenty-one games, Pennock and Bush nineteen, Hoyt seventeen, and Shawkey sixteen, and the team finished fourteen games ahead of second-place Detroit. There wasn't a weakness on the squad. It looked solid for years to come.

At the 1923 World Series—for the third year in a row—it was the Yankees versus the Giants. But this time McGraw's brain power could pull off no miracles for his team. The Yankees steamrollered their old rivals four games to two. Pennock won two games and saved another. Ruth hit three home runs, a triple and a double, batted .368, and scared the Giants' pitchers half to death, although Meusel actually provided more of the clutch hitting. When it was over the Yankees felt they had finally shaken the McGraw monkey off their backs. They were the champs of the world. Even Colonel Ruppert unbent long enough to join in the riotous clubhouse party.

Before the Series McGraw had boasted, "I've said it before, and I'll say it again—we pitch to better hitters than Ruth in the National League." Now the sportswriters made him eat his words. "Ere the sun had set on McGraw's rash and impetuous words, the Babe had flashed across the sky fiery portents which should have been sufficient to strike terror and conviction into the hearts of all infidels," wrote Heywood Broun, making a special return to the sports pages after years of more literary endeavors. He summed up the action with the kind of phrase that made sportswriting of his day what it

was. "The Ruth is mighty," he wrote, "and shall pre-
vail."

And after the second game, in which Ruth hit two
homers, Runyon began his story: "It has been written that
the World's Series of 1923 is a struggle between Brute
Force and a Master Mind, the first represented by Babe
Ruth, huge, ponderous, formidable: the second by John
J. McGraw, pudgy, gray, and crafty.

"That being true, it must be set down that the score
of the second game at the Polo Grounds yesterday afternoon was
>   Brute Force 4
>   Master Mind 2."

By 1923 Christy Walsh had been given full range to
exploit the Babe's popularity. He began by assembling a
list of the manufacturers of every item with which his
client could be associated in the public eye. Then he set
about convincing them of the benefits to be gained by
Babe's endorsement of their products. Before long ads
for modish men's wear, alligator shoes, hunting and fishing equipment, baseball gear, smoking paraphernalia,
and racy automobiles featuring the unqualified endorsement of the Behemoth of Biff were appearing regularly
in the New York papers.

The fact that Ruth had endorsed Cadillac Automobiles in New York in no way precluded him from trum-
peting the virtues of Packards in Boston, or Reos in St.
Louis. In each new city Walsh put Babe up for grabs to
the highest bidder, and if he happened to be plumping
for a competitor of the product he had endorsed the day
before somewhere else, well, who cared? If he spoke
out in favor of Dr. Reed's Cushion Shoes in one town, it
was only fair that he put in a good word for Crawford's
Orthopedics in the next.

Walsh's first endorsement tries were successful
enough that he decided to franchise the Ruth name.
Starting in 1922 and continuing over a span of
several years, a series of Babe Ruth sweaters, caps, scoring aids, cheroots, dolls, socks, gloves, and uniforms hit

the market. None of the lines really fulfilled Walsh's hopes, however, probably because the quality and design of the goods were usually inferior.

Walsh was particularly disappointed by the failure in 1922 of the Babe Ruth Scorer. This was a celluloid rectangle measuring one and a half by three inches and containing slots for runs, hits, errors, and outs for both teams, which Walsh felt would certainly add to a fan's enjoyment of a game. Since all of its number changes had to be operated manually by means of little wheels behind the slots, it was a relatively complicated little gismo. Maybe for that reason, maybe because a fan could much more easily get the same information just by glancing at the scoreboard, the Babe Ruth Scorer proved to be a resounding dud.

One of Walsh's more inspired ideas which took shape in the same season involved the guest-editing of sports pages. For a not insignificant fee Babe would appear in the newsroom of a paper, be photographed with the editors, and "guest edit" the next day's sports section. Out-of-town papers, particularly in non-major-league cities, found the gimmick a sure attention-getter. The publisher, editors, and sportswriters also got to hobnob briefly with the great man, as well as collect an autograph and photographs of themselves in his company that would decorate their homes and offices from then on. The "editing" job consisted of little more than a ghostwritten inside-baseball story, plus an interview, but it must have been worth it to the newspapers, for there was always competition for the honor among the local papers when Ruth showed up in a new town.

One of the commonplaces of Babe's barnstorming appearances, along with the inevitable lodge smokers, hospital visits, and ceremonies at city hall, was an autographed-ball hunt. The agency sponsoring Ruth's visit would hide a hundred or so autographed balls around the city, setting off a frenzied search among the male youth of the area. The lucky finders would get to meet their hero personally, or at least view him up close. Ruth actually put his pen to relatively few of the balls.

Walsh employed a squad of surrogate signers, the most adroit of whom was Al Woods, the Yankee trainer. Probably ninety percent of the extant autographs of Ruth were actually signed by Woods or one of his cohorts.

The free and easy days of sportswriters collecting the fee for producing Ruth at a function also ended as soon as Walsh got wind of what had been happening. They might still take him to charity affairs, but now if a commercial enterprise wanted an appearance by baseball's greatest drawing card, it could contact his manager, and be ready to pay an appropriate fee for the privilege. The fee could be as little as $250, or as high as ten thousand dollars, but the one sure factor was that Walsh would squeeze out the last penny they could afford. He booked Babe into banquets, grand openings, smokers, founders' days, municipal picnics, country fairs, boxing and wrestling matches, celebrity golf tournaments—wherever there was money available.

From the first Walsh also recognized the importance of playing down Ruth's confrontations with the authorities. He made sure that Babe's good deeds received adequate publicity, and threw in plenty of charity appearances wherever he went. (The Yankee management aided all it could in this respect. "What's Babe Ruth doing today?" Ed Barrow was asked by a *Sun* reporter in 1924. "Oh, I suppose he's helping out some worthy cause," replied the general manager. "He usually is.")

If a little flamboyance found its way into the Sunday rotogravure sections, that never hurt. In the first year of Walsh's stewardship alone—besides innumerable hospital, safety-fair, and church benefit appearances—Ruth caught a baseball dropped from an airplane for charity and another thrown from the roof of the Cohan Theater on Broadway to aid widows of policemen, received a gold brick from Marshal Foch on behalf of the Knights of Columbus during the war hero's triumphant American tour, refereed a large number of boxing and wrestling matches, "guest-quarterbacked" for at least six college football teams, received the keys to an unknown

but substantial number of cities, showed a slightly be-
mused General Alphonse Jacques, the chief of the Bel-
gian general staff during World War I, how to hit them
out of the park, sat for his first radio interviews, and
played a theatrical benefit for the Foot Clinic of New
York.

Despite the profusion of great players on Yankee rosters during the twenties, in merchandising terms Ruth
was the franchise. Other superstars existed in the league,
but until the advent of Joe DiMaggio in 1936, no other
player owned by the Yankees had even a fraction of his
drawing power. (Gehrig, though he was popular with
his teammates and with sportswriters, had little appeal
at the gate. In an effort to inject some color into Gehrig's on-field personality, Barrow and Huggins urged
him to make some of his plays look spectacular by
flashy one-handed stabs, and to dive after balls even if
he knew he couldn't reach them, but the placid first
basement didn't go for such tricks.) The fans wanted
Ruth, and nobody else would do.

"I remember one time during an exhibition game in
Pittsburgh, and remember, Pittsburgh is a National
League town," says Shore. "I don't remember who was
pitching—some rookie, I think. On his third time up
Babe hit a ball over the fence in right field—only the
second time it had ever been done. As soon as
the ball had cleared the fence at least a third of the
crowd got up and walked out, just as if someone had
pushed a button."

Out-of-town promoters demanded assurance of
Ruth's appearance before they would sign the Yankees
for exhibition games. A clause was inserted requiring his
presence and indemnifying them should he fail to appear. When Ruth became ill and had to withdraw from
an exhibition game in Chicago, seventeen thousand disappointed fans exercised their right to a refund. A similar incident in New Haven is mentioned by Barrow in
his autobiography, *My Fifty Years in Baseball*. That
time, however, the Yankees were simply told not to

bother showing up without Ruth, and the club convinced Babe to rise from his sickbed and put in an appearance. Barrow states that Ruth actually missed only
one exhibition game in his life. That seems unlikely in
view of his frequent ailments, but certainly every effort
was made to get him to the park for each game since
Yankee profit margins depended in large part on his
presence in the lineup. (Barrow estimated that thirty-six
percent of the Yankees' total trade came from the
team's out-of-town appearances.)

There is no way of knowing exactly when and how
the subject was first raised, but at some point fairly early
in his career with the Yankees Babe began receiving
special recompense for his presence in exhibition games.
Walsh undoubtedly had a hand in the arrangements, and
he was equal to Barrow's penny-pinching tactics. According to a study of baseball economics by Paul Gregory, at first Ruth received ten percent of the gate receipts
of exhibition games. In later years his cut rose to a guarantee of twenty-five hundred dollars against fifteen percent of the gate. Over the years sportswriters often paid
tribute to Ruth's devotion to his fans when he ignored illness and injury to play in exhibitions; they seldom mentioned the fact that he might have other motives as well.

As for the regularly scheduled games, comparative attendance figures for 1919 and 1920 demonstrate his value to the Yankees. The 1919 team drew a total of
619,164 fans to the Polo Grounds. In the following
year, with Ruth belting them out at a record pace,
attendance rose to 1,289,422, a new American League
record. And when Yankee Stadium, with its enormous
seating capacity, opened for business in 1923, Fred Lieb
labeled it "The House that Ruth Built," and no one denied the judiciousness of that description.

Other American League owners had cried foul at the
time of Ruth's transfer to the Yankees, but after the deed
was done they were eager for their share. When Ruth
came to town they were almost certain of good attendance
figures, so there was extensive scheming and juggling by
owners around the league to make sure that no suspen-

sion of the King of Clout took place when the Yankees were playing their team. It looked as if Ruth might be set down for a lengthy period after the Dinneen incident in 1922, but Calvin Griffith of the Senators pointedly reminded Ban Johnson, via the newspapers, that baseball simply couldn't afford to keep Ruth out of action for very long.

Even his salary battles with the Yankees were good for baseball. For weeks prior to his meetings with Ruppert, the sports pages resounded with quotes from Babe as to his worth, his good intentions, and his rock-bottom figures. These were followed by quotes of Barrow's dark mutterings over the immorality of one man valuing himself so highly, Colonel Ruppert's indignation over Ruth's attempts to put him in the poor house, opinions from fans, and various learned comments from the sportswriters. The writers knew it was just part of the off-season hype, but fans around the nation followed closely the haggling over sums which to them bordered on fantasy: twenty thousand in 1920, thirty thousand in 1921, fifty-two thousand in 1922, seventy thousand in 1927, and finally a peak of eighty thousand dollars in 1930–31. Even in the dismal early depths of the depression, when Ruth was receiving a salary that would have fed and housed fifty out-of-work families, no one begrudged him his extravagances. As long as the Babe was making it pay, there was hope for all of us.

Ruth's salary in the fourteen years he spent with the Yankees totaled approximately $850,000. His World Series shares, exhibition-game cuts, and barnstorming-tour fees must have brought his total baseball earnings to between one and a quarter and one and a half million dollars. According to sportswriter Joe Williams, who was close to Walsh and often worked for him, Babe's nonbaseball earnings during that same period came to something over two million dollars. A more common estimate is one million in off-field recompense, but the higher figure seems a more realistic guess, making a total in the neighborhood of three million dollars for what

McGeehan called Ruth's "arduous labors" in the twenties and early thirties. That averages out to slightly more than two hundred thousand dollars a year, no trivial sum today, but a monumental amount fifty years ago.

As to Walsh's share, again, there are no specific figures available. But it was well known among sportswriters of the time that under certain circumstances Christy's percentage went considerably higher than the normal ten percent. In cases when he himself was doing the actual promoting, such as the barnstorming tour of 1927, or in newspaper syndication work, in effect Ruth became his employee, rather than the reverse. And on occasions when Ruth had lucrative offers that conflicted with promotions Walsh was working up, Walsh's plans took precedence. In 1931 Lieb organized a post-season tour of Japan. The Tokyo newspaper magnates who were sponsoring the tour pleaded for Ruth, promising Lieb anything necessary to deliver him, but Walsh had a West Coast tour planned and refused to let the Babe go. (In that instance he may well have acted in Ruth's best interests. On that tour Ruth picked up $10,500 for a single appearance at a Los Angeles charity game organized by Marion Davies, a fee schedule that might have left even a Japanese newsprint baron slightly shaken.)

Despite his colossal earnings, Ruth never became a rich man. Ignoring Walsh's best arguments, he spent his money so fast that it was all Walsh could do to keep it coming in fast enough to cover expenses, not to mention Ruth's gambling losses. Realizing that Babe's spendthrift ways would never leave any capital for investment, Walsh concluded that the best way to insure Ruth's future solvency would be to stick every cent of Ruth's money he could into untouchable annuities. With the aid of Ruth's lawyer, Melvyn Lowenstein, over the years he built up something on the order of a quarter of a million dollars' worth of such funds, often over the bitter resistance of his client. His foresight proved to be the best thing that ever happened to Ruth. After Babe retired he, and later his widow, received a substantial yearly income from the annuities (although nothing like the cash flow of his playing days).

Still, Walsh's Calvinist spirit must have mourned for what might have been. Other men had taken advantage of the limitless opportunities of the times and parlayed far smaller incomes into fortunes. Cobb, whose combined earnings in the first fifteen years of his career barely approached the income of one of Ruth's better years, was a multimillionaire by the time he quit the game in 1928. ("You know, Ty practically begged me to buy Coca Cola with him," laughs Larry Gardner sixty years after the fact. "That was when practically nobody ever heard of it and it was selling at twelve. I knew I should have listened to him.") But Cobb really belonged to the thrifty nineteenth century and Babe to the profligate twenties. (Cobb's millions made his life no happier, anyway. He died a bitter, lonely alcoholic in 1961.)

Walsh had done his best by Babe and made himself a rich man in the bargain. If he had remained a quiet, unobtrusive figure in the background—well, that was the way he preferred it. When he went back to California in the late thirties he could look back on the kind of business career in sports few people had even believed possible before he had come on the scene—and on the satisfying fact that he had saved America's greatest sports hero from the financial misfortunes that had ruined the lives of so many other athletes.

8

Hitting Bottom

DURING THE 1923 season someone introduced Babe to a pretty, young, part-time model and aspiring actress named Claire Hodgson. She was the daughter of a prominent Georgia lawyer, James Merritt, who among his other duties handled the legal affairs of fellow Georgian Ty Cobb. In New York Claire had dated Cobb occasionally and through him met many of the Yankee players. At the time she and Ruth were introduced she was considered the girl friend of one of the pitchers. As she tells it in her autobiography, *The Babe and I,* Ruth initiated their "courtship" by sending her a note and was soon actively chasing her. As many of the players remember it, the reverse would be a more apt description.

Claire had always known her own mind. At the age of fourteen she had eloped with the most eligible bachelor in her home town of Athens, Georgia, a thirtyish gentleman by the name of Frank Hodgson. She had a child by him the next year, obtained a divorce not long after that, and in 1920, seventeen years old, arrived in New York with her daughter and a Negro maid to make herself a career in the big town.

To the Yankee ballplayers this new girl, who was appearing with increasing frequency at Ruth's apartment, seemed quite a different proposition from Ruth's wife. Where Helen was quiet and retiring, Mrs. Hodgson never hesitated to speak up at any time. In contrast to Helen's frequent inability to make up her mind, Claire was a shrewd, tenacious young woman who was capable of getting what she went after. She was also sharply attuned to business affairs. ("You will find in the book that I have a remarkable awareness of the value of a dollar, plus at least a normal fondness for money," she remarks in *The Babe and I*.) Finally, where Helen had not seemed to have the desire, or perhaps the know-how, to influence Babe, Claire was not bashful about trying to change some of his uncouth ways.

But officially Babe was still married to Helen and would be for some time. There was strong pressure from business and religious advisors for them to keep up appearances. So the Ruths continued to attend various public events together and Helen came to the games when she was in New York. To the public, which was judging by the pictures in the rotogravure sections of Babe and Helen working at various chores on the farm, they were the happiest of couples.

If Helen knew about Babe's new interest she didn't seem to care. Now considerably recovered in health, slimmer and less haggard-looking, brimming with what for her was unusual energy, she was full of plans of her own. "I remember she was talking about opening up an antique shop in Sudbury," recalls Grace Monroe. "She showed me the store she wanted to rent. It never came to anything, though."

Another of Helen's new interests was Dr. Edward Kinder, a dentist from nearby Watertown. A good-natured, generous fellow in his late twenties. Helen had met him as a patient at some point in 1923 or 1924. Each saw in the other something that they needed, and in a short time the two were spending a great deal of time together. As in Ruth's affair with Mrs. Hodgson, protocol required that Dr. Kinder and Helen's relationship be carried on quietly. But it became obvious to those who knew her and Babe that something would soon have to give.

In 1924 Ruth's famous appetite was catching up with him. He set out earlier than usual for Hot Springs, arriving at the Arkansas resort on February 12 with Helen and an entourage of New York writers assigned to chart each pound as it was shed. The next day he launched into his usual exuberant but disorganized attack on the problem of getting into shape: lots of hot baths, carousing around and working out in equal measure.

"Right away he got pneumonia, because he would turn the heat up in the baths to the highest possible temperature, then immediately run out and go horseback riding," recalls Bob Shawkey, who had been sent to Hot Springs with some of the Yankee pitchers at the same time as Ruth.

Such illnesses seldom kept Ruth out of action long, and for a "sick" man he played pretty well in the exhibition games after repairing to New Orleans for the start of spring training. Ed Barrow, interviewed by a *Sun* reporter, professed to see a new attitude on Ruth's part: "The Babe used to be just a big kid who thought only of two things, playing ball and having a good time," he asserted. "But in the last year a change has come over him . . . now he has become serious, with his eye on the future."

Barrow's optimism was echoed by the crowds who turned out as the team traveled the South for exhibition games. In Mobile a sports-minded judge adjourned his court so that he and the participants could walk over to the park to catch the Babe as he came through. Although Babe was sneezing and coughing from a heavy cold that day, he struggled into his uniform and hit a home run for the judge. On other stops equally excited crowds cheered for their hero and usually inspired some kind of memorable response. Once he got solidly back on his feet, the writers agreed, he could be expected to take up right where he had left off in 1923.

The Yankees were overwhelming favorites to take their fourth straight pennant, but the unsmiling Huggins wasn't quite so confident. His players did not look sharp.

Something was always coming up to worry him. Joe Bush's arm had temporarily gone lame, Sam Jones was getting knocked around, Whitey Witt had slowed down. And all you had to do was look at the record to see that the World Champions were getting a little long in the tooth. Schang was thirty-five, Shawkey thirty-four, Jones, Bush, Scott, and Pipp all thirty-two. All of them had spent more than ten full years in the majors, and the wear and tear of that many seasons' service was bound to start having an effect soon.

The immediate problem was center field. Since neither Meusel nor Ruth was noted for his range, the man who played between the two in the spacious acres of the Yankee Stadium outfield had to be able to cover a great deal of territory. Casting around for a replacement for Witt, Barrow decided to buy a twenty-three-year-old center fielder who in 1923 had torn apart the American Association while playing for Louisville. He was a country boy from the back hills of Kentucky by the name of Earle Combs, and as good a prospect as Barrow had ever seen in all his years of flushing young flashes out of the sticks.

When Barrow ordered his new find to report to the Yankees' camp, Combs told him to go jump in the lake. The Kentucky hillbilly turned out to be a college graduate, a schoolteacher in the off-season, an individualist with a sense of his own worth who had no intention of allowing himself to be sold to a major league team unless he received a fair portion of the fee. When Barrow recovered from the shock of having a minor leaguer make such demands, he took the position that since he had paid the asking price, Louisville had to settle with Combs. When the minor league team balked at that interpretation, Barrow resorted to a carrot-and-stick policy, alternately threatening Combs with dire consequences to his career and wooing him with visions of the good life as a Yankee. But the young man remained adamant. In the end, probably to his own amazement, Barrow capitulated. Even more surprising, from that moment he became an all-out admirer of Combs.

Barrow's players shared his high opinion of the new-comer. The rookie was almost the equal of Tris Speaker in the field, a consistantly strong hitter at the plate, and a fine baserunner. And, like Herb Pennock, he contrib-uted his own brand of dignity to the team. He was a strict teetotaler, a Bible reader, an even-tempered, self-possessed man who sometimes seemed like the embodi-ment of an earlier, more innocent America. ("He used to come through the train on road trips asking if anyone wanted to play hearts for fun," laughs a teammate.) To round it off, Combs was a graceful, dashing figure of a man, almost universally considered the handsomest guy in baseball, and was married to a woman no less bright and appealing.

On opening day in Yankee Stadium Combs won his first game before the home folks with a home run. "Of course, the headlines all said 'Ruth Goes Hitless, Yanks Win Anyway,' " he recalls today with a rueful grin. (He and his wife, Ruth, went back to Kentucky after his baseball career ended. They live in an 1821 white-washed brick plantation house in the hills, not far from a hamlet called Paint Lick. A long drive, passing under arching oaks and by a peaceful pond where cattle graze, leads up to the splendidly restored house. The Combs are in pretty good health, despite serious operations in recent years, friendly and gracious people who go out of their way to make strangers feel comfortable. Earle was elected to the Hall of Fame a few years ago, their children and grandchildren live nearby, and they would probably be the first to admit they've been pretty lucky.)

Before coming to Yankee Stadium the team had opened the season in Boston. Prior to that game, Babe posed at home plate with a spate of local dignitaries, and "The Sudbury Farmers' Association presented its neighboring agriculturist with one hundred prize chicks," according to the *Sun*. "[The presentation was made because] the Babe . . . takes greater interest in poultry than any other phase of rural activities." (At least, there were a bunch of chickens around the farm.)

Ruth's recurrent illnesses nagged at him, but he seemed in good spirits, buoyed up by the knowledge that his popularity was greater than ever. The *Herald* devoted a column to a description of one of his autograph sessions for deserving boys on the windswept Cleveland waterfront. And on May 14 Commissioner Landis, Ban Johnson, and a U.S. Navy band gathered at home plate before the game to present Babe with the MVP award he had won the previous year. Ruth shook hands with the two baseball bosses and said, "Thanks, Commish," and "Thanks, Prez." He held no grudges.

But fans began to notice that the team, though winning regularly enough to be in the thick of the early season battle for the league lead with Washington, Detroit, and St. Louis, was not playing with the authority of a year before. The pitchers struggled through one sloppy performance after another, and most of the hitters seemed to be marking time. Only Ruth and the newcomer Combs were hitting. Babe's average hovered around .360, and he was slugging home runs at a pace nearly equal to that of 1921 ("When Ruth is on his game he is more than a match for any pitcher in baseball," cheered one reporter.) Combs was among the league leaders in batting average, stealing bases right and left, and gobbling up virtually everything hit into the outfield. ("Huggins told me to go after every ball I could get, no matter how far into left or right it was," Combs recalls.)

But early in June Combs chased a fly ball one step too far, crashed headlong into the left center-field wall at Yankee Stadium, and crumpled up in pain that could be sensed as far away as the press box. The crowd held its breath as he was carried off the field on a stretcher. When the news came back that the star rookie was out for the season with a badly broken leg, a large part of the Yankees' hopes went with him.

Working under real pressure now, Ruth did his best to take up the slack. Noboby ever seemed to give him a good ball to hit, but he managed to murder the bad ones. At the end of July he led the league in hitting with a .389 average and had belted thirty-three home runs. In the next few days he improved on those marks, getting up to .406, with thirty-eight homers, by August 11.

But the other contenders, especially Washington, refused to fold. Veterans Walter Johnson and Roger Peckinpaugh of the Senators were playing like possessed men. They wanted to win so badly that they could practically taste it—Johnson because in all his years as a major league star he had never played in a World Series, Peckinpaugh because he had something to prove to the Yankees, who had traded him three years earlier. The unexpected competition made the Yankees jittery.

During batting practice before the first game of a critical series in Detroit on a muggy early September day, several players on both teams began to exchange insults. Suddenly Bob Meusel led a charge of Yankees toward the Tiger dugout. The Detroit players, led by Ty Cobb, rushed out to meet them. Men in the outfield threw their gloves aside and raced in. In a moment the entire rosters of both teams had met around home plate and were swinging wildly at each other, kicking up clouds of dust and scattering equipment around in a wide circle. The fans leaped to their feet, shouting encouragement to the Tigers. A large number got carried away. They ran down the aisles to the box seats and vaulted over the low walls onto the field. Soon more than a thousand persons were milling about in the infield, shouting at each other and looking around for someone to assault.

Ruth, who had been in the Yankee dugout when the trouble started, hurried out to join in but got caught up in the mass of pushers and shovers around home plate and soon became indistinguishable from the rest. (He was fined fifty dollars for his role in the fight, as were most of the other players.) No one really got hurt, but the encounter seemed to throw the Yankees' nervous systems completely out of balance. When the series finally started they played like sandlotters, lost all three games, and virtually gave the pennant to the Senators.

Even though Ruth ended the year leading the league in hitting with .378 and in home runs with forty-six, some people put on him part of the blame for the team's collapse. When Cliff Markle, a little-used relief pitcher, was sent down to the minors in early September, his caustic remarks about the team were widely quoted: "I didn't knuckle down to Babe Ruth and his pets so nobody spoke to me," he stated. "You know Ruth runs the Yankees. To me the attention paid to Miller Huggins is pitiful. . . . Those birds have been in so many World Series they remind me of a lot of Wall Street brokers. . . . From the time the game starts they sit on the bench razzing one another. Ruth has a few cronies who are ace high with him and therefore ace high with the club. They take orders from him. . . ."

Insiders knew that much of what Markle charged couldn't be passed off as just sour grapes. The practice of vigorously riding their opponents was a new one for the once lordly Yankees. Various personal antagonisms had pervaded the clubhouse throughout the year. Men like Joe Dugan and Whitey Witt often did hit the hot spots with Babe in defiance of curfews and training regulations. And Ruth, as always, had run roughshod over every rule Huggins tried to enforce, overtly encouraged his pals to do the same, and dared the manager to do something about it. All in all, despite its second-place finish, the team was aging rather ungracefully.

As usual, Babe showed no sign of being aware of the team's problems; he was still on top. He put the season behind him and moved on to more pleasant topics. After "reporting" on the World Series between the Senators and the Giants (McGraw had won his fourth straight pennant), along with several other experts for Walsh's syndicate, his business manager sent him off on a mammoth barnstorming tour across the northern Midwest to the West Coast—a trip that (according to Walsh) encompassed eighty-five hundred miles, fifteen cities, 125,000 spectators, twenty-two speeches, five thousand balls autographed, four parades led, eighteen hospitals visited, and distance records established at five minor league parks.

Babe, not unreasonably, decided he had put in a good

year's work and deserved a rest. He may have been especially eager to get away from Boston, since his relationship with Helen had entered a final stage of deterioration. In spite of his unfortunate experiences there in 1920, he selected Cuba as a vacation spot. The denizens of Havana's *demimonde* had not forgotten him; soon after the ship pulled into the harbor, Babe was up to his neck in the usual crowd of tourist-pleasers, all eager to try for whatever they could get from the expansive and easily led *Norteamericano*.

Wild rumors somehow made their way back to New York: Ruth had gotten into terrible shape; Ruth was desperately sick; Ruth had been injured in a barroom fight; Ruth was in hock to gamblers for vast amounts; Ruth's life was being threatened if he did not pay up. A story asserting that the Yankees had been forced to advance him his entire next year's salary to cover his Havana gambling debts circulated so widely that Barrow felt impelled to make a statement in the *Evening Post:* "As for the assertion that Ruth is 'broke' and a physical wreck, I cannot deny them too vigorously. I know that the Babe has worked more faithfully than ever this year . . . to put himself into condition for what he hopes will be one of his best years."

But on the first day of spring training the writers and Ruth's teammates could see the truth for themselves. The Yankees had moved their camp to St. Petersburg, Florida, and when Babe made his appearance there he looked worse than they had ever seen him—a good thirty pounds overweight, run down and haggard, with a puffy, flaccid-looking face and sunken, bloodshot eyes. His foul mood (and Barrow's tacit admission of the fact to intimates who promptly told everyone else) showed that the stories about his gambling losses had not been exaggerated. Ruth had indeed gambled away his year's salary.

The Yankees counted on the serene atmosphere of St. Petersburg to help restore Babe's health and spirits. Even in 1925 the town was famous as a retirement center ("The city of the living dead," one writer called it).

The slow pace of its elderly citizens as they strolled past the white frame stores and stucco banks with their slightly chipped pink arches extending out over the sidewalks seemed to reduce everything to slow motion. Waterfront Park, where the Yankees trained, was nestled right against the water. From second base you could see the tops of sailboat sails as they glided out to sea and watch the gulls floating over the fence and back. It was as calm and relaxing a place as anyone could want.

(The Yankees still train at St. Petersburg, and the downtown is still pretty much the same—a little seedier, a little more chipped, but still charmingly open and bright and full of greenery. One of the old-timers who lives there today is Fred Lieb. Now eighty-six, a widower, he lives in one of those huge Victorian boarding houses right across the street from where the old Yankees used to stay. He looks very much as he did sixty years ago, allowing for the inevitable changes of age. He walks and talks much more slowly than he did, but he's still a sharp and witty observer of the world. "Talk about getting old," he says. "How about a man with a sixty-two-year-old daughter?")

Babe started off his training by catching the flu. Then he broke a finger in a silly clubhouse accident. He was now past thirty; he had subjected his body to eleven years of ceaseless abuse—even a superman had to run down some time. Bill McGeehan, the most optimistic of his writer fans, reported hopefully that although "he is putting on weight and slowing up, he still packs a punch." But Rice ruminated about Ruth's lack of condition in "Sport Light." and a *Post* reporter darkly commented, "Apparently the Bambino will never take the lesson of moderation to heart. . . . He cannot be temperate in eating or smoking. That such a giant as he should have influenza practically every spring is a bad sign."

The team was also showing some bad signs. Everett Scott had slowed to a walk at shortstop. Wally Pipp's swing had lost its power. The aches and pains of age were afflicting Wally Schang. Aaron Ward could no longer make the plays in the field to compensate for his anemic batting average. Bob Shawkey was through as a starter. Several first-rate players remained, of course, and Barrow had helped the pitching staff by trading Joe Bush to St. Louis for spitballer Urban Shocker, but the Yankees no longer looked like the same champion team.

The team was housed at the Princess Martha Hotel, a rambling, homey establishment on Third Avenue, a few blocks from Waterfront Park, but Ruth chose to stay at the Don Cesar, an expensive, pink, neo-Moorish San Simeon on the water a few miles out of town. The Don Cesar was the center of the winter high life in the St. Pete area, something like the old Majestic Hotel in Hot Springs but ten times more extravagant and wide open. From the elaborate roof gardens to the tiled arches on the ground floor, the Don Cesar always had something going on. There Babe could be insulated from the criticism of the Yankees and the questioning glances of the writers.

Unable to shake off his various maladies, angry over his inability to get in shape, he still insisted upon dressing for every exhibition game. "The Babe can't disappoint his fans," he informed the writers. At the dinner table he gorged himself and drank as much whiskey and beer as he could force down his throat, at the same time complaining loudly about the pangs of indigestion racking him half the night. But when Barrow or Huggins told him to go to bed he responded by ordering two or three new girls sent up to his room and carousing all evening with them—no matter how lousy he felt.

As the team packed up and began its exhibition tour north, Ruth went on a rampage at the plate. He would smash a home run far over the fence, then circle the bases half doubled up with abdominal pains. On April 3 the tour reached Nashville, Tennessee, where one thousand orphans were being treated to the game. Ruth looked worse than ever, but he put on his uniform and played. At Knoxville three days later Babe could barely stand, but fifty-five hundred tickets had been sold to the game, and Ruth tottered out to first base, hit two tremendous homers, and received praise in the papers for his "guts and willingness to go to any end to serve his public."

The next day, in Chattanooga, Huggins again ordered him to bed, but the thought of a crowd gathering at the ball park while he lay in a hotel room proved too much for Babe. He took a taxi to the park, pushed through the spectators who stood on the playing field watching the teams warm up, and fell into the dugout. Huggins' gnomelike face expressed his annoyance, but he let the King of Clout play five innings at first base before substituting Gehrig.

His complaints over aches and pains had become so regular that no one paid much attention to them, but as he and Steve O'Neill, a reserve catcher, alighted from the pullman car at Asheville, North Carolina, Babe's face turned gray, he started breathing heavily, and his eyes closed. After tottering precariously for a moment, he pitched forward, face first, toward the cement platform. O'Neill caught him just before he hit, saving him from a possible cracked skull. But it looked bad—very bad. "I thought he was dead," recalls Lieb, who was standing close by.

Local volunteers and players carried Babe to his hotel room. The press corps raced alongside the fallen idol, trying to see if he was still breathing. The inadequate facilities of the Asheville telegraph office spouted forth dire reports: Babe Ruth had collapsed; he was in a coma. The story grew in proportion to the distance that it was transmitted. Readers on the West Coast learned that the Sultan of Swat was at death's door. In London sports fans received the news that Babe had actually crossed the grim threshold and should now be referred to as the late Behemoth of Biff.

Back in Asheville, a doctor hurried into the hotel room to examine Ruth. He looked down at the sweaty, gross, gray-faced man lying in the bed, took his pulse and blood pressure, listened to his heartbeat, fiddled around a bit more, then relaxed. He informed Huggins and Barrow that their star would live a while longer, then gave Babe some medicine to relieve the stomach pains, and strongly suggested that Ruth undergo a series of tests when he got back to New York to determine if the problem might be somewhere else besides Babe's stomach.

Meanwhile, the writers paced back and forth in the hall outside his door. In the street outside townspeople gathered to look up toward Babe's room. "Holy Cow, is Babe Ruth going to die in Asheville?" they asked each other, not sure whether that was a good thing or a bad thing for the town.

Finally Barrow emerged to reassure everyone. The writers hastened to inform the world that Babe had already shaken off the coma and was out of danger. Then, faced with the necessity of filling in the story, they went to work inventing interviews with the half-conscious Babe. The *World* found itself in the embarrassing position of having run one of Babe's ghostwritten "detailed analyses" with an Asheville dateline, a story which could only have been written while he was unconscious, as McGeehan gleefully pointed out in his column. The paper solved the problem by issuing a statement by Babe pointing out that he had actually dictated the story on the train just before reaching Asheville. The *Post* reported spotting tears in Babe's eyes because he couldn't play before the swell folks in Asheville. "Don't worry, Babe, I'll show them how you hit them," Bob Meusel allegedly promised at Babe's bedside.

On April 9 Babe was carried onto a train in Asheville. Before it reached New York a relapse threw the medical picture into new confusion. "Ruth has Six Seizures on Train," cried the front page of the *World*. The *Sun* only counted three, but added that he had also fainted twice. The *World's* diagnosis was acute indigestion from a "hearty breakfast of fried potatoes." The *Sun's* medical informants opted for a medley of "concussion of the brain and influenza." The *Herald-Tribune* (The *Herald* and the *Tribune* had recently merged) tended toward the *World's* point of view, but the *Post* agreed with the *Sun*. The *Times* carefully mentioned all the possibilities. In the *American* Runyon knocked out an uncharacteristically solemn front page story about Babe's brush with the "grim outfielder."

Late on the afternoon of the tenth Ruth's train pulled into Penn Station. A mob of reporters, photographers, Yankee officials, medical personnel, policemen, and interested spectators fought one another to meet it. Helen and Walsh, protected by a ring of policemen, forced their way onto the platform, followed by the surging mob. Attendants lifted Ruth's stretcher through an open window. As he was being lowered by the ambulance men outside the car, he was seized by new convulsions. In a daze, he heaved himself back and forth, knocking the attendants off balance. They stumbled back into the policemen who were struggling to keep the crowd back. One of the cops fell over a photographer, upsetting the stretcher. Ruth crashed to the cement floor, staggered to his feet and lurched about, his bathrobe half off and dragging behind him. The attendants grabbed Babe and forced him back to the stretcher. Helen became hysterical and had to be calmed by one of the doctors. While various people shrieked conflicting orders and others pushed bystanders out of the way, the stretcher-bearers ran through the grimy downstairs hall past the bulging eyes of concessionaires, red caps, and arriving passengers and out to the loading ramp, where an ambulance waited. Helen, Walsh, and several attendants finally climbed inside with the barely conscious Babe. As Walsh describes the scene in a memoir, the rescue vehicle sped off toward St. Vincent's Hospital in Greenwich Village, with "Mrs. Ruth squatting down inside the ambulance," and Walsh "clanging the bell in the driver's seat."

At St. Vincent's, Ruth was taken through the emergency doors and rushed to a private room. The doctors went to work. Only Walsh, Helen, and Yankee officials were allowed upstairs; all the reporters could do was hang around the lobby waiting for a bulletin, or stand out on Seventh Avenue looking up at his window. Finally a medical announcement did come. It was a repeat of the Asheville doctors' diagnosis: Ruth was suffering from a combination of influenza and indigestion; there was really nothing to worry about.

But as one wit put it, he found the indigestion story a little hard to swallow. The reporters were becoming skeptical; it would have to have been a monumental case of overeating even for Ruth to have caused all this trouble. "Well, what do you think it is?" Barrow snapped when they approached him with their doubts. "Syph," they responded. The general manager reluctantly conceded that they were correct. "Well, he's just damned lucky it never happened before," someone commented, and Barrow had to agree with that also.

That left them with the problem of what to tell the readers. For a while they hemmed and hawed, speculating about various forms of the grippe and shades of indigestion, taking Babe to task for his reckless behavior and rehashing the 1922 problems. In the end it was Bill McGeehan who got the editorial train back on the right track. In what were to become the best-known lines of his career, he wrote: "Babe Ruth is our national exaggeration. . . . He has lightened the cares of the world and kept it from becoming overserious by his sheer exuberance. . . ." And, summing up, he put a label on Ruth's ailment for all time. "The stomach ache heard round the world," was what McGeehan called Babe's little problem, and so it became.

Walsh took over management of the news flow from the sickroom. He gave out homely stories of Babe's boyish good spirits and his family's devotion. Interviewed by the *World,* Walsh revealed: "Now that Babe has seen his little girl, Dorothy, guess what he wants to see most? The answer is, the big steam shovel just outside the hospital window." Another oddity Walsh commented upon before anyone could make anything of it was the fact that Ruth had a male nurse. He attributed the unusual procedure to Babe's dislike of being fussed over by women. But even in the midst of these precautions, Walsh found a way to pick up some spare change. When the first pictures of his invalid client came out, they

showed him wearing brand new silk pajamas, manufactured by a pajama company with which Walsh had just
signed an endorsement contract.

With their leading hitter out of the picture for the
time being, the Yankees began the season with a succession of losing efforts. On May 16, after a month of play,
their record was 8–16, and the papers were referring to
them as the "Hapless Hugmen." Barrow began to look
longingly toward St. Vincent's Hospital. The doctors
had pronounced Ruth cured but in need of rest, but in
the last week of May Babe left the hospital and began
workouts. While the team played in the West, Babe ran
and took batting practice as best he could in the lonely
acres of Yankee Stadium. On June 1, over the stated
objections of the doctors and the unstated ones of the
players, he returned to the lineup. "The club had to
have a male nurse in the dugout to make sure he didn't
go against the doctor's instructions," says Bob Shawkey.
"You know, he wasn't allowed to shower with the other
players or anything like that." The players didn't take
any chances. They steered as clear of him as possible
and made sure he didn't use any of their towels or
equipment.

If Barrow hoped Ruth's presence would inspire the
sluggish team, he soon found that he had miscalculated.
Some of the players had been blaming the manager's
tactics for their problems, and when Ruth showed up he
was quick to second their complaints. In early June a
Sun headline read, "Poor Showing of Yankees Attributed to Friction between Players and Manager Huggins."
Vila pictured the scene as a clique of rebels defying the
"mite manager," led by "one of his star pitchers," as
well as Ruth. (Hoyt was probably the man he referred
to.) Barrow and Ruppert were forced to deny rumors
that Huggins would soon resign over his inability to handle the team.

On June 3 Huggins removed Wally Pipp from the
lineup. Lou Gehrig, who was not yet ready for the job
but whose hitting power was badly needed, replaced

him. (He would go on to play 2,130 consecutive games at first base for the Yankees.) That same week Barrow picked up from the minors a kid shortstop by the name of Mark Koenig, whom he intended to groom as Scott's successor. The need for change was dramatically demonstrated a week later when the Yankees suffered through a 19–1 slaughter at the hands of Detroit, in which the Tigers scored eleven runs before a single man was retired in the first inning. It was the most ignominious defeat in their history. The following day Ruth hit his first home run of 1925, but the team lost again.

Combs' .366 average could be mentioned with pride, Ben Paschal was doing some good work playing part-time in the outfield, and Meusel was holding his own, but the rest of the team had become a disaster area. Gehrig's weak hitting almost ended his consecutive-game streak before it started. On June 23 he boasted a .278 average and Vila predicted: "One of these days Huggins will decide that Pipp has suffered long enough on the bench."

Ruth was still unable to time a fast ball or chase a long fly. His teammates looked at him objectively and agreed with a sportswriter who wrote: ". . . It is generally believed that Ruth will never regain his form. It is expected he will be out of the league in five years." "Everybody figured he was washed up," Combs comments. "He was just a wreck."

Helen added to his troubles by calling it quits for good. She had suffered a nervous breakdown after learning of the true nature of her husband's ailment. Walsh put her under a doctor's care, sent her back to Boston, and saw to it that she received whatever she needed. He knew the point of no return had been reached between Babe and Helen, and that when she recovered there would be arrangements to make, but he hoped to put it off until the end of the baseball season. But the farm in Sudbury went up for sale in midsummer.

Opposing teams' bench jockeys called Babe a "fat phony" and asked why he didn't send his nurse up to bat for him. Babe responded by breaking furniture in the clubhouse, staying out all night at the whorehouses, and bragging more loudly than ever about his exploits. Barrow put another detective on his tail, but could only shake his head when he received reports indicating that more than once Ruth had had four or five different women in a single night. When Huggins remonstrated with him, Ruth turned his back and spit tobacco juice on the floor. Some of the players wondered if his "indigestion" had affected his eyesight, a point also made by several writers.

To add to the Yankees' troubles, Herb Pennock was reported to be considering retirement. Wally Pipp fumed at his relegation to the bench. Aaron Ward knew his days were numbered when Barrow announced the purchase of another minor league phenomenon in late August. The new kid, whose name was La Zerre, Lezerri, or Lazzeri, depending upon which paper you read, had hit a pile of home runs in the thin air of Salt Lake City, and was as good as conceded the second-base job in the coming year. As the team struggled along deep in the second division, with little likelihood of improvement, morale was as bad as any baseball expert could remember on any recent team.

Near the end of August, the Yankees arrived in St. Louis for a three-game series. Ruth vanished immediately after stepping off the train. He reappeared for the next day's game, played poorly, rushed out of the clubhouse, and did not show up again until minutes before the start of the following game. This time Huggins was waiting for him. As Ruth tore off his shirt and started to get into his uniform, the manager told him not to bother. He'd had it—Babe was suspended indefinitely and fined five thousand dollars. Ruth blew his stack. Combs recalls Ruth shouting, "You can't do that to me! I ought to choke you to death!" "If I were fifty pounds heavier you wouldn't try it," Huggins replied hotly. "You've got a yellow streak up your back a yard wide."

Babe stormed out of the clubhouse. His face red with indignation, fists clenched, he denounced the little bastard to anyone who would listen. In graphic, expletive-filled language Ruth accused Huggins of trying to make him the scapegoat for his own managerial failures. He finished up with a steaming statement which, cleaned up, made the front page of every New York newspaper: "If Huggins is manager I am through with the Yankees. I will not play for him. Either he quits or I quit, regardless of my contract, which expires next year."

None of the players volunteered any support, either privately or to the press. Barrow fully supported his manager, and Ban Johnson issued a statement to the effect that "Misconduct, drinking, and staying out all night are things that will not be tolerated by his team and the game." Judge Landis, reached by a Chicago journalist, would only reply that the matter was basically an internal dispute of the Yankees.

Ruth climbed on a train for Chicago to take his case directly to the top. When he arrived at Judge Landis's posh, wood-paneled office, he found that he had made the journey for nothing: the judge had unexpectedly departed for a remote lake in northern Michigan to enjoy a few days' vacation. Ruth agreed to the reporters' requests for a press conference in the Congress Hotel, where he was staying. In a conference room, he planted his feet firmly on the thickly carpeted floor and faced the reporters. His expression became serious and his thick, hoarse voice as earnest as a preacher's as he insisted he had only been out two nights in recent weeks, and then only for an hour and a half. Everybody needed to let his hair down occasionally. He was entitled to a fair break from Colonel Ruppert after all he had done for the Yankees, and he would get it or else.

A reporter read him Ban Johnson's comments. Ruth appeared surprised; he frowned, then shrugged. Another writer asked about his weight and general condition. Ruth insisted that he was getting into shape his way. A third man asked if there was any truth to the rumors that his wife was about to sue for separate maintenance. Ruth refused to comment. That was none of their god-damned business. To his discomfort, more queries along this and other sensitive lines followed. Ruth's stalwart posture seemed to sag more and more as the session went on. Finally he said, "That's enough," and walked out.

The "former Monarch of Swat," as the *Herald-Tribune* called him, stepped wearily off the Twentieth Century Limited at Grand Central Station on the morning of September 1. It had been a hot, dreary, lonely trip. Babe had been by himself the whole time, wrestling with these puzzling new factors the writers had introduced. Three thousand sweaty, sensation-seeking spectators had gathered in expectation of more fireworks around the ramp leading from the track to the central hall with the big clock in it. But an uncertain and subdued Ruth, his usually spiffy clothes wrinkled and dirty, perspiring profusely, barely acknowledged the shouts of his fans and the questions of the reporters. With his head down he walked to the taxi stand, got in the first cab, and drove off.

Later that afternoon he went to see Colonel Ruppert at his offices in the brewery on First Avenue. Reporters could see from his slumping shoulders that he had lost his nerve. The colonel's office door opened after he and Ruth had spent a half hour inside, and a sheepish-looking Bambino followed his smiling employer out the door to face questions. Ruppert, in a convivial mood, told the writers that the fine and suspension would stand. Ruth had agreed to apologize to Huggins and do whatever else the manager felt was necessary to regain his good graces. Babe glumly confirmed that he had been out of line. Ruppert was asked when Babe would return to the lineup; the reply was—when manager Huggins tells him to.

Huggins had called Ruth's bluff; now the press detailed the Bambino's reformation. "Yankee Outfielder, Realizing his Mistakes, Intends to Keep Out of Trouble," announced a *Times* headline. Some observers even felt that the incident would prove beneficial to the Babe's image, since fan interest in him had been slipping before his outburst. Even Vila was gracious enough to express his hope that "Ruth's punishment may bring the big slugger to his senses."

The *Daily News* found a typical sex scandal angle on the affair, blaming it all on Ruth's dallying with Claire, whom it referred to as Ruth's "party hostess." The paper got a bonus of sorts when Helen, near another nervous breakdown, hysterically tried to tear off her wedding ring and had to be hospitalized after nearly amputating a finger. Babe then visited her, took her hand, and swore eternal devotion for the benefit of newsmen, although everyone knew the marriage was done for.

Babe returned to the lineup on September 8, after nine days in disgrace. Huggins said he had to learn where he fit in, and in his second game back, he actually demonstrated his new team spirit by following his manager's instructions to lay down a sacrifice. To everyone's delight, the layoff seemed to have done wonders for his batting eye. He hit safely in nine straight games and brought his home run total up to twenty. He ended the year with twenty-five and a .290 average.

But the fans seemed unimpressed. In Boston, where the Yankees had been playing when he returned, cheers greeted his reappearance. But he was always cheered in Boston. When the team returned to New York only a few thousand fans turned out to see the Yankees demonstrate their continuing ineptness. When Ruth's hitting briefly fell off again, the fact elicited neither cheers nor boos. The question of Babe Ruth seemed to have lost much of its urgency.

In the final standings the Yankees finished in seventh place, with a record of 69 wins and 85 losses. Combs finished the year with a .343 average, but no other regular reached .300. Gehrig hit a disappointing .295; Meusel dropped under .300 for the first time in six years, although he led the league in home runs with thirty-three; and Dugan developed leg problems and played only 102 games. The pitching was a shambles all season, the catching worse, and the vital second base/shortstop axis a travesty. Mark Koenig, rushed in to fill the gap in September, succumbed to a bad case of nerves, hit .205, and fielded as if he were wearing handcuffs.

As for Babe Ruth . . . thirty years old, his marriage finished, his "mental balance" (as the *Herald-Tribune* phrased it) under widespread suspicion, his physical powers sapped, at least temporarily, by venereal disease . . . well, it didn't look promising. Many baseball people felt he would never again be a force to reckon with. Babe, as always, professed to have no worries. He told everyone he'd be back next year, as good as ever. Better, in fact. He'd learned his lesson now. But he didn't make his predictions with the usual zest. He knew they were all looking at him and wondering "Is the Babe Washed Up?" for real this time.

9

Was there Ever a Guy like Ruth

BABE RUTH WAS only thirty-one years old at the start of spring training for the 1926 season, but the intensity of the experiences he had given baseball made it seem to many people as if he had been around forever. Harry Hooper and Larry Gardner had hung up their spikes after the 1925 season; only Tris Speaker, now primarily a manager, and Herb Pennock remained in the league from the Boston Red Sox of his rookie days. The Yankees had released or traded Mays, Pipp, Schang, Scott, Jones, Witt, and Bush. Shawkey and Ward were on their way out. The question on everyone's mind was whether Ruth was about to join the exodus.

The writers' jaws dropped when they took their first look at Babe out at Waterfront Park. What the hell was going on, they asked themselves. Ruth looked like a twenty-year-old kid. His weight was way down, his belly seemed as flat and hard as it would ever be, his toothpick legs had a spring in them reminiscent of his early days with the Red Sox. He was out every morning doing laps in the outfield and even chasing after an occasional long ball. "Ruth in Uniform, Astounds Critics" proclaimed a *Times* headline. When he put on an Alice Wills eyeshade to protect his eyes from the sun, and a heavy rubber shirt, the better to sweat in, he looked a bit like a stuffed cabbage roll with a hat on, in one writer's opinion, but he definitely impressed people with his determination. (The two innovations apparently were more of Ruth's home medicine. Huggins got him to abandon the shirt when it began to reek after a few days.)

Besieged by writers demanding to know what had gotten into him, Babe stopped his exercising long enough to explain his new image. "Working out," he said seriously. "You gotta work out." It turned out that Walsh and his other pals had talked him into enrolling at Artie McGovern's gym, a popular training center on Vanderbilt Avenue opposite Grand Central Station. McGovern, a tough little cookie who was a cousin and look-alike of Terry McGovern, the former featherweight champ, had put Ruth through a rigorous program of calisthenics and whipped him into better off-season shape than he had been in for years. "I'm down to 222," Babe boasted. "You shoulda seen me throw that medicine ball. Umph, right in the gut."

Over the winter Babe had moved from Boston to New York. His new permanent residence was the Hotel Ansonia on Broadway and Seventy-third Street. Off and on in the past he had kept a suite in the cavernous old hodgepodge of a building, which was a center for the sports and gambling action in New York. He felt at home there. The bootleggers and Apple Annies working out of the place greeted him with cheerful hellos as he rushed in and out of the velvet-draped, heavily carpeted lobbies, trailing clots of autograph seekers and "old friends" behind him. Many of the ball teams stayed there when they were playing in New York, so Babe often ran into old teammates in the halls. And he liked the place being so big, too. It had a whole bunch of side exits, so he could avoid the fans when he was in a hurry. In fact, he probably should have moved there years ago.

Babe hardly ever thought about Helen now. Walsh and his lawyer took care of the support arrangements. Dorothy was in some kind of boarding school up there. It was as if Helen were just some girl he had known when he was a kid. Of course she hadn't given him no trouble, which was something. A lot of broads wanted to run your life.

Claire was his new steady girl now. When he felt like company he went over to her and her mother's apartment for supper and that kind of stuff. She even had a daughter, named Julia. When he was on the road or didn't feel homey, there was a world of beautiful, if often expensive, broads to choose from. Lucky thing his religion didn't believe in divorce. He knew a lot of guys who wished they were in his shoes.

(Helen did keep in touch with some of the Yankee players. By this time she knew many of them well and when the team played in Boston she frequently dropped in at their hotel for a chat. "We'd just sit in the coffee shop and have breakfast and talk," Earle Combs remembers. "She'd ask about the other guys and their wives, how they were getting on and things like that. She didn't seem to be carrying a torch or anything on that line.")

At St. Petersburg in the spring of 1926 Babe seemed relieved to have all that stuff behind him. He socked the ball easily. In the field he took off after fly balls with a renewed enthusiasm, and even if he didn't always grab them he looked good trying. And by concentrating on his own conditioning he stayed out of Huggins' way. His opinion of the "little squirt" hadn't changed; but now he was a little afraid of him. Besides, a lot of the guys who used to back him up when he told Huggins off had been dropped from the team this year, and the rest of the old gang were studiously minding their own business.

The two most important replacements for the departed men were a couple of twenty-two-year-old San Franciscans, shortstop Mark Koenig and second baseman Tony Lazzeri. At first Koenig's only distinguishing characteristic was his extreme nervousness. A high-strung, sturdily built young man who had something of the look of a G-man about him, Koenig often acted ready to take on the world when it looked at him in what he felt was a peculiar fashion. But once he relaxed, his bluff good nature became more evident.

Lazzeri was a swarthy, fine-boned, dark-eyed fellow whose slight 165-pound frame disguised a tremendous power. The son of a blacksmith, he worked as a boilermaker in the off-season. His wrists and arms had the strength iron bars. That, added to his experiences in the streets of San Francisco's Italian ghetto, gave him the reputation of being a tough customer—so tough, in fact, that no one on the team ever cared to test the truth of it.

Lazzeri was a lively, outgoing type, full of jokes in the clubhouse and exhortations on the field. He relaxed Koenig, kidded Gehrig out of despondency when he made an error, and encouraged Dugan when his bad knee acted up. Like Pennock and Combs, he quickly became a favorite among everyone connected with the club and helped lend the team a certain depth of character. Since he was known to be epileptic, he also brought out his teammates' protective tendencies, especially on those occasions when he suffered seizures in the dugout or at road-trip hotels.

In the spring of 1926, however, Koenig and Lazzeri were just two untried rookies burdened with an extraordinary amount of pressure. "Give it [the team] a good shortstop and a good second baseman and it will be battling with the best of them. Give it a weak shortstop and a weak second baseman and it will wallow hopelessly in the second division. On the shoulders of messers Koenig and Lazzeri rest the major hopes of Father Knickerbocker," wrote a *Times* reporter. He might have thrown in the rest of the infield as well. It would also be necessary for Gehrig to do better than he had the previous year, Dugan to regain his mobility after an off-season knee operation, and Mike Gazella, the new utility infielder, to show himself ready to step in when necessary if Father Knickerbocker's hopes were indeed to be realized.

Huggins was optimistic. These new men were a good sort, he pointed out to reporters. Gehrig, Combs, Gazella, Lazzeri, Paschal, and Koenig could be counted on not to waste their enegies and careers on the high life. And although Huggins did not actually pronounce the words, every reporter there imagined he could hear the manager's heartfelt "Thank God" in conclusion.

Babe didn't pay much attention to the new guys. Once in a while an impressionable rookie, overwhelmed by the chance of close-up attention from Babe, would become a great "pal" of his. Muscular little Mike Gazella seemed to be one of that kind at first. He was a Catholic, like Babe, and his size meant Babe could playfully shove him around when he felt like it. Gazella had received a fair share of publicity as an All-American halfback at Lehigh University, so he wasn't all that impressed with Babe's fame, but he became a Ruth favorite after a fashion and the butt of many of Ruth's practical jokes. Babe seemed to like little guys around him.

In the second week of practice Ruth came down with a lame ankle. Joe Vila sighed, "Babe Ruth's annual injuries have begun." And though the papers had been commenting that along with Babe's improved physique there was some improvement in deportment, Babe's efforts at staying on the straight and narrow seemed to be flagging. He managed to get himself thrown out of the Don Cesar after he and some lady friends engaged in some late-night bottle smashing that left his suite a shambles and drew protests from the hotel's more conservative clients.

The Chicago Cubs and Brooklyn Robins ran the Yankees off the field in short order in early exhibition games. Babe's performance at the plate didn't seem to match his physical appearance. "Ruth's swing has lost much of its former power," an opposing pitcher told a New York reporter. Koenig and Lazzeri, trying too hard, appeared unlikely ever to make a double-play. Dugan's knee seemed okay, but his hitting did not. Pat Collins, a veteran National League catcher who had only once in his career played more than sixty-three games in a season, but whom Huggins had scheduled to carry the bulk of the load behind the plate, looked as shaky as any of the rookies. The Brooklyn players agreed that the Yankees were a second-division club. The bellhops at the Princess Martha even had the nerve to challenge their guests to an exhibition game.

But as the Yankees and the Robins embarked on their annual northward tour everything suddenly seemed to connect for Babe and his teammates. The new men found their feet, the old guys returned to the form of their best days. Everyone from the batboy on up hit as if his life depended on it. Ruth reached the fences in the minor league parks at least once a day, Gehrig and Meusel nearly as often. Nobody could figure out what it was they were doing right that they'd been doing wrong before, but they were happy about it. The players wore out the seats of their pants sliding into bases and got bruises on their hands from slapping each other on the back.

The Yankees won eighteen straight games from their National League and minor league opposition. They massacred them in Savannah, in Charleston, in Richmond, even back in Brooklyn. Old Wilbert Robinson, the Brooklyn manager, yanked at what was left of his hair and trotted out everyone he could lay his hands on to pitch to the Yankees, but after his team had lost twelve straight to New York, all by huge scores, he just gave up. "The Yankees have the greatest hitting club that has ever been assembled under one tent," he told reporters.

Preseason games didn't mean much to the bookies, however. In the betting parlors Washington, the defending champions, and Philadelphia, sporting such promising newcomers as Mickey Cochrane, Al Simmons, Lefty Grove, and Jimmy Foxx, started the season as 2-1 co-favorites. The Yankees' odds, which had been as high as 20-1, shortened to 9-2, reflecting their impressive preseason play. But no experts gave them more than a good shot at third place.

Opening on the road, New York won four of its first six games against Boston and Washington. That in itself didn't mean much, but the scores they ran up, even in defeat, caused the rest of the league to take notice. In those six games the Yankees scored fifty-one runs on seventy-three hits, including an 18–5 pounding of Walter Johnson and the Senators.

Everybody who was anybody turned out to see what all the commotion was about when the Yankees returned to Yankee Stadium on a prematurely warm April 21. (The temperature got up to seventy-nine degrees that day.) Runyon and Broun, who rarely covered baseball anymore, showed up in the press box. Down in the celebrity section along first base sat Jimmy Walker, elegantly turned out in a trimly cut dark suit, vest, and derby, ready to toss out the first ball. (Beau James was now His Honor, having been elected mayor of New York in the 1925 election.) Flanking him on one side was a beaming Colonel Ruppert, on the other a relaxed, cigar-waving, bow-tied Harry Frazee, now the biggest of all Broadway producers. *No, No, Nanette,* his last year's smash hit, was still going strong on the Great White Way and boasted ten separate road companies in the United States, Canada, and Great Britain.

On signal, the three dignitaries stood and stepped on the field to lead a loosely organized parade of three military bands, state and local officials, Yankee personnel, and the entire rosters of the New York and Detroit teams toward the flag pole 450 feet out in center field. ("The Yankees set a new world record for being out of step," reported the *Times.*) Forty thousand fans cheered as a groundskeeper raised Old Glory, then settled back to watch the newly reconstituted Murderer's Row take the field.

Ruth slammed two doubles and a single to lead the Yankees to an 8–5 victory. Combs and Meusel hit home runs, but as usual their contributions were lost in the excitement over Babe's rejuvenation. The next day the Yankees lost, 9–8, but they made up for that with another string of victories with some impressive scores: 9–1, 8–2, 7–2, 8–6, and 3–0. After the last of these one reporter joked, "The Yankees are in a slump. They reaped only ten hits off Grove." By May 5 the team was in first place with a 13–5 record. In the next three and a

half weeks the Yankees won seventeen while losing only
four for a record of 30–9 on May 29. That left them nine
full games ahead of the second-place Senators. Joe Dugan
had gone through the roof and was leading the league
with a .414 average. Meusel's average was .375, Gehrig's over .330. Lazzeri was hitting .315, and he and Koenig were fielding like old pros. Combs was around
.320. Even old Pat Collins briefly reached the .300 level.

And then there was Babe Ruth—the "huge, ponderous, formidable" fellow who had been given up for dead
at the end of the 1925 season, a casualty of his own lack
of discipline. Babe Ruth's average on May 20 was .397.
He had blasted fourteen home runs in thirty-one games.
He had driven in twice as many runs as anyone else in
the league. He had made one spectacular play after another in the field. He had stolen seven bases in the first
month of the season. Once he had just missed stealing
home. Once he had started a Yankee rally by laying down
a perfect surprise bunt.

On May 21 he hit his fifteenth home run. He trotted
around the bases, stopped at home plate to raise his cap,
run his fingers through his wavy hair, and bow to the
crowd before continuing on to hop-skip down the dugout steps to acknowledge the congratulations of his
teammates. Resting his foot on the steps and looking out
across the dust of the infield to the stands beyond, he listened to the cheers that shook the walls and echoed
along the passageways under the stadium. "How do you
like that, eh, keed?" he exulted to everyone around him.
"Some noise, huh? Ever hear nothing like that?"

Last year some people said he was finished, but he'd
showed them. Let 'em listen to that noise. He could hit
.600 if he wanted to. They'd never keep him down.
Not him. Not the Babe.

Babe had always been an exciting figure—a great hitter and a wild character. Now he entered into the very
fabric of American mythology. His comeback from the
humiliation of the 1925 season made him a symbol of
continuity that now stood above the swirling uncertainties

of the twenties. Everything else was changing, but Babe Ruth had proved that no one need ever grow old, that you could gorge yourself on cake and recover from the "stomach ache" to be greater than ever. Like the country itself, Babe had suffered a mid-twenties depression and lost his bearings for a while. But he had found his way again, just as the country was certain she had.

As if by magic, memories of the "physical wreck," the "exploded phenomenon," the "warped mind" of the immediate past disappeared from the minds of sportswriters. There would be few stories in the future about his treatment of Huggins, his vulgarities, his bad temper, or the manner in which he often antagonized his teammates. But from now on the image of "the idol of the American boy" was above tarnishing. A new generation of sportswriters, more sentimental, more solicitous of the players' reputations, more eager to be their friends than the Runyons, Lardners, and McGeehans, stood ready to exalt his character to their hero-hungry readers.

"For every picture you see of the Babe in a hospital he visits fifty without publicity," said Bill Slocum. "I know. I get him there.

"Every road trip it'll happen three or four times. . . . I'll be going to bed around eleven and I'll meet the Babe. . . . He'll say, 'Bill, I promised some guy I'd go out to a hospital tomorrow morning. St. Something-or-other hospital. Find out which one it is. I'll meet you at eight o'clock here in the lobby.' "

"He is as fond of children as they are of him," wrote John Kieran. "The last man away from the ballpark every day is Babe Ruth. He has to autograph baseballs, score cards, and torn bits of paper for the ragged kids who waylay him outside the dressing room door."

"It was during that early association with boys [at St. Mary's], good, bad and indifferent, that Ruth acquired his tender feeling for kids in general: his understanding of their emotions and problems," wrote Bozeman Bulger in a feature for the *Saturday Evening Post*. "He appreciates thoroughly the cause of rough exteriors and awkwardness in little shavers who have been knocked about.

He also sees through those who show a respect for elders and have been taught little forms of politeness. At heart, he insists, their impulses are the same. . . .

"He is convinced any boy is better for having some sort of religious background. . . .

"After a nice, quiet talk with [Brother Mathias] Ruth again becomes the lovable, good-natured boy who left St. Mary's to go into professional baseball. Those early days have left a deep impression on his mind. . . .

"On the bench there is nothing of the upstage star in Babe Ruth. He is simply another one of the ballplayers, and is so regarded by them. He does not high-hat his associates and probably would not know how to assume a patronizing air. . . . With his teammates he skylarks, argues, jokes and makes suggestions, all participants on an even footing."

The Yankees record had been rising like a Fourth of July skyrocket. But in the middle of the year the rocket suddenly fizzled out and dropped quietly to earth without as much as a bang. Babe kept the Murderer's Row reputation alive by hitting .372 and leading the league in home runs with 47 and RBIs with 155, but Dugan, who had been hitting over .400 when he left the lineup with a split finger in mid-May, never regained his form and finished the year at .288. Meusel and Gehrig's averages dropped to .315 and .313 respectively—presentable enough, but hardly spectacular. Lazzeri ended up at .275, Koenig .271, and Collins .286. Even Combs fell to .299. By September the team that had once been eleven games ahead was hanging on by the skin of its teeth. At one point a late surge by Cleveland brought them to within two games of the lead, but Babe led a last-minute rally and New York won the pennant by three games.

But they were no superteam. In the World Series Grover Alexander, now a thirty-nine-year-old alcoholic playing out his string with the National League champion Cardinals, struck out Tony Lazzeri in the seventh inning of the seventh game with the bases loaded and St.

Louis one run ahead. He shut out the Yankees in the last two innings. (In the ninth Ruth walked, made his notorious break for second when he thought the Cards weren't expecting it, and became the last out of the Series.) Since Alexander had also started and won two of the other Series games, he became the new Series hero. Ruth had hit three home runs in one game and a fourth in another, but he wasn't a major factor in the other contests and ended up on the losing side, anyway.

But fate wasn't letting Babe take a back seat to anyone—not in 1926. After the first Series game in St. Louis, a well-connected businessman in Essex Fells, New Jersey, had managed to get in touch with someone in Ruth's entourage. He told them a story about his young son (or nephew, no one was ever quite sure), who was an avid fan of Babe's. The boy, Johnny Sylvester, seemed to have lost the will to live after undergoing a serious operation. (A great deal of confusion has always existed over the nature of his ailment. *The Times* called it a sinus condition, the *World* a "spinal fusion." In his book about Ruth, Tom Meany described it as a "head operation." *The Babe Ruth Story* refers to a back problem.) The caller pleaded for some personal word from the Babe to Johnny—anything would do. He knew it sounded crazy, but they were desperate—the boy was dying.

Later that day a telegram from Ruth arrived at the boy's hospital bedside; in it Babe promised to hit a home run for Johnny. The next day he hit three. Johnny Sylvester, listening to the game on the radio, lifted his head for the first time in days and miraculously began to recover, while his parents wept for joy and called it a miracle.

The papers gave the story a tremendous play. When the team returned to New York, Babe was driven out to the hospital to shake hands with his young worshipper. Paul Gallico reported the meeting of Babe and Johnny in the *Daily News*. His words were to become the most famous of all descriptions of Ruth: ". . . It was God himself who walked into the room, straight from his glittering throne. God dressed in a camel's hair polo coat and flat camel's hair cap, God with a big flat nose and little piggy eyes and a big grin, with a fat, black cigar sticking out the side of it . . ." Now Ruth had really reached the heights; in all the millions of words written about various baseball heroes, no one before had ever been equated with the Almighty himself.

After the Series Walsh and Babe once again took on the vaudeville circuit. This time his contract called for $8,333 per week for twelve weeks, the highest weekly salary in the history of vaudeville to that time. Not even W. C. Fields, Fanny Brice, Anna Held, or Babe's "childhood pal," Al Jolson, had ever made that kind of money.

Show biz treated Babe less seriously than some of the sportswriters did, however. In Portland, Oregon, along with the awards dinners, hospital visits, and the rest, Babe performed a baseball act with a chimpanzee at the Music Box Theater. When he reached San Francisco, Koenig and Lazzeri went to see the show. "It was at the Pantages Theater. I'll never forget it. He came on stage by jumping through a huge tissue-paper hoop," laughs Koenig. Later in the act Babe blew a few squeaks on a saxophone, but for the most part he threw a baseball around and made cracks about the game. "It was boring as hell," Koenig says succinctly. As in 1922, the tour did not live up to the organizer's expectations at the box office. If kids could have afforded tickets it might have been different.

During the tour, which stopped at most of the major cities from New York to San Francisco, Babe endorsed Oldsmobiles, Reos, Auburns, Chevrolets, Cadillacs, Packards, Studebakers, and Chryslers, among other old favorites. Walsh also sold Babe's name to manufacturers and promoters of such un-Ruthian products as pure milk, home appliances, boarding kennels, housing developments, and—in what must have been another first for any celebrity—the view from Point Aery outside San Diego. And when the tour ended in Los Angeles, Babe barely had time to take a deep breath before plunging into rehearsals for *The Babe Comes Home,* his First National Pictures feature with Anna Q. Nilsson.

By this time radio was established as a major cultural force, and stations all over the nation clamored for the privilege of putting the Sultan of Swat's thick, gravelly tones on the air. But Walsh recognized that off-the-cuff interviews were fraught with pitfalls of grammar and bad taste for his client; even if his lines were typed out in large print and handed to him before the show, Ruth was likely to blow them, so Walsh kept a firm limit on such appearances.

(One of Grantland Rice's NBC sports shows demonstrated Walsh's foresight: "At one point the Babe was supposed to refer to the Duke of Wellington's historic remark that the battle of Waterloo had been won on the playing fields of Eton," Rice wrote in his autobiography, *The Tumult and the Shouting.* "Babe managed to come out with this gem:

" 'As Duke Ellington once said, the battle of Waterloo was won on the playing field of Elkton.'

"Later I asked Babe how he could louse up one short statement so completely.

" 'About that Wellington guy I wouldn't know,' he replied. 'Ellington, yes. As for that Eton business—well, I married my first wife in Elkton (Maryland), and I always hated the goddamned place. It musta stuck.' "

Since it was highly unlikely that Babe had ever heard of Duke Ellington, and the town where he and Helen were married was Ellicott City, not Elkton, there is reason to doubt Rice's details. But Ruth's confusion seems real enough.)

Ruth appeared exhilarated in the Yankees' 1927 training camp. It had been a hell of an off-season; vaudeville, Hollywood, broads, booze, money—you name it, he was rolling in it. Before the year started he signed a new contract with Colonel Ruppert calling for seventy thousand dollars per year for the next three years. He was on top of the world. All spring he murdered the

ball. On opening day the Hearst organization gave him
an award as the nation's Most Popular Player. The
newspaper guys wrote prideful, joshing articles about his
Hollywood stardom. "G. Herman Ruth, popular star of
the silver screen," they called him. When he went hitless
in one early game, then recovered to bang out three
hits in the next, a *Times* reporter joked, "It was
feared . . . that the lights of Hollywood had affected
his vision, giving him an ailment known as klieg eyes."

When the Yankees traveled to the outback for exhibition games, he set off a new kind of mass phenomenon;
now the entire population of outlying towns would show
up to memorize his every move and hold their breaths at
his legendary swing. Huge swarms of fans, enough to
have set major league attendance records only a few
years earlier, fought their way into uncomfortable bush
league parks to see the great man. In late May, thirty-
five thousand Fort Wayne fans crammed into the rickety
bleachers of their local park for a chance to watch Ruth
play first base for a few innings against the Lincoln
Lifes, a local sandlot team. "My God," says Koenig.
"The way people would come from all over to see him.
You had to be there to believe it." And even now, sitting in the living room of his ranch-style bungalow in a
back canyon north of San Francisco, a hearty, beetle-
browed man with a growing spare tire, his wife inter-
rupting to say how much she hates baseball (she is his
second wife; they were married long after he left the
game), he still shakes his head almost in surprise as he
thinks about it.

If 1926 had been Ruth's year, 1927 was to belong to
the whole team. The Yankees started the new season
just as they had a year earlier, but this time the slugging
spree lasted straight through the year. By mid-June fans
across the nation were beginning to call the 1927 Yankees one of the great teams of all time. On a sunny, hot
July 5, seventy-four thousand fans poured into Yankee
Stadium to see the Yankees play Washington, their
nearest rivals, in what was laughingly billed as a "cru-
cial" doubleheader. (New York was twelve games in the

lead at that point.) The Yankees took the first game 12–1, the second 21–1, and when the last Senator blushed his way off the field no one anywhere in America had any further reservations.

The final statistics told the story: the Yankees won a record 110 games, lost 44, and came in an unheard-of nineteen and a half games ahead of second-place Philadelphia. (The latter ironically finished with a record identical to that of New York in 1926.) The team batting average was .307. The regulars averaged .320. Four men (Ruth, Gehrig, Meusel, and Lazzeri) drove in more than one hundred runs each. Ruth and Gehrig between them hit almost twenty-five percent of the home runs in the entire league that year—more than any other team's combined total. Combs hit .356 and led the league in total hits and triples; Gehrig hit .373 and led in runs batted in and in doubles; Ruth hit .356 and was first in runs scored and home runs; Meusel hit .337, Lazzeri .309; Hoyt had the season's best pitching percentage. No other team in baseball history had dominated the competition in that way. No one was surprised when the Yankees trampled the Pirates in four straight games in the World Series. Any other result would have been a shock.

Lou Gehrig had finally come into his own. In the first half of the season it was Gehrig's hitting more than any other factor that demoralized the rest of the league and carried the Yankees to their incredible lead. Holy crap, opponents said, one Ruth was bad enough, but to have another guy hitting like that just wasn't fair. Gehrig began the month of June at .415. When Meusel, who had also been hitting around .400, hurt his leg and went to the bench, and Ruth, who had been hitting home runs in bunches, fell into a brief slump, Gehrig took up the slack. By the end of the month his average was still near .400, and his home run total had surpassed Ruth's.

So in the papers now it was "Babe Ruth, Lou Gehrig and Company." The press found it convenient to invent a hard and fast friendship between the two sluggers.

Photos of them poised on the dugout steps before a game or shaking hands after consecutive home runs flooded the sports pages. On days off Walsh sometimes got Lou to tag along on fishing expeditions, and the two were snapped out on Long Island Sound with reels in their hands. "The rival Yankee sluggers are good-natured rivals and exchange merry quips as the occasion warrants," a *Times* reporter informed his readers.

Gehrig in 1927 was a soft-hearted, naive young fellow who lived in a modest apartment on West 133rd Street with his cheerful, bustling mother and slightly dim father. (His father had received a head injury while working in a steel mill and never quite recovered.) Mama Gehrig managed both her husband and her son with an iron hand. She packed homemade pickled eels for Lou to munch on in the clubhouse and invited the boys to her house for one of her sumptuous German spreads as often as she could get them to come. She saw to it that her son stayed away from dangerous companions, especially single young women. "He was just hopeless," laughs Mike Gazella. "When a woman would ask him for an autograph he would be absolutely paralyzed with embarrassment." When some of the boys, during a road trip, sent a prostitute up to his room as a practical joke, he suffered agonies of embarrassment that kept the clubhouse in stitches for weeks afterwards.

Mama had apparently never spoken a harsh word to "her Louie," and the young player just folded up when someone yelled at him. "Once, while I was managing the club, he picked up a bad habit of not touching the bag after a throw on a grounder," says Shawkey. "I warned him it would cost us a ball game some time. One day in Chicago we lost 1–0 because an umpire caught him at it. 'Well, there's that game I told you about,' I told him. He went right to the bench and burst out crying."

But Gehrig's teammates were eventually won over by his unabashed sweetness of character. His unusual talent and stoical determination (as a Columbia University fullback in 1922 he played the entire second half of a

214 BABE RUTH & THE AMERICAN DREAM

game against Colgate with a broken collarbone) didn't hurt, of course. As the years passed and he remained the same man he had always been despite the temptations of wealth and fame, he achieved a position of respect unequaled by any of his fellow players. They might not be up to emulating his steadfast devotion to family, friends, and team, but they still admired him for it.

But it would be years before Gehrig became the "Pride of the Yankees." In 1927 neither Babe nor the fans took Gehrig seriously as a threat to the big boy's position. After watching the keed steal some of his thunder with his midsummer burst of home run hitting, Babe revved up the old "mauling stick" (as one reporter called it) and calmly knocked out seventeen homers in the last month of the season. When he finished with sixty for the year, every home run record in the books lay in ruins and Gehrig, who had hit forty-seven, was forgotten. ("Lou Gehrig, Lou Gehrig," mused F.P.A. "Wasn't he the guy who hit all those home runs the year Ruth broke the record?")

For Babe the new record was the icing on the cake. Now he had done it all. Not that anyone was surprised. Babe Ruth could do anything. Next year he might hit seventy. Next year he might raise a whole hospital of kids from the dead. Next year the whole state of Missouri might turn out for one of his games. There were no limits—not in America in 1927. Sixty home runs— what a man! What a team! What a year!

The stock market was going up, up, up. Everyone was getting rich. Lindberg flew the Atlantic in May. Warner Brothers presented *The Jazz Singer*. Dempsey and Tunney fought the battle of the long count. And Babe Ruth had capped the succession of sensational events with his sixtieth home run.

Ruth, Walsh, and Gehrig prepared to set off on the barnstorming tour to end all barnstorming tours—the tour that chugged away from an early morning crowd of cheering New Yorkers at Penn Station, the tour in which he would travel more than eight thousand miles, cross eighteen states, perform before more than two hundred thousand screaming, adoring fans, pull in tens of thousands of dollars, give out five thousand autographs, encounter the assembled mayors, farmers, doctors, orphans, sandlotters, housewives, cowboys, Indians, miners, soldiers, social workers, editors, Rotarians, cow ponies, and champion egg-laying hens of the greatest country on the face of God's green earth, be carried in delirious triumph through the streets of the small towns and the boulevards of the big ones. John Kieran's famous rhetorical question caught the mood of the nation when it thought of Ruth better than anything before or since:

> With vim and verve he walloped the curve
> From Texas to Duluth;
> Which is no small task, and I rise to ask;
> Was there ever a guy like Ruth?

10

The Payoff that Never Came

AFTER THE TOUR, Babe spent the winter of 1927–28 just taking it easy—hunting, fishing, playing cards, doing all the things he liked to do. Walsh was willing to let things coast for a while; it was all he could do to sort out the various offers that now poured in unsolicited. He wouldn't have to worry about publicity gimmicks again, either. It seemed as if every week Babe's mug appeared on the cover of one of the national magazines. The rotogravure sections of dailies, weeklies, monthlies, ethnic newspapers and foreign periodicals, as well as the newsreels and sports films, were full of him. His name appeared in footnotes of learned quarterlies and doctoral theses. By this time only a confirmed recluse could have avoided knowing about Babe Ruth.

Babe didn't seem to mind the royal treatment. He knew he was bestowing a great favor by granting his presence at a banquet, grand opening, or benefit, and that awareness made it easier for him to be gracious. He took off for an extended hunting trip down South in midwinter ("shooting peasant," in his words to an acquaintance). And when the Goldsboro, North Carolina, K of C invited him to dinner, he patiently let the entire complement of local big shots pump his hand until his arm felt like a length of rubber hose.

Babe wasn't the only one who felt good. At the Yankees' training camp that year you could feel the confid-

216

ence in the air. Hell, if the team played only half as well as last season they would still waltz home first. And there was no reason why they shouldn't be just as good, or even better. The pitching staff, featuring Pennock, Hoyt, Shocker, George Pipgras, and last year's late-blooming rookie find, Wilcey Moore, might be getting a bit elderly (excluding Pipgras, their median age was thirty-two), but they were still a super group. The new infield stars were still climbing toward their full potential. And Babe looked fit and relaxed. (Claire came down with him that year. She took a room on a different floor of the Don Cesar.)

A popular pastime of the players this year was keeping up with their new financial interests, which now ranged from real estate back home to clothing stores and service station dealerships. Many players opened the *St. Petersburg Times* to the financial page as soon as they sat down to breakfast. The great bull market of 1928–29 was carrying more than one Yankee's fortune up with it. Ruth, under Walsh's guidance, invested sixty-five thousand dollars in some waterfront property near St. Petersburg. ("Ruth a Landowner," read a headline in the *Sun*.)

But they put in plenty of time working out, and when the season started it looked like a replay of 1927. By July 1 the team had zoomed to a record of 50–16 and was cruising along eleven and a half games ahead of second-place Philadelphia. Ruth had slammed an incredible thirty-eight home runs, Gehrig's average was .363, Lazzeri and Koenig's each .347, Combs and Meusel were both well over .300. The fans and writers nodded knowingly and sat back to enjoy the slaughter.

The men were in top spirits. Ruth led the horseplay in the clubhouse, exercising his privilege to play practical jokes without fear of reprisal. He ripped the shirt off one guy's back and tore it to shreds. Every straw hat he could get his hands on he smashed in, laughing at the pained reactions of the owners. On the road it was "the drinks are on me" for anyone who volunteered to make the late-night rounds with him.

Sometimes a few of the boys—Koenig, Gazella, reserve catcher Benny Bengough, a few others—would spend an evening in his hotel suite playing poker. "He used to always have a woman waiting in the bedroom," Gazella recalls. "When twelve o'clock came he'd shoo us out."

For a while a brash young reserve infielder by the name of Leo Durocher hit the hot spots with Babe. Finally, however, the rookie's biting, truculent manner started to tick Babe off and they stopped being friends. (In that he was joined by every other member of the team. No one liked Durocher.) And during this period Babe made another movie appearance. This time he played himself in a cameo role in Harold Lloyd's comedy *Speedy,* in a scene in which Lloyd takes a job as a taxi driver and Ruth is one of his fares.

Halfway through the season the team ran into trouble on the mound. Wilcey Moore disappointed everyone by proving to be a one-shot sensation who couldn't seem to get anyone out; Urban Shocker, an eighteen-game winner in 1927, had left the team earlier in the season (playing minor league ball in Denver, he had caught pneumonia, which aggravated a heart condition, and the veteran spitballer died in a Colorado hospital on September 9); and in August, on his way to what looked like his greatest season, Herb Pennock's arm went dead. That left only George Pipgras and Waite Hoyt remaining from what had been considered one of the finest pitching staffs ever.

Then Ruth's batting eye mysteriously clouded over. No one could account for it, but between July 1 and August 15 he hit only six home runs. The others continued to belt the ball, but with the decline in pitching it wasn't enough. The team's big lead gradually evaporated. Philadelphia, sensing its chance, began to play like the team it was supposed to have been in 1926 and 1927. Led by Simmons and Foxx, they won seventeen of eighteen games in the last half of July. The Yankee lead dropped to eight games on July 21, four games by mid-August, and by the beginning of September it had disappeared completely.

A week later, when the A's came to town for a critical series, New York was actually trailing by a half game. But their fans hadn't deserted them. A record crowd of over eighty thousand cheering supporters jammed Yankee Stadium to urge them on. (According to the *Times,* a hundred thousand additional fans were turned away, and another five thousand took their lives in their hands and watched the proceedings from the roofs of apartments overlooking the low center-field bleachers.) Perhaps inspired by that show of support, the Yankees took the opening doubleheader behind the pitching of Pipgras and Hoyt and the slugging of Meusel. The next day a reinvigorated Babe won the third game of the series with one of his classic home runs. Though Philadelphia crept close again later in the month, the Yankees managed to hang on to eke out a two-and-one-half-game margin over Connie Mack's team at the end of the year.

Some observers, including at least one Yankee, felt that their final victory had been due partly to poor tactics on Mack's part. "Hell, the A's would have won if Mack hadn't played Cobb and Speaker in the outfield instead of Mule Haas and Bing Miller," says Koenig. "Those guys were just too old by then." (The two stars had been released by their old teams because of their alleged involvement in a ten-year-old betting scandal that had recently come to light. Mack had picked them up as a gesture of support. But after 1928 neither ever had anything to do with baseball again.)

The main thing to the fans was that the Yankees had come through with their third straight pennant. And despite Philadelphia's impressive comeback, the Yanks ended up with some pretty good statistics. Ruth's average dropped to .323, the lowest he had ever hit in a full season of play, but he still drove in 142 runs and led both leagues with fifty-four homers. For Gehrig it was another good year. He hit .374 and tied Babe's RBI to-

tal. Combs and Meusel hit slightly under their averages
with .310 and .297 respectively, but Lazzeri and Koenig
made up for them with marks of .332 and .319. And
Pipgras and Hoyt won forty-seven games between them.
    The National-League-champion St. Louis Cardinals
didn't approach the World Series with anything like the
same awe that had so unnerved the Pirates in the pre-
ceeding year, however. The Cards' roster was full of
brash, confident stars such as Frank Frisch, Jim Bottomly, and Rabbit Maranville. Besides, the Yankees
were in terrible physical shape. When they limped onto
the Yankee Stadium field for the first game they looked
more like a pickup team from the accident ward at Mt.
Sinai than the world champions. Both Ruth and Dugan
were hobbling around on bad knees. Pennock had no
feeling in his throwing arm. Lazzeri could hardly lift his
right arm due to a shoulder injury. And if that were not
enough, Combs was on the bench after flying into his
old nemesis, the Yankee Stadium left-field wall, just before the season ended, and breaking a bone in his wrist.
    New York won the first game 4–1, behind Hoyt's
three-hit pitching and a Meusel home run. But that
didn't bother the Cardinals. Then the Yankees took the
second game 9–3, with Gehrig hitting a home run, and
the third game 7–3, as Gehrig hit two home runs. By the
start of the fourth game, in St. Louis, the Cards' fans
were looking very unhappy. Complaints to the effect
that their team had choked up echoed from every corner
of Sportsman's Park.
    So far Gehrig and Meusel had done most of the dam-
age. Ruth had banged out seven base hits and scored six
runs, nothing exceptional. But now the Big Bambino
seemed to decide that it was time for him to brush aside
the bit players. In the fourth inning of the fourth game
he made his first gesture toward recapturing the spot-
light: with the Yankees trailing 1–0, he belted a long
home run off Willie Sherdel, the Cards' ace left-hander.
    St. Louis scored in their half of the inning to take a
2–1 lead; then Sherdel held the Yankees scoreless for
two more frames. By the time Babe came to bat again in

the top of the seventh, tension was high. Sherdel was pitching a beautiful game, mowing down the Yankees one after another. Everyone in the park knew that this was the big one. If he got Ruth out, the Big Bambino might not even come up to bat again, and the Cards would be sitting pretty.

The murmur of the crowd rose as Babe lumbered up to the plate. He took his time, joking with the umpire, waving his big bat around in slow, menacing practice swings. Finally he stepped into the batter's box. Sherdel, a slight wiry veteran with pinpoint control, wound up and threw his tantalizing "dew drop" curve ball right past Babe. The plate umpire, Charles Pfirman, raised his right hand for a strike. Ruth coolly nodded, giving his approval to the call. It was a damned good pitch, he seemed to say. Now Sherdel wound up again and came back with another slow curve. This one seemed to break outside before it reached the plate, but Pfirman called strike two. Ruth turned back to protest. "What the fuck kind of strike was that?" he demanded. As the two men argued, catcher Earl Smith casually tossed the ball back to Sherdel, who snatched it out of the air with his foot on the rubber and fired it back without as much as the smallest stretch. The ball cut the plate waist high—a perfect strike. The St. Louis fans burst into cheers.

Ruth looked around in surprise. "That don't count! That's a quick pitch!" he exclaimed. The umpire agreed with him and refused to allow it as a strike. Smith's face clouded up and manager Bill McKechnie raced out of the dugout, hollering at the top of his lungs. Sherdel, Frisch, Maranville, and Bottomly charged over. Smith slammed his mask to the ground. The Cardinals made a circle around the umpire, pleading and raging, kicking the dirt, clutching their temples.

Pfirman held his ground. They knew damned well Landis had banned the quick pitch for the Series, he shouted at the Cards. (The maneuver was still legal at that time in the National League.) The fans, in ignorance of the commissioner's directive, howled for Pfirman's scalp.

After several minutes of this the red-faced umpire succeeded in ordering the Cards back to their positions, amid thunderous booing from the crowd, and the game got underway again. Sherdel, upset, threw two low curves wide. The crowd watched intently as he wound up again. This was the pitch. Wee Willie would toss it right past Ruth's fat belly. Studying the plate, Sherdel watched the big bastard's bat waving over his shoulder, then wound up and threw as hard as he could. An instant later the ball had reversed directions and was soaring with even greater speed in a high arc toward right field. The fans rose to their feet to catch a final glimpse of the incredible blow disappearing over the right-field grandstand (a sight few of them had witnessed before). When they turned their gaze back to the infield Ruth was trotting toward second base, a wide grin on his face, and Sherdel was staring at the ground. As Babe completed his circuit a funereal silence settled over the stadium. The Cards were finished, and everyone knew it.

Almost predictably, Gehrig followed with his own home run (his fourth of the Series). Before the inning ended the Yankees had scored twice more, knocking Sherdel out of the box. In the eighth inning Ruth came up again and hit an even more tremendous blast over the right-field stand. The final score was 7–3.

Babe had put the Cardinals in their place and in doing so set a new Series batting record of .625—ten hits in sixteen times at bat, including three doubles and three home runs. In all he had broken or tied thirteen World Series records, ranging from most walks in a career to most home runs in a game.

Times changed, presidents retired, aviators fell into the ocean, revolutions swept foreign lands, but Babe Ruth went on forever. This year the inevitable post-season barnstorming tour started at Dexter Park in Brooklyn, then headed north of the border to Montreal before moving west to Omaha. The same stories of Babe's devotion to children, his purchase and casual abandonment of new cars, his golf game, his stage, screen, and speaking appearances, and the ups and downs of his attempts to stay in shape filled the same columns in the same newspapers and magazines. As the country celebrated the new year there was no reason to suspect that the pattern would ever change short of retirement—almost everything that could happen to a man had already happened to Ruth. What could be left for him in 1929?

On January 14 the answer to that question appeared in large headlines in all the New York newspapers. Three days earlier, in Watertown, Massachusetts, a house fire had incinerated a woman known to her neighbors as Mrs. Helen Kinder. A passerby had rushed to give the alarm, but the woman expired as she was being carried out of the house. The family made hurried preparations for a quiet funeral, but the police became interested in the case, and the story broke wide open.

"Her identification as Mrs. Ruth was not made until today [January 14], a few hours before she was to have been buried as Mrs. Helen Kinder," reported the *Times*. "She was known and accepted by residents of the neighborhood as the wife of the dentist." After filling in its readers on the details of the Ruths' estranged marriage, the paper added that Dr. Kinder himself had disappeared and ". . . The police admitted tonight they would like to examine him to clear up a few phases of the investigation. . . ."

Rumors of all sorts spread quickly. One version had Helen poisoned; another claimed the body contained several knife wounds. There had been something funny about the death—no one had any doubt of that. The Watertown police denied any evidence of foul play, but expressed their desire to interrogate Dr. Kinder—to learn, for one thing, why Helen's death had been concealed for three days. Public speculation mounted when the county coroner announced that a special autopsy would be performed.

Babe didn't learn of the tragedy until the evening of the fourteenth. Walsh, Dugan, Gazella, and a few others went to his Hotel Ansonia apartment to offer their condolences. Babe took it hard. He broke down and cried.

He seemed to forget that he and Helen had been estranged for some time and that he'd been quite happy to
leave it that way. He went on about the great times
they'd had together. He felt awful. She had been a wonderful woman. He prayed to God she would get what
she deserved in heaven.

A distraught Dr. Kinder showed up at headquarters
and gave a rather garbled explanation for his absence,
including the unlikely claim that he had wanted to break
the news to Babe first. The newspapers continued to run
breathless hints of revelations to come and in the meantime rehashed Helen's background. Reporters managed
to discover from neighbors that she had been living as
Dr. Kinder's wife for about eighteen months, and that
Dorothy, now away in a boarding school, was thought to
have been adopted by the doctor. (For a while the
Kinder family maintained that the couple had been married in Montreal the previous year, but that pretense
was eventually discarded.)

When the autopsy finally took place it was an anticli-
max. The coroner's report included no basis for any suspicion of dark doings. It stated definitively that Helen
had died in a fire that she herself had caused when she
fell asleep smoking a cigarette. People familiar with
Helen's history suspected that she had been doped
up when she'd set the fire, but the report made no mention of needle tracks, and the police were willing to let
the matter drop. On January 18 she was buried. She was
thirty-one years old when she died. Babe attended the
funeral service, at which a grief-stricken Dr. Kinder
handed to him his wife's favorite brooch as a melodra-
matic but apparently heartfelt gesture of good will.

Helen's final gesture toward Babe was quite different.
When her will was read, in addition to the expected
statement leaving the bulk of her fifty-thousand-dollar
estate to Dorothy, there was a clause setting aside the
sum of five dollars for George Herman Ruth. Her life
with Babe had not been an easy one; the five-dollar be-
quest was the only way she ever found to get back at
him.

With Helen gone there were no obstacles standing in the way of Babe's marriage to Claire Hodgson, and the two lost no time in making plans. On April 17, three months after Helen's burial, Claire became Mrs. Babe Ruth in a simple service at St. Gregory's Catholic Church in Manhattan. Shortly after that she and Babe formally adopted Dorothy, and the nine-year-old girl came to New York to live. It now turned out that she was definitely not Helen's child (though she was her legal ward).

In his years with Helen, Babe had never allowed being a husband and father to cramp his style. But now with Claire things began to change. As the second Mrs. Ruth put it in her autobiography: "I freely, in fact proudly, admit I moved in and changed a lot of the Babe's habits after we married." No one would disagree with that. "She really clamped down on him," one former teammate says. "He was really under her thumb."

Once they had tied the knot, the new Mrs. Ruth accompanied her husband on all road trips. This was fine with the Yankee management, who welcomed anything that provided another check on Babe's activities. (She and Ed Barrow did not get along, however. Discussing the general manager's decision to keep Babe in the outfield back in 1919, her autobiography states: "If for nothing else, the Babe and his friends can always be grateful [to him] for having the courage of his convictions. And, frankly, I can think of nothing else to be grateful to Ed for." To judge from the tone of Barrow's comments on Mrs. Ruth in his autobiography, the feeling was mutual.)

The old habit of inviting the boys up for a good time ended abruptly. Mrs. Ruth did not seem to want much to do with the other players and their families. "I only met his second wife once," recalls Jane Pennock, whose husband remained with the Yankees until 1934. "That was when I went up and introduced myself to her in a hotel lobby."

(Not that Babe immediately became a model husband. There were still plenty of "men only" affairs for him to attend, and sometimes even on road trips he eluded her vigilance.)

In her book Mrs. Ruth claims that Babe was broke when they married. Since Walsh was a pretty good manager, that is probably somewhat of an overstatement, but in any case she took charge of dispensing money. From 1929 on Babe was allowed fifty dollars at a crack and no more—although there were a great many such cracks, and Babe kept a secret account with the barber at the Hotel Ansonia. Walsh could not have been entirely happy to see someone else moving in on what had been his territory, but he kept his thoughts to himself.

In an interview with Gordon Cobbledick of the *Cleveland Plain Dealer* early in 1929, Miller Huggins surprised baseball people with the candid way he expressed his apprehensions: the Yankees didn't have a prayer of beating a super team like Philadelphia, was his opinion. The team just wasn't good enough this year.

Huggins was right, as usual. It was a repeat of the team's problems in 1924; too many players had passed their prime. Pennock's arm would never recover; he was reduced to the status of relief pitcher. Hoyt had lost his stuff. Meusel, after nine years in which he had averaged around .315, could no longer hit a fast ball. Dugan had been released after the World Series of 1928. Leo Durocher, his replacement (Koenig actually moved to third and Durocher played shortstop), couldn't hit any kind of pitch. Late in the season Koenig himself developed eye trouble, and his promising career in effect ended. Even Gehrig inexplicably slumped, ending the season with a .300 average.

Philadelphia finished sixteen games ahead of the second-place Yankees. Babe hit .345, with forty-six home runs and 154 RBIs. Lazzeri raised his average to .354; Combs went back up to .345; and Bill Dickey, the finest catcher ever to play in a Yankee uniform, took over behind the plate. But as Huggins had foreseen, the Athletics were just too good. Five of the Philadelphia regulars hit .327 or better, and the pitching staff, led by Lefty

Grove and George Earnshaw, dominated the rest of the league.

The "mite manager" was not around to see his unhappy predictions fulfilled. He had looked unwell all year. His normally wizened face had become even more shrunken-looking and his body even frailer and thinner than usual. Barrow, coaches Art Fletcher and Charlie O'Leary, and his family all urged him to see a doctor, but Huggins never seemed to have time. All he had was a boil or something on his cheek, anyway, he insisted. On September 20 he trudged home after a game at Yankee Stadium and lay down on a couch. Five days later he was dead of erysipelas, a strep skin infection no one on the team had ever heard of before. His death at the age of forty-nine stunned the Yankees. He had been with the team for twelve years, longer than any of the others. You couldn't picture Yankee Stadium without his scrawny figure perched on the top step of the dugout, his head turning slowly as he took in everything on the field. They just couldn't believe it had happened.

Two days later the players, Yankee employees, league officials, writers, and relatives crowded into the flower-decked, L-shaped sanctuary of the Little Church Around the Corner in mid-Manhattan for a memorial service. Among those shedding tears was Ruth. As the nattily dressed Bambino knelt next to his teammates, he was heard to murmur to those around him what a great guy Hug had been and how much he and the rest of the players were going to miss him. This was too much for one member of the Huggins family, who afterward commented angrily to Fred Lieb: "He took five years off Miller's life." The statement didn't make much sense in view of the way Huggins had died, though Lieb knew what she meant. But life moved on; even as the service was ending an impatient wedding party burst through the closed doors at the rear of the chapel, leaving a bad taste in everyone's mouth.

Coach Art Fletcher took over Huggins' job for the remainder of the season. As expected, Barrow and Ruppert offered him the post for the next year, but Fletcher confounded everyone by choosing to remain a coach. His earlier experience as a manager in the National League apparently had led him to prefer the less tumultuous life of the coaching box. Next Barrow and Ruppert sounded out Eddie Collins, but he had expressed hopes of succeeding Mack at Philadelphia and didn't relish the idea of taking over such a high-pressure job in any event. Donie Bush, the Pittsburgh manager, also did not choose to run.

It was Babe himself, encouraged by his new wife, who broached the notion: why shouldn't he be manager? That was the logical step. Almost every other major star of his time—Cobb, Speaker, Johnson, Mathewson, Sisler, Hornsby, Wagner, Lajoie, Collins, anybody you could think of, except maybe drunken old Pete Alexander— had had his chance to direct a club. Babe had played more positions than any of them, his baseball instincts were famous, and he sure knew about the pitfalls that could endanger a young player. He had everything it took.

No one seemed to take him seriously, though. In the shocked aftermath of Huggins' death, various strange notions were bandied about, but Ruth as the successor to his old antagonist—that was too much to swallow. In recent years there had been occasional newspaper items devoted to Ruth's "secret ambition" to become a big-league manager, but such commentary was usually intended as a laugh-getter. Back in 1925, the Baseball Writers' Dinner had featured a skit entitled "If Babe Ruth Were Manager of the Yankees," in which a whiskey-drinking Ruth plotted his strategy against Cleveland during a 3 A.M. poker game, only to get to the park the next day and discover that the team was in St. Louis.

Colonel Ruppert kept his thoughts to himself when Babe stated his case to the Yankee owner, although he promised to give the slugger every consideration. But the generally cool reception his idea had received seemed to dampen Babe's ardor somewhat, and when Ruppert and Barrow announced their choice for the job,

Babe did not seem particularly upset that he wasn't the man.

Like everyone else, however, the identity of the new manager caught him by surprise. It was Bob Shawkey —Bob the Gob, of all people. On reflection, the choice had its merits. Shawkey was a smart baseball man—he had managed the Yankee farm team at Newark for the last couple of years. He had been in the New York organization for fifteen years and he knew the Yankee personnel well. He wasn't the most easygoing guy, but maybe the two years in Newark had mellowed him. He deserved the chance.

Babe's impending contract negotiations got his mind off his disappointment. His three-year contract at seventy thousand dollars per year had run out. This year he was shooting for the moon—one hundred grand. Almost as soon as the 1929 season ended, Babe and Ruppert launched their traditional debate in the press over his worth. Readers were anxious for a sign that the ominous collapse of Wall Street in October and November was merely a temporary setback for the nation's economy. As usual, they could take heart from the Babe. In the end he and the Colonel agreed on a two-year contract at eighty thousand per year. It wasn't all he had asked, but it was still a fabulous deal and Babe felt content. He had given them another record to shoot at. Let's see if anyone ever came close to this one.

The 1930 season got underway with Shawkey determined to lead a renaissance in Yankee fortunes. Bob Meusel had been waived out of the league, but the rest of the lineup was relatively unchanged. Barrow was dickering with the Red Sox for Red Ruffing (he joined the team in May), who would help the pitching, and if Shawkey could coax a good year out of Gehrig, the team would have a chance to catch Philadelphia. But a cold, wet spring at St. Petersburg hampered conditioning, and although the team worked hard under their new manager, difficulties soon arose in Shawkey's relationships with the players. Men used to the gentle hand of

Huggins did not take kindly to open criticism from a former teammate. "He was too much of a hothead," says Combs, who had an uncharacteristic blowup with his new boss. "He'd criticize players and second guess them in front of everyone." Curiously, according to Shawkey, Ruth was one of those with whom he never had any trouble—possibly because he had no alternative but to let Babe go his own way.

At the plate the Yankees remained as tough as ever. Babe hit .359, led the league in homers as usual with forty-nine, and drove in 154 runs. Gehrig climbed back up to .379 and led in RBIs with 174. Combs hit .344, Dickey .339, Lazzeri .303. But even with Ruffing the pitching had gone to hell, Koenig's departure had left a hole at shortstop, and third base was still a problem. Besides, nothing short of a resurrection of the 1927 Yankees had a chance of stopping the Athletics. They again matched the Yankees at the plate with five .300 hitters, and their pitching was still far superior. The Yankees finished in third place, sixteen games behind Philadelphia and eight behind Washington.

Soon after the season ended Shawkey was fired. He pointed out in his own defense that this team's record has been virtually identical to that of the Huggins-led 1929 team, but no one wanted to listen. (Bitter over the affair, he got out of organized baseball and took a coaching job at Syracuse University, where he spent the rest of his working life. Today, a robust man in his mid-eighties, fuller-faced and sturdier than he was in his playing days, he and his wife live in an apartment tower twenty stories above the Syracuse campus, from which you can look out over half the city. He hasn't lost any of his old bluntness. He's still annoyed at things that happened fifty and sixty years ago, and put out at some of the recent "old-timers" choices for the Hall of Fame. But he's still active, still gets out to hunt and visit quite a bit, and all in all feels pretty good about life.)

Now Babe set out in earnest after the manager's job. As he looked around the dugout and around the league he couldn't help noticing things were different somehow.

The thirties had crept up on him. Cobb, Speaker, Johnson, and Alexander were out of baseball. The young boys who were learning the game on America's sandlot diamonds had never even heard of Harry Hooper or Home-Run Baker or Smokey Joe Wood. Christy Mathewson had been dead for five years, for God's sake. It was enough to make a man pause and think about his future. After all, as his acquaintances pointed out to him, he now had six persons to support—in addition to Claire, Dorothy, and Claire's daughter Julia, there were Claire's mother and brother, who had moved in with them.

It was hard work to keep the old stomach in trim; every year spring training was more of an effort. The same injuries came back every year, and one day he might get hit with a major one. He would soon be ready to give up playing and start showing these new fellows how to play. When he took over as manager of the Yankees he'd stay active as long as he could help the club, then retire to run things from the bench. No one could argue with that program, could they?

He had played his heart out for the team. He'd made Barrow rich and Ruppert even richer. The Yankees owed it to him. They were nothing without him. Oh, a few times he'd pulled some dumb stunts and caused a little trouble, but nobody took that stuff seriously. If Shawkey had deserved the job, so did he.

Babe soon made his desires known to the press. Practically every day on one sports page or another Ruppert and Barrow, not to mention ordinary fans, could read a quote on the subject from the Behemoth of Biff, or find a comment in one of the columns. And just in case the Yankee management missed the signs, Babe again went directly to Ruppert and outlined his qualifications in detail. He didn't want anyone to think he wasn't interested. He wanted the job as badly as he had ever wanted anything.

The columnists pussyfooted around a bit. In print they acknowledged Ruth's ambitions, but in private they asked the obvious question—how the hell could Ruth manage a ball team when he couldn't even manage himself? Not a single writer could honestly say that if he were running the Yankees, Ruth would be his choice. They had to admit that Ruth would supply an endless stream of good copy—but not as manager of their team, please.

Most of the players shuddered at the thought of playing under Ruth. What would happen the first time Babe had to administer disciplinary action? How would he ever know if someone got in after curfew? As the saying went—"If he can't manage himself . . ."

"Well, I don't know about the not managing himself stuff," says Combs today, with forty years to reflect on it. "He did know a lot about baseball. But he would have found it hard not to play favorites. That would have been the biggest problem, I think."

A few men even defend the idea. Koenig thinks Babe should have been given a chance: "He could manage himself at least as well as a lot of the other assholes who became managers," he points out. "Christ, half of them were drunks and worse. They should have given him a chance just to be fair. All the other big stars got the opportunity; there's no reason he shouldn't have."

Unknown to anyone else, Ruppert and Barrow had made their decision early in the 1930 season. Joe Mc-Carthy, manager of the Chicago Cubs and an old friend of Ruppert's, had one more year to go on his contract with the National League team. But relations between McCarthy and Cubs' owner Bill Veeck were strained and the manager had decided to leave the team at the end of the season. Very early in the year Ruppert began discreet negotiations with him; the matter was effectively settled by midyear. As for Ruth's chances for the job, Barrow summed up the front-office feeling in his autobiography: "At no time during the years he was with the club, from 1920 to 1934, was Ruth ever considered a candidate for manager of the Yankees." And that was that.

The players were not especially impressed when they met Joe McCarthy at spring training in 1931. The new manager was a stocky, dour-faced man who seldom revealed any emotion except disapproval. "Cold efficiency" described his approach. He had no use for the clubhouse antics that had enlivened the Yankee teams in the twenties. He wanted single-minded concentration. Card playing was out. Even shaving in the locker room was proscribed. And God help the player who failed to show up for a team meeting or obey a training rule laid down by the manager.

There were some murmurs of discontent. The players didn't all relish being turned into "businessmen in monkey suits," in the words of one sportswriter. Least of all Babe Ruth. He'd had his troubles with Huggins, but the squirt's good humor had eventually forced a truce. And Hug didn't go around saying you couldn't have a quick game of poker. No third-rate former minor leaguer (McCarthy had never played in the majors) who had copped Babe's rightful job just because he was friends with the boss was going to tell Ruth what to do.

McCarthy preferred not to make an issue of their differences, especially in his first year with the new club. For the most part he just let Ruth go his own way. He rarely even spoke to Babe, and kept his mouth closed about him to anyone else. Babe didn't hesitate to give out his opinion, though—to fellow players, reporters, management, and anyone else who cared to listen. McCarthy just didn't know what he was doing. All he could do was make rules. Even Mrs. Ruth, who by now could be relied on to champion her man at every opportunity, entered the fray. According to Barrow's book, she and Mrs. McCarthy soon began feuding on their own on those unavoidable occasions when they were thrown together.

Babe's bad temper was not helped by his physical state. He was now up to around 230 pounds. Before each game he heaved his bulk up on the training table to have his weak ankles taped, and during a game he frequently repaired to the medicine cabinet seeking relief from various gastric upsets, colds, sore throats, and other aches and pains. But his batting eye remained as sharp as ever. In 1931 he hit .373, his highest average

2ak

in eight years, and tied with Gehrig for the lead in home runs with forty-six—his twelfth and last home run championship. But defensively he had slowed almost to a walk. "Sometimes he wouldn't even chase balls in the field," Combs recalls, with a trace of the fine craftsman's distaste for unprofessional behavior in his voice.

There was talk in the clubhouse about Ruth being washed up, how he hurt the team in the field as much as he helped it at the plate. Once when he heard his name mentioned he turned around angrily and demanded to know who was shooting his mouth off. Ben Chapman, a new outfielder, coolly identified himself. Babe didn't know how to take this direct challenge; he muttered something under his breath and turned away. But he was beginning to be made painfully aware of a certain impatience with his performance on the part of some teammates.

The public didn't seem aware of Babe's problems. To them he was still the same old Babe, still the greatest idol the game had ever known. After the 1931 season Walsh sent him on the exhibition trail to the West Coast again, and in spite of the fact that a quarter of the country was out of work, people emptied piggy banks or somehow dug up the cash to get a glimpse of the great man. It was during this tour that Ruth received $10,500 for a single game in Los Angeles. When the tour concluded Walsh and Babe stayed around Hollywood to make a series of five baseball comedy shorts for Universal Pictures, which Walsh co-produced. The films, which starred Babe and Franklin Pangborn as a prissy school teacher, seem to involve Babe's causing chaos in Pangborn's classrooms by his presence on the local sandlots, and have Babe spending a lot of time playing ball with the kids. One of the shorts, entitled "Fancy Curves," had him playing with a girls' team. No one remembers having actually seen one of these films in a theater, but they must have played somewhere.

The depression didn't put a halt to endorsement offers, either. Mrs. Ruth mentions one cigarette company that continued to pay him five thousand dollars a year for the use of his name on their product, even though everyone in the world knew by now that Babe only smoked big black stogies.

Walsh was having problems with Mrs. Ruth. She had made clear from the first her concern with money matters; now she wanted a greater say in the management of Babe's income. She and Walsh began to have strenuous disagreements over how Babe's funds should be handled, especially as to how much was to be put into annuities. "Walsh was banking the money, and she wanted more of it," is the way one person close to the scene puts it. Walsh's habit of sometimes taking more than the standard agent's fee may also have irked her.

(The disagreements continued until Walsh finally threw in the towel around the time Ruth retired from active play in 1935. A 1936 feature story in the *Boston Post* quotes Mrs. Ruth as reporting, "We have turned down about $100,000 in contracts since he quit," and went on to affirm that "Mrs. Ruth has sole charge of the Babe's finances and investments." In later years Mrs. Ruth attempted to downgrade Walsh's role in Babe's career. According to Fred Lieb, when he came to ghostwrite *The Babe Ruth Story* in 1947 she tried unsuccessfully to convince him to leave Walsh out of it entirely. When she published her own autobiography in 1959, she had apparently changed her mind and spoke warmly of Walsh.)

When Babe signed his 1932 contract, news photos showed Claire sitting side-by-side with Babe and Ruppert, the first time a third person had been in the ceremonial signing scene since Ruth and Stuffy McInnis had posed with Harry Frazee in 1918. Sometimes Claire even joined Babe at Artie McGovern's gym, where the newspaper photographers caught her in a fetching shorts outfit. In a story in the *Philadelphia Public Ledger* in 1932, the writer devoted a good deal of space to ". . . his charming wife, from whom the baseball star takes his orders and obeys them, a habit that has saved him thousands of dollars that formerly were scattered to the winds."

A *Boston Globe* feature stated, "Mrs. Ruth takes care of the daily mountain of pleas and says 'no'—she protects him from the telephone pest, too." ("She really kept him on a tight leash," laughs Shawkey. "I remember I played a round of golf with him once and he had to borrow money to get home.")

In 1932, his nineteenth year in baseball, Ruth was thirty-eight years old. It was a long career for any man, and given Babe's abuse of his body, a very long one. His failing physical powers became too evident for him and his fans to ignore. He found increasing difficulty in rebounding from the usual injuries, and in 1932 he played in only 133 games. The marvelous reflexes at the plate had also begun to decline. His average fell from .341 in 1932 to .301 the following year, and .288 the season after that. His famous home runs dropped from forty-one to thirty-four and finally twenty-two. Fight it as he would, it looked like the end of the line for the Sultan of Swat.

To add to his indignation, a reduction in salary (seventy-two thousand dollars in 1932, fifty-two thousand in 1933, and thirty-five thousand the next year) went with the decline in skill. He protested against each cut, but the Colonel reminded him that the country was in the grip of a depression. "Times are changing, Ruth," he said sternly. Everyone had to tighten his belt. Anyway, he still received the highest salary in baseball. Gehrig hadn't made even half of what he had in 1933, despite his years of stardom. Combs had never made more than $13,500 for a season. Babe should have nothing to complain about.

Well, maybe Ruppert was right, Babe finally conceded. It looked like something was going on in the country. There were a lot of men out of work, breadlines all over, a lot more people on street corners bumming dimes, a lot of property up for sale in the towns where the team played. In Florida you could see ragged fellows hopping off the rails every day and people just drifting around, looking for something to do. Land was a lot cheaper, too. And there were plenty of stores in St. Pete boarded up these days. The Gulf Coast sure didn't seem to have the spark it used to. Even getting rid of prohibition hadn't seemed to help.

Times were changing at home, too. The family now lived in a large apartment on lower Riverside Drive, which was filled almost to bursting with trophies, plaques, and photographs. Claire's grand piano also took up a deal of room. Dorothy was a teenager now and Julia practically a grown woman. She was pretty, like her mother, and every weekend clean-cut young guys came to the door to call for her, were introduced to her famous father and shook hands respectfully with the old man. Babe eyed them all suspiciously. A lot of them looked like punks. *Young* punks. They were practically babies. Just looking at them reminded him how old he was getting.

They were flabby, too. When he'd been their age his body had been like a god's or something. Not perfect in physique maybe, but nobody had ever had his coordination. When he wound up and threw, or stood up at the plate and swung at a fast ball coming right down the pipe, he felt practically as if he were standing outside his body and watching as it sprang to smooth, powerful life all by itself. "Strike," the umpire would call, or "crack" would ring out as the ball shot away from the bat. Days and weeks went by in which every step he took, every motion he made, seemed to be a part of a flawless sequence. None of these kids, no one except another great athlete, could ever know how it felt to be a perfect machine. The trouble was he didn't get that feeling much on the ballfield anymore. Mostly it came when he made a good golf shot, when it came at all.

His manager was waiting for the day he would be gone. Even Babe could feel that. One sportswriter had pointed out that McCarthy's policy of letting him do what he chose could also be called "giving him enough rope to hang himself." On the bench sat fresh-faced kids, like the ones dating Julia, giving him glances that seemed to ask when he would get his big ass out of there. He wasn't even the star any longer. Gehrig did the big hitting now. (Although not big enough to win the team many pennants.) And that guy Foxx in Philadelphia led the league in home runs.

Once in a while a kid came along to whom Babe took a shine, and they became pals for a while. For a few years the Yankees carried a little utility infielder by the name of Jimmy Reese, who followed at Babe's heels almost like a puppy. "Grabbing hold of little Jimmy Reese, a boy who worshipped him, he would stow Jimmy in his locker and turn the key. The boy loved being the object of such special personal attention from his idol," wrote Martin Weldon in his biography of Ruth. Few of Babe's other teammates found such personal attention enticing, however. Good-natured youngsters like Lefty Gomez sometimes joked around with Ruth, but for the most part he and the others had little to say to each other.

A social event in 1933 that took everyone in baseball by surprise led indirectly to more troubles for Babe. Lou Gehrig, the shy and supposedly confirmed bachelor of the team, got married. "I couldn't believe my ears when I heard about it," says Koenig. (No one was more shocked than Mama Gehrig. Not surprisingly, she and her Louie's new wife did not get along.) It soon turned out that Lou's bride, like Claire Ruth, had a mind of her own. ("She even insisted on being called Mrs. *Eleanor* Gehrig," a disgusted Joe Wood commented years later.) Friction soon developed between the wives of the two Yankee sluggers. In her book, Mrs. Ruth attributes the trouble to a slighting remark over how Dorothy was dressed, but most people assumed that jealousy over the relative positions of their husbands was more the reason. Before long Babe and Lou had ceased speaking to each other. They did not shake hands or even look at each other when Babe concluded one of his home run trots around the bases and Lou waited at home plate to come up next. Babe knew that none of the other players had any sympathy for his side; they had always liked Gehrig.

Babe and Claire's close friends were all from outside

baseball, or at least had never been athletes themselves. They were businessmen like Paul and Ben Carey; Mel Lowenstein, his attorney; sportswriters Ford Frick, Charlie Segar, and Bob Considine and their wives. Perhaps coincidentally, they were all men who solicitously fronted for Babe in one way or another—as financial or legal advisors, ghostwriters, social guides, and general image protectors. Babe felt comfortable with them.

Sometimes everything would come together for him and he would start slugging them out for a while. When Philadelphia unaccountably faltered in 1932 after winning three straight pennants, Babe helped the team to another championship. And in the World Series against Chicago there was the famous "called shot" home run. Those closest to the scene that day—pitcher, catcher, and coaches—have always considered the incident an on-the-spot invention of a radio broadcaster by the name of Ted Husing. The description they give, in one form or another, is that Ruth, in the course of a shouting match with the Chicago bench jockeys, happened to point his finger in the general direction of the mound either to indicate that he still had one strike left, or to warn one of the Chicago pitchers riding him from the bench that *he* would be out there the next day. But in the press box, Husing and a few sportswriters interpreted the gesture as "calling his shot," and when Babe slammed the next pitch into the center-field bleachers, they considered it a prophesy fulfilled. Accounts of the dramatic event went out over the air and the wire services, and by nightfall another ingredient had been added to the Ruth legend.

In later years Ruth came to believe the story and reminisced about how foolish he would have looked had he failed to hit the next pitch out. Charlie Root, the Chicago pitcher that day, used to blow his top when he heard that particular line. He even refused to recreate the moment for Hollywood. "That next pitch wouldn't have been anywhere near the plate if Ruth had really called his shot," he'd sputter indignantly. But the story was too good to be dampened by such objections.

In 1933 Babe was chosen for the first All-Star Game. He liked that. Entering the clubhouse at Comisky Park in Chicago on July 6 in an expansive mood, he reached into the inside pocket of his custom-tailored gray suit jacket, pulled out a sleek leather billfold, flipped it open, extracted ten one-hundred-dollar bills, and handed them to Ephraim Colledge, the clubhouse manager. "Take care of the boys," he boomed. "This one's on me." Then he went out and blasted a line drive into the right field seats, the first All-Star Game home run, to lead the American League to a 4–2 victory. Forty-nine thousand fans, many of them old Yankee haters, stood up and gave him an ovation that lasted a couple of minutes. He still had some of the old stuff left.

The writers watched Babe's playing career stumble to a close, and speculated in print about his future. What would baseball do with its greatest hero ever? Would someone give him a chance to manage a major-league team? What about the Yankees? After all, for over a dozen years he had been the heart of the franchise. And he had made his wishes known on the subject. Would Ruppert and Barrow accede to Babe's continued demands to get rid of McCarthy and install him in his place?

The Yankee management wasn't talking, but even as they filled their stories with such questions, the writers knew the answers. The Yankees had spent huge amounts of time and money over the years protecting Babe from the consequences of his conduct; they weren't likely to hand him the job of looking after their interests.

But it wasn't just Babe's past escapades that stood in the way. The fact was that neither Barrow nor Ruppert had ever worked up much personal respect for their star. They had tried, but Babe was like a character out of some fantastic, primal, animated cartoon. You could have fun with Popeye, ooh and aah at his prodigious strength, and even introduce him as your friend, but you didn't pick him to run your business. They knew that twenty years in the majors had taught Ruth nothing about understanding the problems of others; he had spent every second of that time concentrating on his own emotional needs.

If the players had been polled they would have responded much the same way. The notion of talking over a personal problem with Ruth, or of getting an intelligent hearing from him over a disciplinary problem, made most of them laugh. To the newer men especially, Ruth hardly seemed a member of the team—his celebrity's life had very little to do with the game they played for a living.

So the question remained; what to do with this fat, aging dinosaur? The Yankees had to make some gesture, if only to keep up appearances. In 1934 Colonel Ruppert offered Babe a chance to take over the team's number-one farm club in Newark. There he could learn the ropes, Ruppert explained, and see how he liked working on the bench. The Yankees would even supply a driver to take him to and from his Riverside Drive apartment each day. Only a few years before Shawkey had used the Newark job as a steppingstone to the majors. All in all, the Yankee owner advised, it would be a good deal for Babe.

The writers, who recognized the offer as little more than an excuse to get Ruth off the backs of McCarthy and the Colonel, came to his defense. They pointed out that nobody had ever had the nerve to suggest to Cobb or Mathewson or any of the other superstars that they "learn the ropes" in the minors. Twenty-six-year-old kids like Joe Cronin of Washington were managing in the American League. They were unanimous in their support of Babe when he rejected the offer, and they showed it in their stories. Tom Meany wrote, "The Babe turned it down, stating with simple dignity: 'I've always been a big leaguer.'"

Babe confided his worries about the future to Earle Combs. "I had only one serious conversation with him in all the years we played together," Combs recalls. "Just before he quit in 1934. He seemed to have something on his mind and I asked him what it was. He said,

'You fellows won't appreciate me until I'm gone.' I said I didn't agree with that. 'Listen, keed,' he said. 'I got you big salaries. When I'm gone you won't draw nobody. I'm expecting baseball to degrade!' I said I thought baseball was bigger than any one man, but he didn't seem to agree. He really sounded worried about what he would do with himself after he quit."

Some of his acquaintances speculated on whether at heart he felt up to the responsibility of managing a club. It was safe to demand a job that he must have suspected Ruppert would never give him. When a real opportunity to take over a big-league club did arise—the only such opportunity he would ever get—he didn't take it up.

In late 1933, Frank Navin, looking around for something to hype up his uninspired fifth-place Tigers in the next year, decided to offer the manager's job to Ruth —having Babe around would at least increase attendance at Navin Field. Barrow willingly gave him permission to talk to the discontented slugger. Babe was preparing to depart for one more of those barnstorming tours that seemed to have become a permanent feature of his life, this time to the West Coast and Hawaii. Navin telephoned him with a request that he stop off in Detroit on his way west to settle matters, and Barrow went to the trouble to personally urge Babe to be sure to keep the appointment. He couldn't emphasize how important it was that he see Navin now. Babe listened, promised to follow Barrow's advice, but never got off the train. In the new year, after he returned from the tour and called Navin, the Detroit owner curtly informed him he had already signed Mickey Cochrane.

(He had one more half-chance at managing, though he never knew it. After the 1934 season Connie Mack organized a tour of American League All Stars in Japan. Babe and Claire decided to go along. Before the tour Mack, who was then seventy-two years old, had given serious thought to retiring to the front office and hiring Babe as the Athletics' field manager. But after observing the Sultan of Swat up close for several weeks he changed his mind. According to Tom Meany, Mack explained his change of heart to another sportswriter the following spring: "I couldn't have made Babe manager," he said. "His wife would have been running the club in a month." Since Mrs. Ruth, in discussing that Oriental tour in her book, refers to Mack as nothing more than a "figurehead," the Philadelphia owner probably saved himself a good deal of trouble by dropping the idea when he did.)

Ironically, Detroit, under its new manager, Mickey Cochrane, took the pennant in 1934. The Yankees finished second. In the All-Star Game, to which he had been selected mostly for old times' sake, Babe became part of a record string of strikeouts by National League pitcher Carl Hubbell. In his own league, kid pitchers struck him out with nothing fast balls and dinky little curves. He saw the pitches, but he just couldn't get around on them, and he finished the year with a .288 average and only twenty-two home runs. If a ball was hit to either side of him in the field, it became an automatic double or triple. He was an embarrassment to everyone.

In the Yankee dugout the players waited for the day he would announce his retirement. It seemed unlikely that Barrow would risk the bad publicity and actually release him. "Yanks Fire the Babe"—you could just see the headlines. Ruth sensed this and tried to force the Yankees' hand in the only way he knew—by deriding Joe McCarthy every chance he got. It was 1921 all over again, but this time instead of pushing Roger Peckinpaugh for manager Ruth was pushing himself. McCarthy doesn't know what he's doing, Ruth said. All he can do is finish second. I'd shake things up if I was managing this club.

Babe confided to the reporters that this would be his last season as a regular. The Red Sox and Boston fan clubs, assuming that he meant full retirement, gave Ruth a "Farewell Appearance Day" during the Yankees' last series in Fenway Park, but no suggestions of the usual "day" for a retiring hero came from the New York bosses.

Babe's career with the New York Yankees—the team

he had led to seven pennants, in whose uniform he had
revolutionized the game of baseball and rewritten the
record books—came to an uneasy end on a dull late-
September Monday. There was a chill in the air. Only
two thousand fans showed up to see him trot slowly out
onto the field for the last time. Out in left field the conversation of the few bleacher spectators echoed off the
empty seats. Silence seemed the order of the day. Babe
did nothing at the plate and ". . . the final passing of
the great man Ruth . . . was shorn of all the dramatics
that usually associate themselves with this illustrious
character of the game," wrote John Drebinger of the
Times.

Ruth dressed quickly after the game, hung up his
sweaty pinstripes with the number 3 on the back, and
hurried out of the dressing room. The other players
averted their gaze as he passed. Not even Combs and
Lazzeri, the two men besides Gehrig remaining from the
old days, had anything to say.

Babe "covered" the World Series between Detroit and
the St. Louis Cardinals for Walsh's syndicate. His relationship with the Yankees was left ambiguous. In St.
Louis's crowded, smoke-filled Union Station, waiting for
the train to begin the trip back to Detroit for the third
game, Babe let slip to sportswriter Joe Williams that
he'd had it with the Yankees. He wasn't spending another day in the New York organization unless he was
manager. Williams, hoping against hope that Babe met
no other sportswriter in the next hour or so, strolled
back to his train compartment, ripped up the story he
had already prepared for that day, and sat down to type
up his scoop. The story made the front page of the
World-Telegram and caused a minor sensation. (Also
among publishers of those papers that were paying Walsh for Ruth's exclusive comments on the Series.)
Babe had made his challenge to Ruppert and Barrow in
typical Ruth fashion—take it or leave it.

Babe and Claire then took off on their trip to the Orient with Connie Mack. When they returned three months later they found that the Yankees had chosen to leave it. On February 26, Ruppert invited the press to a meeting at his brewery offices. Babe was present, as was Judge Emil Fuchs, the pudgy wheeler-dealer owner of the Boston Braves of the National League, all three dressed to the nines in well-cut blue suits. Ruppert first handed a small slip of paper to Babe, which read:

> Mr. George H. Ruth:
> You are hereby notified as follows:
>   1. That you are unconditionally released.
>   (Signed) Jacob Ruppert

"It was a dark day outside," reported John Kieran, "fitting weather for what was a sad occasion in New York. The wind was wailing and the skies were weeping." But for Ruppert and Barrow the sun was shining. They were damned glad it was over.

His release by the Yankees didn't mean the end of Babe's baseball career, however. For a month negotiations between Babe, the Yankees, and Judge Fuchs had been taking place, and the three were now happy to announce that an agreement had been reached. Babe was being released to "better himself" as a member of the Braves. Fuchs explained that Babe was to become a vice-president of the club, as well as a part-time player and assistant manager, the only such three-headed phenomenon in the history of baseball. After all, Boston was his first home in the majors and they still loved him there, Fuchs pointed out. Ruppert broke in to say that he wanted it understood that the Yankees had asked no remuneration for Ruth's release. They weren't making a cent on the deal. Reporters asked Babe what his front-office duties would be. He didn't really seem to have much idea. Fuchs mentioned something about an "advisory capacity." Somewhere in the background the reporters thought they heard murmurs about Babe becoming manager after a while, but Fuchs was careful to make no hard promises. The session ended with the photographers snapping pictures of the three men shaking hands.

A few days later, as they viewed the frenzy of promotion that preceded Ruth's arrival for spring training in Florida, many of the writers felt certain that Babe was being taken for a ride. The Braves had long been a second-division club, and it took no genius to see that Fuchs, a fast-talking promoter type heretofore noted mainly for being the best big-stakes bridge player in baseball, intended to milk every last ounce of drawing power out of his tottering ex-superstar. He probably figured that if the Braves were lucky their new attraction might last a couple of seasons. If not, at least once around the circuit.

Opening day in Boston brought out a crowd of over twenty thousand, the largest in many years for the Braves, to welcome the Babe home. The governors of several New England states, the Mayor of Boston, and scads of less august local dignitaries took their places at Braves Field. Ruth responded in his best style, snapping his reluctant body around on a Carl Hubbell fast ball and driving it into the right-field bleachers for his first National League home run. A few weeks later, in Pittsburgh, the old passion flared again and he hit three tremendous home runs, the last being one of the few balls ever hit over the right-field grandstand in Forbes Field. But it was a strain. "He could barely move around the field," remembers Lloyd Waner, who as Pirate right fielder that day watched all three balls disappear over his head. "When he hit them he went around the bases with a fast walk. Afterwards someone brought him a chair and he sat outside the field signing autographs for kids until ten o'clock. He seemed to know it might be the last time."

Despite those two good days, after twenty-eight games Babe's overall batting average was only .181. It hadn't worked. He was too old. By the end of May Fuchs decided he had gotten whatever mileage he was going to get out of Ruth. Since in signing Babe he had put him in a management category, he could safely void the contract without facing legal repercussions. On June 2 Fuchs sent out a news release in which he fired Ruth, and reporters broke the news to Babe in the clubhouse.

Babe went home to Riverside Drive to lick his wounds. For the rest of the season he stayed pretty much out of sight, surfacing only to make a few personal appearances and play a few exhibitions with semipro teams. Once he played against a Negro team in Yankee Stadium. On Labor Day he spent the evening at Zack's Bay Front Stage in Coney Island, where the big attraction was a chance to watch him bat out phosphorescent baseballs to a crowd of holiday revelers. And he closed out the season at Dykeman Oval in the Bronx, playing with a pick-up team of minor leaguers against the New York Cubans. He could still draw a crowd; nine thousand fans filled the unkempt public park to watch the Babe do his stuff against dark-skinned, gold-toothed men named Tiant and Spearman and Gonsalves.

For the first time since he had learned to swing a bat at St. Mary's, no one wanted him. He couldn't understand it. Hell, he was only forty-one years old. He was the greatest attraction the game had ever seen. It was crazy. But despite the cries of "shame" from the writers, the game wasn't interested in Ruth.

So Babe stayed away from baseball, and baseball returned the favor. After 1935 he seldom went back to watch a game at Yankee Stadium or anywhere else. The players assumed his bitterness kept him away, but they didn't really know or care. The Yankees had a new hero now, anyway. In 1936 a graceful, striking-looking young Italian kid arrived from the West Coast on the wings of a tremendous publicity campaign. Even his name—Joe DiMaggio—met the standard of mellifluous charm a real hero's name needed. He turned out to be the real thing. In a short time he had resurrected the Yankee tradition and the team was winning pennants with the regularity of old. The fans would never forget Babe Ruth, but the new man's name was the one on their lips now.

Babe's life took the form of that of a gentleman of lei-
sure or retired British colonel. During the day he bowled,
hunted, fished, and played endless rounds of golf with
his circle of solicitous friends; at night he stayed home
with Claire or they played cards with the same people.
Sometimes they traveled; one year they toured Europe,
but no one on the Continent seemed to have heard of
baseball or him and he did not much enjoy the trip. In
the winter they went south, stopping off at the same
hunting lodges and resorts he had always frequented.

Once in a while he went on an old-time bender, but
not often. Occasionally he played in an exhibition game
or participated in a promotional stunt. Every so often a
newspaper or magazine would do a feature on the Babe
in retirement, in which Claire described how well they
were doing financially, Babe expressed his desire to get
back into baseball, and both of them renewed their complaints of Babe's mistreatment by the baseball brass.
Sometimes ghostwritten articles with his byline ran in
various magazines. *Liberty* magazine printed one in
1936, entitled "How it Feels to Be a Has-Been." Julia
got married and Babe put on a frock coat, top hat and
tails to escort her down the aisle. And there were always
the invitations to dinners and smokers—he could have
attended a different one every night of the week if he
had so chosen. He always showed up at the Baseball
Writers' Dinner, where each year he asked the boys why
the hell he couldn't get back in, and they replied they
just didn't know.

In late 1936 Warner Brothers starred him in a baseball short, but it did nothing in the theaters, and his
movie career ended at that point. Part of the problem
may have been that by now Babe's weight had neared
250, and he no longer bore much resemblance to an
athlete. The CBS network put him in a comedy spot on
the "Kate Smith Show" that same year. *Variety* reported, "Kate and the Babe slated . . . if it clicks, he will be
a regular feature." But after the first few shows nothing
more was heard of that idea.

The next year CBS tried a different tack: Babe became a baseball "dopester." His regularly scheduled broadcasts, in which he analysed games, made predictions, interviewed various sports figures, and told a few jokes, ran from 10:30 to 10:45 Wednesday and Friday evenings. A network publicity release presented a glossy close-up and a caption saying that though Babe perspired freely during a broadcast, he was gradually getting over his "mike" fright. The *Variety* reviewer reported, "Babe Ruth is playing the comic in his baseball spiels for Sinclair on WABC these nights. Has the same frog-voiced delivery and his interviewing will never grab a Pulitzer prize. . . ." That show was also dropped.

In 1938 Larry McPhail, the general manager of the Brooklyn Dodgers, approached Babe at midseason with a coaching-job offer and Babe signed. It looked like Boston all over again to some people; the Dodgers were mired in seventh place, going nowhere, and their sagging gate needed a boost. Babe played in a number of exhibition games that proved lucrative for the club. But when managerial possibilities came up no one seemed eager to speak up, and Babe again studiously avoided asking for a commitment.

In those few months with the Dodgers Babe recovered a bit of the old feeling. Mike Gazella, who was managing a Moline club in the Three-I League, recalls Babe picking him up to play in an exhibition game: "When I got back to my room Babe had put my bed and everything else out in the hall as a practical joke," laughs Gazella. "I remember I talked to him about getting old. He said he didn't mind as long as he could still get a woman."

Mostly he felt like a fifth wheel on the Dodgers. Leo Durocher was their captain. Before Babe had spent half a dozen games in the coaching box the two had come near blows over Babe's alleged incompetence. As far as that went, Durocher had a point. Babe couldn't coach —he couldn't even remember the signs. At the end of the season he and the Dodgers said goodbye with little regret on either side. Durocher got the manager's job shortly afterward.

Too old to be any use in the field, too young to be venerated as a legendary old-timer, Babe remained an embarrassment as he still hung on at the fringes of the game, appearing at the opening of the Hall of Fame in Cooperstown, in occasional exhibitions and celebrity gold tournaments—always a bit maudlin in his speech, always a bit baffled at his continuing exclusion from the only activity in which he had ever felt comfortable.

At the centennial gathering at Cooperstown in 1939 (baseball had been founded there a hundred years before by Abner Doubleday, went the popular mythology), Babe posed with the rest of baseball's all-time greats: Tris Speaker, Ty Cobb, Honus Wagner, Nap Lajoie, Cy Young, Walter Johnson, George Sisler, and Grover Alexander. All of them except Sisler were over fifty years old, and all had been out of baseball at least nine seasons and showed little desire to get back in. Babe, at the relatively young age of forty-four, seemed out of step with the others.

In April 1939 Lou Gehrig quit, his disease-racked body a travesty of its once gargantuan strength. He had played 2,130 consecutive games since that June day in 1925 when he had replaced Wally Pipp. The spontaneous outpouring of sentiment from everyone from Colonel Ruppert to the youngest fan must have surprised Ruth. Nobody had even bothered to say goodbye when he quit the team. At Lou Gehrig Appreciation Day, held on July 4, 1939, Ruth made one of his rare appearances at Yankee Stadium. As he stood in a line with a group of former teammates to honor the man he hadn't spoken to in six years and gazed up at the huge crowd, he must have wondered where his appreciation day had been. But he still retained his showman's instinct. Ignoring the old feud, he walked up to Gehrig and threw his arm around him while the cheers of sixty thousand people shook the stadium. Gehrig smiled graciously as always, and the photo of Ruth embracing his old "sidekick" became the sports picture of the year.

Two years later, at the age of thirty-seven, Lou was dead of amyotrophic lateral sclerosis. Babe willingly ac-

cepted RKO Pictures' request that he play himself in
Pride of the Yankees, the movie to be made of Gehrig's
life. At least he would be in uniform again. He threw
himself a little too exuberantly into a locker-room scene
in his anxiety to get things right and stuck his arm
through a glass window, cutting himself badly. Not that
it mattered. On screen Gary Cooper's presence dominated everything. It made a good movie, though in usual
Hollywood style it bore little resemblance to Lou's actual life with the Yankees.

During the war years Babe appeared occasionally at
benefits and war-bond sales. Once in a great while his
name came to the attention of a country now involved in
things more important than baseball. In 1942 he
wrecked his car and was hospitalized, apparently more
for shock than for physical injuries received. In 1944
NBC tried once more to revive the sportscaster idea,
with no more success than previously. And there was a
story making the rounds of the columns about how Jap
soldiers, as they stormed American-held islands early in
the war, had tried to demoralize the Yanks by screaming
what they thought was the ultimate insult—"to hell with
Babe Ruth."

By the war's end Babe had become a living relic.
Only twenty-five years had passed since Harry Frazee
had sent the new home run king down to New York
(and been hung in effigy for his trouble). But to Americans, the concentration of events in those years made
them seem like a century. The roaring twenties, the Depression, and World War Two had crowded in on each
other in such a way that it seemed only a professor of
history could reconstruct in his mind all that had happened in that time.

If Babe had chosen to drive up to Yankee Stadium
for a game he wouldn't have recognized the players anymore. Only a couple of men on the 1946 Yankee roster
had been in the league in his last years. Lazzeri, Gehrig,
Huggins, Ruppert, Ban Johnson, and McGraw were in
their graves. (Tony had fallen down a flight of stairs dur-

ing an epileptic fit and died as a result of his injuries.)
Barrow and Landis had retired. Lardner, McGeehan,
Vila, and half of those other sportswriting guys were
gone.

Sometimes he heard about his old teammates. They
were mostly doing well. Joe Wood coached at Yale.
Shawkey was athletic director at Syracuse, Gardner at
the University of Vermont. That sounded pretty impressive. Ernie Shore had entered politics back home in
North Carolina and been elected sheriff of Winston-Salem. Combs had coached with the Yankees for a while,
then gone back to his mansion in Kentucky. Ty Cobb was
a millionaire living somewhere in California. Hooper
was postmaster at some small town out there, too. Duffy
Lewis was the Braves' road secretary. Pennock, Meusel,
Dugan, Koenig—they'd all gone back home to stay.
Only Babe had hung around the big town.

As the country began to settle down after the war, a
place actually seemed to be opening up for Babe. In the
exuberant atmosphere of victory, the country was ready
to celebrate its heroes again. Babe's name had always
been magic—that had never changed. Major-league
baseball might never want him, but the game of baseball
itself, the game of kids in vacant lots, of newly formed
little leagues and American Legion ball, was ready to re-
claim its own.

A whole new generation of kids, who might not even
recognize his funny face anymore but to whom he was
still a god, was waiting for him. When in early 1947 the
Ford Motor Company approached Ruth, now fifty-two
years old, with an opportunity for him to be the nominal
head of their American Legion junior baseball program,
it seemed as if the right role had come along at last. He
would tour the country, letting the kids see him, encour-
aging them to play ball, reminding them what the game
was all about.

Babe liked the idea of playing elder statesman. Claire
also approved. But, as it turned out, it was too late for
that. In 1946 frequent moments of blinding pain had
sent him to the hospital, where he was discovered to

have cancer of the throat. The doctors immediately operated, but even after he had been released from the hospital it was obvious to onlookers that the cancer remained inside him. It was only a matter of time.

Now baseball found the time to pay him tribute. Commissioner "Happy" Chandler, a new man uninvolved in the controversies of Ruth's playing days, set aside April 27, 1947 as "Babe Ruth Day." Simultaneous ceremonies were held in all major-league ball parks where games were being played. In Yankee Stadium a crowd almost as large as the one that had wept for Lou Gehrig eight years before cheered like demons when he walked uncertainly out to home plate. He was a shrunken, sunken-eyed figure now, whose topcoat hung baggily on his stooped shoulders. He was barely able to speak after his operation. From the stands it seemed as if there were almost nothing left of Babe Ruth.

Hollywood hurried to make a movie of his life. A publishing house contracted for his autobiography. A Babe Ruth Foundation was set up to aid underprivileged kids. But it was all a little too late. The day at Yankee Stadium had been decreed by a man Ruth didn't even know, not by one of his old associates. The film didn't star Gary Cooper or Jimmy Stewart, or even Paul Douglas, Mrs. Ruth's choice. William Bendix, Chester Riley himself, a low comedian who had to be shown how to swing a bat properly, was chosen to portray Ruth in *The Babe Ruth Story*. (The gossip was that all Hollywood cared about was tying the movie's release as near as possible to the day Ruth croaked.) The book and the foundation were just frills for a dying man. None of them seemed to be honoring Babe Ruth the person or Babe Ruth the ballplayer. They were, rather, monuments to his drawing power, a last chance to capitalize on the golden name.

Babe died on the evening of August 16, 1948, in Memorial Hospital in Manhattan. His wife, his two adopted daughters, and a few friends were with him in his last hours. He was in some pain at the end, but it came quickly. The nation had been expecting bad news for a couple of days, and when it came, older Americans stopped for a moment to remember the flamboyant, round-faced athlete who had kept the spirit of youth alive in their imaginations long after they had grown a few gray hairs and become less flexible in body. "I saw him play once," they said to each other. "God, I'll never forget it."

Two days later eighty thousand people—kids, old-timers, lawyers, washerwomen, train porters. former teammates, curiosity seekers—mostly just plain people—moved slowly by the body as it lay in state in the lobby of Yankee Stadium. Many wept, crossed themselves, and prayed for his soul. Editorials expressed the sorrow of New York publishers. Letters to the Editor recalled a moment or two when the great man's presence had touched the correspondents' lives. Sylvan Levin, music director of station WOR, composed a five-part symphonic suite in his memory. The first three movements were each called "Success," the fourth "The Called Home Run," and the fifth "In Memorium." Plans were set in motion for plaques, historical markers, and the like.

"Babe Ruth was above all a great American . . . He typified the fair play, honesty, and clean sportsmanship that exemplifies American sport," said Governor Thomas E. Dewey.

"Ruth was a great figure in the game. He was colorful . . . How colorful we will realize when today's [memorial ceremony] attendance returns to normal," commented Judge Fuchs.

"Because of him millions of kids . . . went out to build bodies, occupy their minds during days of temptation, learn cooperation and sportsmanship. . . .

"The pictures of him lying under the crucifix and kids standing and watching and kneeling and praying showed him as he was to the end. . . .

"He was a killer of slimy things that breed in the crooked gambling slums of big cities. He was a crusader with a bat instead of a lance. He was the Great Babe," eulogized Father Daniel A. Lord, S.J., in a preface to one of the many Catholic tracts that appeared after Babe's death.

In the columns the writers rehashed the old stories, once more condemned baseball for ignoring the Babe, and came up with a few new tales about the kind of guy they believed, or wanted to believe, he really was. One involved a conversation between two pallbearers on the steaming hot August day he was buried: "Lord," whispered Joe Dugan, in Roger Kahn's version, ". . . I'd give my right arm for an ice-cold beer." Waite Hoyt, the former pitcher, grunted under the burden of the coffin and turned slightly. "Joe," he murmured, "so would the Babe."

Hoyt's sentimental quip probably came closer to the real truth than any of the sanctimonious tributes. Death is a fact of life, a serious matter that has to be faced eventually, and the central enigma of Babe's fifty-three years was that he always found such things beyond his grasp. Year after year his associates watched him, wondering when he would grow up, expecting that he would eventually have to learn to face facts as they themselves had had to learn, that he would start behaving in a manner consistent with the adulation he received from millions of worshipful kids, but he managed to fool them all. He just stayed Babe Ruth—a wary, self-centered, exuberant, ignorant boy who by an accident of physical coordination happened to be the most exciting figure of his time.

Bibliography

American and Local History:

Allen, Frederick Lewis. *The Big Change.* New York, 1952.
————. *Only Yesterday.* New York, 1964.
Collier's Magazine. "The Baltimore Fire." Special Issue, Spring 1904.
Dos Passos, John. *Mid-Century.* Boston, 1961.
Dulles, Foster Rhea. *America Learns to Play.* Gloucester, Mass., 1963.
Fowler, Gene. *Skyline.* New York, 1961.
Hollander, John. *A Professor Holds Forth.* Baltimore, 1930.
Keats, John. *You Might as Well Live.* New York, 1970.
Laurie, Joe, Jr. *Vaudeville.* New York, 1953.
Lord, Walter. *The Good Years.* New York, 1960.
Mencken, H. L. *Newspaper Days.* New York, 1941.
Rogers, Agnes. *I Distinctly Remember.* New York, 1947.
Spenser, Edward. *The Baltimore Sesquicentennial Memorial Volume.* Baltimore, 1880.

Baseball History:

Allen, Lee. *The American League Story.* New York, 1961.
————. *The National League Story.* New York, 1962.
Allen, Mel. *You Can't Beat the Hours.* New York, 1964.
Asinof, Eliot. *Eight Men Out.* New York, 1963.
Bready, James. *The Home Team.* Baltimore, 1958.
Danzig, Allison and Brandwein, Peter, eds. *Sports Golden Age.* New York, 1948.
Einstein, Charles, ed. *Fireside Book of Baseball.* 3 vols., New York, 1956, 1958, 1968.
Farrell, James T. *My Baseball Diary.* New York, 1957.
Graham, Frank. *The New York Yankees.* New York, 1943.
Gregory, Paul. *The Baseball Player, An Economic Study.* Washington, D.C., 1956.
Kahn, James M. *The Umpire Story.* New York, 1953.

Lieb, Frederick. *The Baseball Story.* New York, 1950.
───────. *The St. Louis Cardinals.* New York, 1944.
───────. *The Story of The World Series.* New York, 1949.
───────. *The Boston Red Sox.* New York, 1947.
Mann, Jack, *The Decline and Fall of the New York Yankees,* New York, 1967.
Seymour, Harold. *Baseball: The Early Years.* New York, 1960.
───────. *Baseball: The Golden Age.* New York, 1971.
Smith, Robert. *Baseball.* New York, 1947.
Spears, Jack. "Baseball on the Screen." *Films in Review,*
Voight, David Quenten. *American Baseball.* Norman, Oklahoma, 1966.
Walsh, Christy, ed. *Baseball's Greatest Lineup.* New York, 1952.

Biography and Autobiography:
Barrow, Ed. *My Fifty Years in Baseball.* New York, 1951.
Cobb, Ty. *My Life in Baseball.* New York, 1961.
Durso, Joseph. *In the Days of Mr. McGraw.* Englewood Cliffs, New Jersey, 1969.
Elder, Donald. *Ring Lardner.* New York, 1956.
Fowler, Gene. *Beau James.* New York, 1949.
───────. *The Great Mouthpiece.* New York, 1931.
Fowler, Will. *The Young Man From Denver.* New York, 1962.
Freeland, Michael. *Al Jolson.* London, 1972.
Gallico, Paul. *Farewell to Sport.* New York, 1938.
Grimm, Charles. *Jolly Cholly's Story.* Chicago, 1958.
Hoyt, Edwin P. *A Gentleman of Broadway.* Boston, 1964.
Pilat, Oliver. *Pegler, Angry Man of the Press.* Boston, 1963.
Rice, Grantland. *The Tumult and the Shouting.* New York, 1954.
Ritter, Lawrence. *The Glory of Their Times.* New York, 1966.
Spink, J. G. Taylor. *Judge Landis and Twenty-five Years of Baseball.* New York, 1947.
Walsh, Christy. *Adios to Ghosts.* New York, 1937.

Ruth:
Bulger, Bozeman. "Along Came Ruth." *Saturday Evening Post,* November 1931.
Father Ted, S.S.P. *"King of Swat."* Youngstown, Ohio, 1948.
Gallico, Paul. *The Golden People.* New York, 1965.
Holland, Gerald. "The Babe Ruth Papers." *Sports Illustrated,* December 21, 1959.
Hoyt, Waite. *Babe Ruth as I Knew Him.* New York, 1948.
Kahn, Roger. "The Real Babe Ruth." *Esquire,* August 1959.

Leisman, Louis J. *I Was with Babe Ruth at St. Mary's*. Baltimore, 1956.
Meany, Tom. *Babe Ruth*. New York, 1947.
O'Day, Marie. "They Reared Babe Ruth." *Catholic Digest*, September 1938.
Powers, Jimmy. *Baseball Personalities*. New York, 1949.
Ruth, Babe. *The Babe Ruth Story*. New York, 1948.
—————. "How It Feels to Be a Has-Been." *Liberty Magazine*, June, 1936.
Ruth, Claire. *The Babe and I*. New York, 1959.
Spink, J. G. Taylor. "The Babe." *Esquire,* December, 1959.
Weldon, Martin. *Babe Ruth*. New York, 1948.
Williams, Joe. In *Baseball's Greatest Lineup,* edited by Christy Walsh. New York, 1952.

Fiction:

Grey, Zane. *The Red-Headed Outfield and Other Baseball Stories*. New York, 1920.
Lardner, Ring. *You Know Me, Al*. New York, 1916.
Runyon, Damon. *A Treasury of Damon Runyon*. New York, 1958.
Ruth, Babe. *The Home-Run King, or How Pep Pindar Won His Title*. New York, 1920.

Newspapers:

I have listed those sportswriters who figure prominently in the text under the newspapers for which they wrote. Not all those listed under one paper necessarily worked for that paper at the same time, and many moved from one paper to another during the course of their careers. In general, however, they did their most important work for the papers under which they are mentioned.

New York American
"Bugs" Baer
Gene Fowler
Ring Lardner
Damon Runyon

New York Daily News
Paul Gallico

New York Evening Mail
New York Evening Post
New York Evening World (later *World-Telegram*)
Franklin Pierce Adams

Heywood Broun
Hugh Fullerton

New York Herald (later *Herald-Tribune)*

New York Sun
William Hanna
Frank O'Neill
William Slocum
Joe Vila

New York Telegram (later *World-Telegram)*
Dan Daniel
Fred Lieb
Tom Meany
Joe Williams

New York Times
John Kieran

New York Tribune
John Kieran
William Macbeth
W. O. McGeehan
Grantland Rice

Boston Daily Advertiser

Boston Evening Globe

Boston Morning Globe
Tim Murnane
Edward Martin

Boston Record

Baltimore Sun
H. L. Mencken

Chicago Tribune

Cleveland Plain Dealer

Des Moines Register

Kansas City Star

Los Angeles Times

Marysville (Calif.) *Appeal-Democrat*

Philadelphia Public Ledger

San Francisco Chronicle

United Press

Associated Press

Variety

The Sporting News

Baseball Magazine

Miscellaneous:

Christy Walsh's scrapbooks—National Baseball Library, Cooperstown, New York.
These encompass twelve volumes of clippings, photographs, advertisements, posters, telegrams, and other Ruth memorabilia saved by Walsh from 1921–35.

Swales Collection—New York Public Library
According to the index cards, this collection contains over five hundred volumes of newspaper clippings, rosters, etc. from the 1870s to 1919. Unfortunately most of it seems to be lost, though some valuable material remains.

St. Mary's Industrial School Annual Reports and additional loose material—Enoch Pratt Free Library, Baltimore, Maryland.

CBS, NBC, Universal Pictures' publicity releases and stills book from 1931 Babe Ruth one-reelers—The Library of the Performing Arts, Lincoln Center, New York.

Films—*Heading Home,* Baumann and Kessel, 1920, distributed by Cine-Vintage Films, Bridgeport, Conn.
The Babe Ruth Story
The Al Jolson Story
Pride of the Yankees
(See the late show.)

Index

261

About the Author

Ken Sobol was born and raised in Cleveland, Ohio,
and attended Oberlin College. He spent several
years in Los Angeles working for various animation studios and first
began writing about sports and other peculiarities of American culture
in *The Village Voice.* He is married, has three children,
and currently lives in Toronto.